A Violent Peace

A Violent Peace

Media, Truth, and Power at the League of Nations

CAROLYN N. BILTOFT

The University of Chicago Press
Chicago and London

The University of Chicago Press, Chicago 60637
The University of Chicago Press, Ltd., London
© 2021 by The University of Chicago
All rights reserved. No part of this book may be used or reproduced in any manner whatsoever without written permission, except in the case of brief quotations in critical articles and reviews. For more information, contact the University of Chicago Press, 1427 E. 60th St., Chicago, IL 60637.
Published 2021
Printed in the United States of America

30 29 28 27 26 25 24 23 22 21   1 2 3 4 5

ISBN-13: 978-0-226-76639-3 (cloth)
ISBN-13: 978-0-226-76642-3 (paper)
ISBN-13: 978-0-226-76656-0 (e-book)
DOI: https://doi.org/10.7208/chicago/9780226766560.001.0001

Library of Congress Cataloging-in-Publication Data

Names: Biltoft, Carolyn N., 1978– author.
Title: A violent peace : media, truth, and power at the League of Nations / Carolyn N. Biltoft.
Other titles: Media, truth, and power at the League of Nations
Description: Chicago ; London : The University of Chicago Press, 2021. | Includes bibliographical references and index.
Identifiers: LCCN 2020038271 | ISBN 9780226766393 (cloth) | ISBN 9780226766423 (paperback) | ISBN 9780226766560 (ebook)
Subjects: LCSH: League of Nations—History. | History, Modern—20th century. | Europe—History—1918–1945.
Classification: LCC JZ4871 .B55 2021 | DDC 341.22—dc23
LC record available at https://lccn.loc.gov/2020038271

*For my daughter, Eden (who has lived ten out of her twenty magical years
in the shadow of this book)—I have never ceased to be amazed
at your ability to welcome even the most disquieting of muses.*

Contents

Preface: Truth, Lies, and Violence, Then and Now ix

1	As Seen at the League of Nations: Global Media, Competing Truths, and the Allure of Fascism	1
2	Rebranding the World (Picture)	17
3	On True and False Tongues	40
4	Fabricating Currencies: Paper, Gold, and Other Facsimiles	60
5	Fiat Lux? False News and Hidden Flesh	89
6	The Word and the Sword Revisited	113

Acknowledgments 121
Notes 123
Bibliography 153
Index 183

Preface:
Truth, Lies, and Violence, Then and Now

I began writing this manuscript years before the present populist and "fake news" pathogens began taking root and multiplying around 2015. I was revising just as many began drawing sharp comparisons between the violence of the 1930s that came after the economic crash of 1929, and the support for far-right political discourses that began increasing after the financial crisis of 2008. I am not so sure those comparisons hold in the devil's kingdom of fine details. If they do hold, it is not as replication, but rather as a series of uncanny sounds. Throughout this book, I suggest that those resonances endure in part because of the ways in which the historical emergence and expansion of information systems have—in each subsequent iteration—interacted with our preexisting longings for absolute power and absolute certainty. In a world where international media networks carry multiple, competing, and destabilizing versions of the "truth," we can perceive transhistorical patterns of reactive popular support for the supposedly more concrete certainties of firm borders, xenophobia, racism, and sexism.

None of this is to merely restate that truth itself is multiple, subjective, or difficult to access. Rather, I am more interested in how human beings have picked up and made use of radically different versions of "truth" and "reality," in order to soothe their niggling fears and anxieties.[1] Then as more and more versions of reality—either spiritual or empirical—have begun to circulate with greater speed and volume and ever further afield, some have responded to those confusions with a storied insistence on the better because more orderly truths of a totalizing variety.[2] Many absolutes, absolutists, and absolutisms were born of the simplest urge to bring appeasing order to disturbing confusion, the way we ascribe human faces to the swirling grains in lacquered wood, or see animals in cloud formations. The world of information systems has brought more variables, more clouds, more confusion—and so many minds have worked busily to shield themselves with simpler tales.[3] Out of the chaos of both small and big data, we wove and continue to weave fables in algorithmic pentameter. Fables of a world of superior gods, of superior races, of superior genders, or of superior ways of life, and on and on. Any suggestion of the need for a scientifically rooted but humanistic intersubjectivity, in darker times, gets labeled as something like a dangerous relativism, which might take us away from the importance of objective truth.[4]

It is in the outlines of those impulses that the events of the 1930s and the Second World War are again troubling us these days. We know that National Socialism and other totalitarian regimes used mass media to spread lies and whip up violent contempt against a whole range of "others." They even tried through conquests and mass graves to lay claim to the world itself, grafting the skin of just one people onto the earth's surface. Even now we have not recovered from the events that followed the dissemination of prevarications—the creation of caricaturized scapegoats—in the service of hate. Nor have we moved past the tendency of some to deny they ever happened at all. In our own moment, it has been startling to see world leaders fear mongering on social media, deeming as fake anything that challenges them. At the same time, we are faced with grisly scenes of young men walking into synagogues, mosques, and churches and opening fire, often goaded by conspiracy theories of one kind or another.

There is perhaps a reason that discussions about the violent reverberations between the past and the present are collating partly once again around the media-driven difficulty of discerning what is true and what is false among all facts circulating about local and global affairs. Maybe the common denominator remains the extent to which various media platforms have often interacted with and amplified what the French historian Marc Bloch, in 1921, called the social "broth," containing collective but divergent prejudices, fears and strong emotions.[5]

In this book I set out to examine several different but linked batches of social broth simmering via information networks in the interwar crisis. It might strike the reader as strange that I follow these patterns through the world's first permanent multigovernment political organization, the League of Nations. And yet, as I hope to make clear, it is precisely because that organization emerged as an information-driven political, cultural, and economic project meant to encompass the "whole world" (even if it did not) that we can use its records to see the both local and global relationship between mass media and mass violence anew. That said, this book sets out neither to evaluate the League's successes or failures nor to trace its accomplishments as such.

I take no position either for or against the importance of international governance. Instead, here the League is simply a place where we can observe the bewilderments of a world where the media served both efforts at cosmopolitan conversations and those of military mobilizations and ethnic cleansings.

Anyone who knows the fuller mixed history of humanitarian efforts, religious or secular, will not be surprised to learn that sometimes the League's mission of peace devolved into violent power struggles. Even this is not the point. The idea I am tracing is how, as the paths of markets and empires began to play out—through space-time compression—on a planetary scale, impossible desires and fantasies for one single, "total" reality vied for primacy. The League's goal of influencing something called "world public opinion," provides a unique opportunity to explore how global webs of signals and wires carried and amplified those desires. What is more, those competing truths circulated in a world crisscrossed with local and global imbalances of power and inequitable distributions of resources. And yet every quest for *totality* not only was in itself impossible but also eventually broke down.[6] Information systems have undermined as often as they have supported totalitarian fantasies and projects.

In its most parable-like register, this book suggests that sometimes urges to "fix" things (as in to resolve or to solve them) grow from or lead to rigid desires for "fixity" (as in to make things static, unmoving, and final). Perhaps resisting fascisms of all varieties comes down to simply attending to forms of life—past or present—whose twists and turns defy the categories used to simplify them, even if only to render them more intelligible. *This* is the only "lesson" you will find in this book: that there is something to be said at least intellectually for surrendering to, rather than seeking to halt, the "ceaseless flux of phenomena."[7]

Alors, on y va mais seulement si t'il plait.[8]

1

As Seen at the League of Nations: Global Media, Competing Truths, and the Allure of Fascism

> An international word. Just a word, and the word a movement. Dada world war without end, dada revolution without beginning, you friends and also—poets, esteemed sirs, manufactures, and evangelists. . . . In plain language: the hospitality of the Swiss is something to be profoundly appreciated.
>
> HUGO BALL, *Dadaist Manifesto*, 1916

Old Longings, New Mediums

In 1928, the Swiss psychoanalyst Carl Gustav Jung ruminated on the First World War's enduring psychological impact.[1] Jung might have focused on the unprecedented violence of that episode, which constituted a collective and indeed global trauma.[2] After all, sixty million people spanning the continents waged war for four years with the nascent technologies of gas, machine guns, and aerial bombardment.[3] At the time of the armistice on November 11, 1918, thirty million people were dead, wounded, or missing.[4] Instead, he focused his attention more precisely on other effects of that conflagration. Namely, he claimed, the dislocations of the trenches and their turbulent aftermath had finally and fully dispossessed "modern man" of "all the metaphysical certainties of his medieval brother."[5] By medieval certainty, Jung painted something of an idealized picture of the assurances of feudal "chains of being," where everyone knew their place in the cosmic and earthly order of things—God, then the angels, then the king and his divine right, then the various classes, in descending order, from the highest to the lowest.[6] Whatever their shortcomings, those hierarchical systems, which linked the worldly order to otherworldly principles, also offered tremendous peace of mind.[7] In such a system, one could know both where one stood in this lifetime and also where one was going after death.

While these rather static forms of spiritual and earthly certitude had long been in decline, Jung described the post–World War I period as another and particularly dramatic episode in a generalized loss of mental quietude.[8] He stated, "The upheaval of our world and the upheaval of our consciousness are one and the same."[9] More specifically, he explained, "the revolution in our conscious outlook, brought about by the catastrophic results of the World War, shows itself in our inner life by the shattering of our faith in ourselves and our own worth."[10] Amid that collective self-doubt, Jung observed a human race caught up in seeking radical new sources of reassurance and new experiences in a wide variety of domains: "It shows itself in the ideal of internationalism and super-nationalism, embodied in the League of Nations and the like; we see it also in sport and, significantly, in cinema and jazz."[11] For Jung, though, none of these pursuits were likely candidates for restoring humankind's lost certainties. As he specified: "And while man, hesitant and questioning, contemplates a world that is distracted with treaties of peace and pacts of friendship, with democracy and dictatorship, capitalism and Bolshevism, his spirit yearns for an answer that will allay the turmoil of doubt and uncertainty."[12] By 1935, Jung added fascism and its reanimated atavisms to his list of modernity's mixture of efforts and ailments. He decried the revival of "the medieval persecutions of the Jews," spurred on by the symbolism of the "the Roman fasces," "the tramp of legions," and the "archaic swastika."[13] The desire for absolute certainty (and absolutist forms of power) seemed to have come home to roost in an acutely brutal form.

In linking the League of Nations, cinema, jazz, capitalism, bolshevism, and fascism as divergent but shared responses to a generalized crisis, Jung opened the door for thinking transversally about the interwar moment.[14] While Jung observed systemic connections among seemingly disparate phenomena, however, he didn't attend specifically to *how* they were connected. Why, after all, should we put jazz, cinema, and bolshevism side by side, as if each somehow mirrored the deeper impulses of the others?[15]

If we consider that question in a historical rather than strictly psychoanalytic register, then we need to ask if there might indeed have been some traceable forms of correlation between the political specters and cultural phenomena that Jung raised.[16] To that end, this book suggests that by standing *inside* the League of Nations, it becomes possible to attain an admittedly partial but still significant view of the extensive connective tissue of interwar crises that eluded Jung's grasp. For if indeed "the upheaval of the world" and the "upheaval of human consciousness" cotranspired as Jung suggested, perhaps we should not overlook the role of telegraphs, telephones, stock tickers, money transfers, radios, and cinema reels in forging—rather than merely reflecting—those intersecting lines.[17] Writing the history of these convergences, even in a single period, is beyond the scope of this book.[18] However, the League does offer a compendium of resources for rethinking the interwar liaisons between mass media, mass markets, and mass violence.[19] For one, like all international organizations, the League was an artifact of the bundle of processes known collectively—if reductively—as globalization.[20] As such, its records are full of fragmented yet fulsome traces of the growth, intensification, and use of global communications grids and their multidirectional effects.[21] They are also full of documents that allow us to observe how a myriad of different actors perceived and talked about those phenomena.

That said, what follows is neither an institutional history of the League of Nations nor a descriptive history of how networks of transnational experts helped "wire" the world.[22] It does not set out to trace the League's impact or its reception, for good or for ill, either in the realms of media and communications or in the arenas of peacemaking and peacekeeping. Rather here, I use the tools of intellectual history, cultural studies, and critical theory to focus *transversally* on what that organizational *site* reveals about the structures and mentalities of the conjuncture in which it coalesced and then unraveled.[23] In other words, I am more interested in what the League reflected about its moment than in what it "accomplished" in discrete terms.

In this sense, we might think of the League as a global *planetarium*.[24] For, projected in its public and private meetings rooms and reproduced in its voluminous broadcasts and publications, we can observe the constellations that emerged within what Marshall McLuhan has called the "Gutenberg galaxy."[25] The constellations that interest me most are the points conjoining quests for total, worldwide economic and political answers to those of other dark and inhuman "final solutions."[26]

Viewed in this way, the League also offers flashes and fragments of the structural, infrastructural, and conceptual DNA of what Robert O. Paxton has called "the anatomy of fascism."[27] To clarify, by fascism I do not refer exclusively to the political regimes that seized power in the 1920s and 1930s. Rather, I refer more broadly to what Umberto Eco called Ur-fascism, which he described as an often contradictory bundle of public and private attitudes that existed—and continue to exist—worldwide.[28] More specifically, I am interested in the range of fascist mentalities and fantasies that come both from the right and from the left and tend to extoll the values of absolute certainty and total control.[29] While impulses toward absolutism have been evident throughout world history, in the interwar moment uneven global media flows interacted with and helped transform these urges in new ways, which also underwrote totalitarian political projects.

Paxton's classic text still offers a useful way of understanding why fascist regimes frequently mobilized the tools of mass media. He argued that the distinguishing characteristic of political fascism was its instrumental definition of the truth. In Paxton's own words: "The truth was whatever permitted the new fascist man (and woman) to dominate others, and whatever made the chosen people triumph."[30] Of course, those regimes used diverse media to disseminate and propagate their truth claims about the so-called science of racial purity or the spiritual sacrosanctity of the people.[31] Often such regimes persuaded their populations that those totalizing visions were worth giving up rights for, dying for, and ultimately killing for. "Media"—bright images, bold texts, and stirring sounds—helped carry those so-called truths into living rooms and packed auditoriums (theaters, sporting events, political rallies) where people consumed them and then reproduced them to various degrees.[32]

While fascist regimes clearly exhibited an instrumental and media-dependent relationship to the truth, it is not as if such a relationship constituted a rare or isolated phenomenon. For, in the age of spin, where crafting narratives had become a rather mundane tool for wielding power and accumulating capital, questions of truth and reality were a matter of continual private and public conflict in many societies *worldwide*.[33] Simply decrying the political manipulation of facts not only overlooks the difficulty of extracting the truth from many competing interpretations but also ignores the crucial difference between facts and that more elusive psychological state called certainty.[34]

Here then, my hypothesis is that the popular appeal of fascist rhetoric may have been less about mass manipulation and more about the complex ways in which information systems both transformed the dynamics of power and profit and also disrupted existential forms of certitude to begin with.[35] Following Jung, we might consider how political narratives of absolute power were in some ways connected to profound desires for the "metaphysical certainties" of one total, homogenous reality. In that vein, *totalitarianism*—especially the most racist, xenophobic, and violent variants—used the media to spread promises of tangible and simple paths away from the discomforts of economic, political, and existential indeterminacy.

Through this frame we can also revisit the common threads between bolshevism, fascism, and the League of Nations that Jung identified but never explicitly defined. At their heart, each constituted a political project that in some way offered—each to very different degrees and toward different ends—a set of truths that were meant to make sense of everything and everyone, *everywhere*. Whatever else the League did or did not accomplish, I posit that it became one center (among many others) for the production and dissemination of "regimes of truth," which corresponded to a specific global "order of things."[36] It was not necessarily even that the League was the most important or most impactful truth-production center in the interwar moment. It is simply that there are things we can see through that organization's windows that we might not be able to see, at least not in the same light, from another vantage point. Sustaining these assertions, however, requires a recasting of the organization's historical role and significance on the world stage.

Into the Planetarium

The past decade has seen a resurgence of scholarly interest in the League of Nations.[37] As Susan Pedersen has argued, this still growing body of work has transcended the tendency to obsess over why the League failed to prevent World War II. By moving past that question, League scholars have recovered a lush archive that was neglected during an era when political historians were uninterested in histories of "failure." We now have fuller and more fine-grained historical portraits of the League's work in diverse domain, such as economics, health, human trafficking, scientific management, imperial observation, environmental protection, and disarmament.[38] As part of this general trend, several scholars have also begun unearthing the organization's legacy in the domains of media and communications. One strand of this literature has focused on how the League contributed to efforts to improve, regulate, or control international communications and transportation networks and infrastructures.[39] Others have focused more broadly on how the League used a variety of media to pursue the (never fully achieved) aspiration of creating a global public sphere.[40] Mostly importantly, this literature makes it abundantly clear that whatever the results, a significant percentage of the organization's work turned in some way on the production, management, or diffusion of information.[41]

There is still some room, however, to explore the League's informational dimensions from a qualitatively different perspective, including by attending to the discourse surrounding the birth of that would-be global body politic. While the League's varied architects disagreed on many technical points, there seemed to be at least a public-facing consensus in the background that *words* might replace *weapons* as the primary tool of international relations. In a speech delivered at the Sorbonne on December 21, 1918, American president Woodrow Wilson insisted that if the Central powers had dared sit down and "discuss the purpose of this war for a single fortnight, it never would have happened." He further claimed that if they had been forced to discuss the conflict for a year—as they should have been—war itself would have been rendered permanently inconceivable.⁴² To those ends, the League supplanted the intermittent diplomatic conference system with a permanent bicameral organization.⁴³ As article 3 of the Covenant stated: "The Assembly shall meet at stated intervals and from time to time as occasion may require at the Seat of the League or at such other place as may be decided upon."⁴⁴ The General Assembly met annually, while the more executive and exclusive Council met more frequently.⁴⁵ The Council additionally played the role of mediator or arbitrator in the event of a dispute between states, thus providing another guarantee that politics could progress without resort to arms. In the opening Assembly of the League of Nations in Geneva in 1920, the Belgian envoy Paul Hymans praised the novelty of such "frequent and friendly intercourse between independent states" that would provide "ties which lead to mutual understanding and sympathy."⁴⁶

There was also more to the League's informational mandate than discussion and arbitration. The final and ostensibly most important weapon in the League's nonviolent arsenal included the force of "world public opinion."⁴⁷ In 1918, Ray Stannard Baker, Woodrow Wilson's press secretary, had already reminded the League's potential critics that the statesmen who created the world's first "parliament of man" were no wiser than their forefathers. However, he asserted confidently that they were fortuitously armed with "more mechanisms for the annihilation of space and time."⁴⁸ Variations on that sentiment got repeated again and again, especially in the first decade of the organization's life. In the historic First Assembly, the British politician turned South African delegate Lord Robert Cecil reminded his colleagues that both the League's success and lasting peace required securing "the confidence of the world."⁴⁹ For it was "the organized opinion of mankind" that would sustain the League system and, by extension, make it possible for states to spare the sword "to the lowest point consistent with national safety."⁵⁰ Ten years later, a pamphlet produced by the League's Information Section stated: "Before the existence of the League, there were only national public opinions expressed by the national press." However, with a great deal of effort, the League had created a "multinational public opinion, whose influence is increasing."⁵¹ And indeed, the League became something of a multimedia organization with a veritable army of technologies and personnel dedicated to the production and dissemination of all manner of information.⁵²

What sense then might we make of the League's emphasis on the power of the word? There are already several existing theories. Perhaps the oldest (and most discredited) is that the League's wordiness was a function of its bleary-eyed cosmopolitan idealism.⁵³ For decades, historians and social scientists presented the League's emphasis on talk and opinion making as the reason for its failure to prevent the Second World War. E. H. Carr's influential *Twenty Years' Crisis*, published in 1939 with the world on the brink of another war, took the opportunity to attack the League's utopianism in general and its faith in public opinion in particular.[54] More specifically, Carr decried the League's "belief that public opinion can be relied on to judge rightly on any question rationally presented to it, combined with the assumption that it will act in accordance with this right judgment."[55] Current historical scholarship has moved on from the realism/idealism debate, choosing instead to focus on the League's mixed record of technical errors and accomplishments.[56] However, by moving on, those interpretations may have missed an opportunity to further historicize and contextualize not only the League's faith in public opinion, but also the interwar variant of the realist/idealist binary.

The interwar moment was one important inflection point in a much longer set of structural and conceptual transformations wherein information revolutions had called into question the nature of reality itself. Of course, those changes accelerated with the printing press in the sixteenth century but in some ways emerged even earlier, with the written alphabet, which allowed words to travel beyond the intimacies of face-to-face interactions.[57] With each successive revolution, words could move faster and further afield, soon through wires and waves and across continents, in the blink of an eye.[58] Increasingly immaterial experiences and forms of exchange led to nascent practices of buying, selling, thinking, feeling, and belonging. They also played a part in the transposition of older philosophical questions about words, names, concepts, and material objects into new registers.[59] Perhaps it is more than coincidental that as (material) information infrastructures facilitated an increase in the volume and kind of (immaterial) signs and messages, other intellectual debates crystalized in turn. Realism/idealism, base/superstructure, nature/nurture: each sought to fix and decide what drove and constituted those original propositions of "what is there," and "how do we know it?"[60]

Of greatest significance for understanding the League's informational contours are the nineteenth- and twentieth-century theories of language, such as semiotics, which emerged just as telegraphs and telephones allowed words to float as seemingly detached from a place or material anchor.[61] In that context, the Swiss linguist Ferdinand de Saussure for one decoupled words (signs, signifiers) and the objects to which they supposedly corresponded (signified).[62] All that once seemed organic and natural came under review: *why should a chair be called a chair?* Saussure suggested that words and the reality that they described were not inherently welded together, that only history and the consensus of the community kept them in place.[63]

The same technologies that helped to make the connection between language and the world seem more arbitrary also raised another set of creative possibilities.[64] Some emergent theories suggested language's power either to constrain one's apperception of reality or to actively shape the world as a potter shapes a lump of clay.[65] I want to suggest that we can see the League's focus on information as bounded to and reflective of this ambient mindset, which increasingly saw signs as capable of fashioning and refashioning the real.[66]

As the League's first functionaries were setting up shop in Geneva, figures such as Edward Sapir, Benjamin Lee Whorf, and Ludwig Wittgenstein (to name just a few) were reimagining the ties between words and the world.[67] Those insights would later lead to the emergence of speech-act theory, which also bestowed on mortal speakers the capacity to call the world into being.[68] Just as God had said, *Let there be light*, and there was light, the judiciary could utter, *I now pronounce you man and wife* and make it so.[69] Beyond the law, there were a myriad of ways in which one might remake reality simply by renaming, renarrating, or redrawing it.[70] Increasingly, to move the world one had to know, in the key phrase of J. L. Austin, "how to do things with words."[71] While "speech acts" were putatively ancient phenomena, the theory itself was a child of the twentieth century and part of a wider corpus of ideas that pondered the impact that words had on the world.

Throughout this book I follow some of these strands first through the League's records, and then back out into the wider world. Rather than situating the League as bound to the linear historical development of international communications institutions (the Universal Postal Union, the International Broadcasting Union, or even multimedia conglomerates) I have chosen other comparative registers. We might, for one, think of the League's annual meetings as the internationalization of the psychoanalytic "talking cure," or the idea that human neurosis (and violence) could be expunged through the therapy of endless discussion. After all, in one sense the League did institutionalize and globalize the posttraumatic therapeutic appointment.[72]

Or, we might picture the League as the inverse mirror image of the Dadaist Cabaret Voltaire, just down the road in Zurich, Switzerland. Both "performative" stages reflected an antipathy for the propaganda-fueled violence of the First World War. Both saw words as creative raw material. In Geneva, words were part of the cocktail of prescriptions for rehabilitating the world after the war. In Zurich, Dadaist performances laid bare the creative illogicality of language. They highlighted sound with or without fury, randomized, and they resignified meaning for a world less orderly, and so, potentially, more poetic.[73]

Of course there were other political and economic variants of these ideas emanating from various centers around the world. It was also in the interwar moment that the Austrian American expert of spin Edward Bernays described the prevalence and effects of this thing called propaganda: "This practice of creating circumstances and of creating pictures in the minds of millions of persons is very common. Virtually no important undertaking is now carried on without it, whether the enterprise be building a cathedral, endowing a university, marketing a moving picture, floating a large bond issue, or electing a president."[74] As Bernays suggested, the age of advertising and that of political publicity emerged together, with the tools of each practice influencing the other.

We know too that both propaganda and war reporting had functioned almost as another front of World War I.[75] In 1922, Walter Lippmann, the contemporary American journalist, confidante to Wilson, and inventor of the term "public opinion," provided an account of the importance of publicity for the Allied victory. Lippmann wrote: "We know first hand from the officer who edited the French communiqué . . . that in the worst moments of Verdun, General Joffre and his cabinet met and argued over the nouns, adjectives, and verbs that were to be printed in the newspapers the next morning."[76] Joffre treated press releases as a vital dimension of military strategy for the age of total war.[77] Lippmann continued: "Within a few hours those two or three hundred words would . . . paint a picture in men's minds of what was happening on the slopes of Verdun, and in front of that picture people would take heart or despair."[78] Given that the production and control of information had been so central to winning the war, it must have seemed rather natural to assume that those tools could be converted toward both securing and keeping international peace.[79]

Presenting the League's information directives as a peer to these other philosophical, economic, and political *linguistic determinisms* actually helps to further historicize what the realist critique had missed, namely that immaterial signs and material reality had become coconstitutive in new ways through the intermingling of media, markets, and power politics. As with the metaphor of the cable and the wire, the structures, infrastructures, and financial architectures of the modern world were both material and immaterial. While messages and funds began to move as quickly as lightning, cables still required tremendous time and resources to construct, install, and maintain.[80] Information flows depended on relay stations and explicit acts of encoding and decoding.[81] In the nineteenth century, the slow agonies of slave labor and the environmental despoliation of gutta-percha, a natural latex used for lining submarine cables, underscored how signals left deep footprints in the material world.[82] Finally just as messages never zipped about truly free of infrastructure, controlling the ethereal world of signs was never an end in itself. As Michael Geyer and Charles Bright asserted, beginning in the late nineteenth century geopolitical conflicts began to shift somewhat away from territory and toward controlling networks or circuits of "money, markets, knowledge."[83] National and global imperial communities grew not only through the tools of what Benedict Anderson called "print capitalism" (including the press, modern literature, public education, propaganda, surveillance, censorship), but also through biopower (demographic statistics, sterilization programs, policing, segregation) and terraforming (enclosures, expropriation of indigenous lands, overseas colonization).[84]

Both at the League and beyond, the production of facts, truths, and information helped seize or maintain specific material ends and vice versa.[85] Here then my proposition is that from its start, the League was tasked with "manufacturing consent" for the post–World War I capitalist and imperial geopolitical *order of things*.[86] In some ways this thesis aligns with the work of Mark Mazower and others who have argued that the League was, from its very inception, a creature of great-power interests.[87] More to the point, Pedersen has argued that the League's emphasis on "talk" and "expertise" generated "legitimizing discourses," which in turn helped influence international norms, often in ways that reinforced the privileges of the great powers.[88] These are important insights.[89] Just a cursory reading of the League's founding documents and opening plenary secessions provides evidence of familiar contradictions, where claims of universal freedom, equality, and progress quickly transmuted into justifications for delaying the extension of rights to certain peoples and certain states.[90] The League also—most pertinently through the work of its Permanent Mandates Commission—presided over an imperial world in which only some peoples had the right to "national self-determination" and thus to statehood.[91] Then, too, in terms of the power-knowledge nexus, the League continually produced volumes of evidence about various nations' so-called progress and so-called backwardness measured via indicators of income, infrastructure, education, and literacy, and so on.[92] Even beyond these variables, the League's institutional structures mirrored other patterns of inclusion and exclusion on the world stage.[93]

This argument, however, is the starting point rather than the end point of what follows. If we are to use the League to understand the media-facilitated allure of interwar fascisms (namely the promise of absolute certainty), we need to explore not only information's nascent *power* but also its inherent *vulnerability*. Information systems not only continually *forged* quests for power and wealth but also continually *threatened* and *disrupted* them. As an example of these vulnerabilities, the tripartite emergence of the telegraph, the telephone, and the stock ticker transformed the rhythms and practices of banking and finance.[94] When people could transfer funds ever more quickly from one bank branch to another, suddenly buying and selling acquired a sense of urgency and immediacy. This new tempo also triggered deeper fears about fraud and the trustworthiness of anonymous transactions. Insider trading, rumors-cum-bank-runs, misrelayed messages or funds—these too hounded those who entered increasingly information-dependent and frenzied market spaces.[95]

With each new node in the global information circuit—from the fifteenth century to the twenty-first—came a glut of what Kenneth Cmiel and John Durham Peters have called "promiscuous knowledge."[96] In these endless streams of fact and counterfact, people had to trust increasingly remote and often conflicting sources of information, as they invested in foreign enterprises, encountered unfamiliar beliefs, and took part in long-distance relationships.[97] The most important insight here is that daily life increasingly required abstract faith in the reality of things, places, events, and criteria that people could not touch or see firsthand.[98] At the same time, those media flows (from books to newspapers to radio broadcasts) also meant that each person and in some sense, even each nation-state suddenly had to face constant comparisons to a sea of "others"—others often more privileged or more powerful.[99]

McLuhan long ago provided some fruitful clues about the sociopsychological impact of these changes: "Mental breakdown of varying degrees is the very common result of uprooting and inundation with new information and endless new patterns of information."[100] Beyond the psychological burdens of information overload, just as networks of knowledge, finance, and power reached out *everywhere*, informational threats could also come from *anywhere*. As a case in point for our story, the volume of information circulating in World War I also meant that the conflict's violence and so its psychological impact reverberated further and further afield. As the war's events circulated via telegraph wires among imperial outposts and places like Verdun, they stretched an awareness of temporal coexistence across unprecedented distances.[101] However, the image of the earth that appeared in 1914 was neither a smooth ecumenical sphere nor a seamless Kantian orb, but rather a febrile grid of intersecting fate lines.[102] The British veteran and poet Robert Graves described World War I retrospectively not as "a clash between flags," but rather "an infection of the earth's common sky."[103] If that common sky had come into being partly through headlines, so had the sickness. War reporting not only became a global point of reference but also made the world's apparent convergence seem more tangible and more dangerous as soldiers from every continent died in the trenches.[104] What is more, evidence of the precarious interdependence of all people on earth continued to circulate in the press in the war's aftermath. The flu pandemic of 1918–19 and the "epidemic" of revolts that seemed to spread from Russia to China, Egypt, and beyond demonstrated that the domino effect was a permanent feature of modern life and politics.[105]

In that tumultuous post–World War I context, the French statesman and former prime minister Leon Bourgeois wrote worriedly: "No local conflict can be confined to some one part of the world as . . . there is such an interdependence in all the relations between nations that . . . every wound inflicted at some point threatens to poison the whole organism."[106] Here, then, we find a way to understand why the League's architects seemed to believe that influencing a unitary, holistic, and fundamentally stable "world opinion" was so crucial and so pressing. Somehow the League's project to stretch *peace* to the far ends of the earth through cosmopolitan discussion, publicity, and international law was tied to a felt need to gain mastery of the whole and always potentially precarious *global public sphere*.[107]

We can hear variants of this concern in other places. In speaking of the necessity of the League, Alfred Zimmern, a member of the League's Committee on International Intellectual Cooperation, stated, "the *res publica* with which it is our duty to concern ourselves, if we wish to retain control over our environment, extends to the ends of the earth."[108] Zimmern claimed that the secret to controlling the international order lay in managing the flow of ideas and information worldwide.[109] While this urge for "control" is indeed an important part of the story, I think of it more as an *effect* of deeper changes in the hegemonic fabric of the world system. In that frame, Zimmern's discourse of *total control* reflected a wider transference wherein a variety of actors transcribed the desire for *absolute certainty* onto the world itself.

As Jo-Anne Pemberton has argued, since the nineteenth century competing visions of the "whole earth" fueled competing quests for "one world."[110] And yet no single worldview could ever cover the full scope of human diversity on the earth's surface. Nor could any ideology or community inhabit a local sphere that was hermetically sealed. The continual instability generated by these two opposed ideals—of total conquest or total isolation—helped to foment what Holly Case has called "the age of questions."[111] And indeed, the information age has been the age of questions: Can there be one nation—or one earth—seamlessly united? Can we live half-slave, half-free? Should we shrink the world down to a single village, or wrap it in a single race, faith, legal code, or economic system?[112] In addition, private questions emerged alongside these varied public ones. What is the nature of truth and reality? How can we be sure of what we know or believe to be true?

While people, states, ideologies, or religions might try, reality would never hold still; information circuits always carried alternative truths, differing political views, and existential doubts into both households and seats of government. There would always be unfamiliar visions and dissonant claims creating doubt and political foment even into the most carefully censored societies. Those heterogeneous struggles to determine truth and reality *once and for all* constitute some of the most persistent ghosts haunting the modern condition.[113]

As it turns out, many of those twentieth-century ghosts frequented the meeting halls of the League of Nations. We find their spectral fingerprints in scattered memos and long-winded speeches.[114] While the League's promised totality was purportedly one of peace, it escaped neither the dynamics of power and profit, nor the more private urges to silence competing pictures and story lines or competing visions of world order.[115] Those competing visions, however, always resurged.

In the 1930s, just as Carr decried the League's idealism, populist sentiments and fascist regimes increasingly reacted against the perversions of "talk" and spoke out for the firmer certainties of blood and soil. The irony that this book comes back to again and again is that claims about the weightier realism of flesh, borders, and swords always circulated (often internationally) via radio broadcasts and cinema reels.[116] No state ripped up the cables, stopped the presses, and retreated to caves and the use of smoke signals (they did try to control the movement of certain peoples). Rather each fought to edit and redact words and images in ways that favored the needs and desires of their own reality, and often in doing so, they mobilized the binary codes of us/them, black/white, savage/civilized, true/false, zero/one.

Because the League was one (if partial and exclusionary) global public discussion forum, it never spoke with a single voice, and it hosted both believers and detractors around its tables. From inside its walls, we can listen to the eerie fugue wherein invocations of perpetual international peace intermingled with calls for *Lebensraum* and a thousand-year Reich.[117] We can detect patterns in the cacophonic coexistence of anthems for the unity of mankind, songs for the solidarity of the proletariat, sputtering Dadaist manifestos, and the dark lullabies of the *Volksgemeinschaft*.[118]

On Method and Orders of Operation

Throughout this book, in looking *through* rather than *at* the League, I am also more interested in the organization's meaning-making functions than its policy-making ones. Despite my theoretical and historical focus on "information," I do not describe the League's specific use of media or communications as such. Instead, I focus widely on the "truth notions" that appear in what Cornelia Vismann would call the League's "files."[119] My primary claim is that the League continually produced not only truth, but also more literally *symbolic capital* for the post–World War I geopolitical order. Thus, memos, circular letters, petitions, and official reports were as integral to that process as newspaper clippings, photographs, or broadcasts.[120] I also frequently put the League's files into conversation with a variety of other interwar texts, including those of philosophers, poets, journalists, filmmakers, or little-known pamphleteers. When read together and diagonally, these sources help reveal how conflicting regimes of truth and power got "synced up" through information systems with heterogeneous fears and desires, which then mutated into calls for real or symbolic violence.[121] Each chapter thus ends by drawing parallels between the League's rhetoric and that of National Socialism. There were, of course, other interwar totalitarian regimes to choose from. However Nazism and its final solutions serve as the recurring referential frame for shedding light on the darkest possibilities encoded in fascist mentalities.

The first chapter is the most League centered, in that it establishes the extent to which the organization itself functioned as a truth and symbolic capital production center. To those ends, it rethinks the very origins of the League as bound to the "credibility crisis" that the violence of World War I created for the (primarily Western) liberal, capitalist, and imperial world order. Rather than the League only influencing "world opinion," I claim that it was also tasked with rebranding something called "Western civilization." Out of all the League's panoply of publicity efforts, the chapter zooms in on the creation of a series of lantern slides, which together made up—to use Martin Heidegger's term—a very specific "world picture." However, not only did those images of the world require constant editing for different audiences; they also met with sharp resistance from those states or groups who objected to their own place or position as depicted within that order of things. Those determined to undo the post–World War I distribution of territory and resources, denied and denounced the truth of League's "world picture," calling instead for the supposedly "higher truths" of blood and earth forged with the sword.

After casting light on the League's verbal and visual truth machinery, I claim that language, money, and the press constituted three of the most important mediums, through which diverse interwar actors competed to establish their preferred version of reality. In one sense, each of these domains offered promising avenues for reengineering human communities, economies, and mentalities. On the other hand, each was also in some way subject to invention, or manipulation, and so to concerns about how to discern the "real" from the "fake."[122] Given the pervading threats of dissimulation, discussions of best language, monetary, or journalistic practice at the League contained subtexts of the search for solid and concrete forms of truth. Often that proposed "solidity," however, appeared in the garb of racial stereotypes or forms of now latent, now patent xenophobia.

The language chapter traces how variants of linguistic determinism emerged inside political projects to remake the world by creating, modifying, or reforming linguistic structures, grammar, or vocabularies. Several of these reform projects ended up being discussed or considered at the League. There were, for instance, debates about the potential merits or threats of international artificial languages, such as Esperanto. At the same time, the League also tracked the use of so-called minority languages, as well as the progression of several national language and alphabet reform movements in a variety of nation-states. Under the guise of progress, however, national language policies and reform efforts frequently sought to expunge foreign influences even as they sought to expand the global reach or prestige of certain mother tongues. Those official programs serve here as a productive background for considering the rise of fascist neologisms, which also sought to use words to press the people's minds into narrow totalitarian channels.

The chapter on money explores how information systems also impacted both national and international programs to stabilize a common medium of exchange. In particular, it demonstrates that fears about the circulation of counterfeit money emerged alongside fears about the glut of paper money and the woes of hyperinflation. International discussions about the ideal monetary standard—gold, fiat, tabular, or chartal—often revealed latent fears about the difficulty of trusting in the "authenticity" or "solidity" of a given currency. The chapter not only explores the League's official discourse on the international gold standard but also looks at the organization's discussion of the problems of counterfeit currency. The chapter then ends with National Socialism's rejection of gold and subsequent decision to counterfeit the currencies of other nations. While metal offered one (symbolically) material anchor for money, the other was state-sanctioned violence.

The final chapter turns to the startlingly relevant question of so-called false news. It opens with the protest suicide of the Jewish intellectual Stefan Lux on the Assembly floor in 1936, and the League's subsequent efforts to minimize the reputational damage of that affair. Ironically, the cover-up of that tragic event took place on the tail of a series of discussions that the League hosted on the dangers of lying and dissimulation in the press. Thus, the chapter moves back and forth between reconstructing Lux's story and a textual analysis of the proceedings of the discussions on "false news." Through this to-and-fro, I show how the story of Lux's life and death got caught up in, reduced, or even erased in the maelstrom of *both* "true" and "false" news. In retrospect, Lux's story appears as a form of writing on the wall, revealing the ways in which informational reductionisms and stereotypes served as a prequel and a handmaiden for the ethnic cleansings to come.

There were also explicit cases where the League cooperated with or turned a blind eye to fascist regimes.[123] However, the goal is not to expose the League's betrayals.[124] Rather, because the League was ostensibly designed for peace, the book also serves as a reminder of the prevalent demon that Michel Foucault famously dubbed the *fascism within*: "The fascism in us all, in our heads and in our everyday behavior, the fascism that causes us to love power, to desire the very thing that dominates and exploits us."[125]

2

Rebranding the World (Picture)

> Impressed by the horrors of the late war and convinced that another of its kind would be productive of still greater disasters for humanity and civilization the High Contracting Parties Unite in constituting a League of Nations.
>
> BRITISH DRAFT OF THE COVENANT, 1918

The World Talks It Over?

Ten years into the League experiment, Burr Price, editor in chief for the European edition of the *New York Herald*, praised the efforts and accomplishments of that novel global public forum. He began by restating a familiar framework: "Centuries ago a great theologian wrote it is more glorious to kill war with words than to slay men with the sword. . . . Finally measures for that strategy are in place." Then, he continued: "In the Assembly representatives speak as delegates from the governments of the world. Back home peoples of the world are watching the proceedings through the medium of their representatives. In this manner the world talks it over."[1]

The League did not actually hold a conversation with the *whole world*.[2] Many sovereign states were initially excluded (Germany, Russia, Turkey), and others were absent by choice (the United States). Then there is the fact that only some peoples had the right to "national self-determination" and thus to statehood to begin with.[3] Even for those states that did enter the League, only some could have a seat on the more exclusive and ostensibly more powerful Council, as opposed to the General Assembly. And finally, while the League's administrative body—the Secretariat—hired a remarkably international staff, most of its members were still largely of European descent.[4] Nevertheless, the League's official discourse claimed to support the principle of the absolute equality of states.[5] Especially during the annual Assembly meetings, the League buildings appeared to contain a vivisection of an increasingly global body politic.[6] Delegates from Haiti, Brazil, Ethiopia, Egypt, China, Poland, and Persia appeared in the Assembly hall next to those from France, Britain, Italy, Japan, and (exceptionally, and with limitations as we will see) even India.[7]

In the foreword to Robert de Traz's famous text *The Spirit of Geneva*, the French author and World War I veteran Andre Maurois described the aesthetic of this novel business of international peace: "Noble Hindus walk about in beard and turban. Abyssinians, sombre and solemn, their white garments covered with black silk capes, invoke the Lion of Judah." He continued to marvel: "This cosmopolitan crowd, diverse in language and color, in demeanor, in gestures and in looks, at fixed hours flows like a wave from the Salle de la Reformation where the Assembly is held to the Secretariat where the commissions sit."[8]

Beyond the not-so-latent orientalism at work in his observations, Maurois also opened the curtain on an elaborately constructed and well-lit global stage, where a diverse cast of characters arrived to deliver their lines. However, reaching "world public opinion," required something beyond merely providing a platform. Hidden behind the Assembly's pageantry, silent armies of stenographers, translators, editors, and technicians assiduously pulled and pushed the leavers and gears of the whole operation.[9] For, at its heart, the League was something of a production company, or an information factory, continually producing words, images, charts, and sound bites. According to one League publication, the 1927 Assembly alone produced more than 2,164 typewritten pages, including seventy communiqués, twenty-two verbatim reports of the plenary meetings, and fifty-six verbatim reports of the eighteen committees, each in both French and English.[10]

For the sake of bringing the *background* into the *foreground*, it is worth pausing to flesh out the inner workings of the League's production process. During the evenings, a certain number of staff wrote, duplicated, printed, and proofread documents, both to record the previous day's happenings and in preparation for the next day's discussion. When day broke, after a long night of fastidious labor, the mountains of documents changed hands like a relay baton. Those reams of paper would travel from the basement "by lift" to the ground floor. Once there, day-shift functionaries retrieved the documents, loaded them onto trolleys, and then delivered the paperwork to their designated destinations.[11] The delegations received their documents in the meeting halls, while the journalists received theirs in an "ante-chamber" containing hundreds of compartments that the League called "pigeon holes."[12] On the other side of the antechamber, there was also large room that contained telephone booths and telegraphs for sending and receiving messages. Some of the Secretariat's external communications would even travel by a pneumatic tube that stretched from the League building all the way to the main post office in the Geneva city center.[13]

Beyond the work of reporting and publishing the goings-on at the League, there were other tasks and other mechanisms of information input and output, knowledge creation and exchange. The library held extensive collections, including most of the world's most prominent newspapers.[14] The League also produced its own publications as a way of keeping the world informed about the League's work as well as about recent developments in a vast number of technical fields. Those publications included (but were certainly not limited to) the *Official Journal*, the *Treaty Series*, *Armaments Year Book*, *Bulletin of Statistics*, *Monthly Epidemiological Report*, and a *Quarterly Bulletin of Information on the Work of the I.L.O.*[15] Finally, the Secretariat had a photography and film department for producing still and moving images, appealing to the world's hearts and minds via that most sensitive occipital nerve.[16]

Perhaps unsurprisingly, the League's archival holdings are also replete with further evidence of this enormous work. In the finding aides, which help the researcher navigate the League's archival collections, there are six files dedicated to "typewriters," thirty-eight to the subject of "radio," twenty-eight to "cinema," twenty to "wireless," and twelve to "broadcasting." Remarkably, the "press" appears in 239 files across the majority of all the League's sections. And too, beyond references to specific mediums, the word "language" appears in the title of forty-three files, "speech" in twenty-two, and "nomenclature" in twenty-four.[17] If we just open a few of those files, we can hear repetitions on the theme of confidence in the power of words to cure the world of the woes of war. In 1920, the League's secretary-general Eric Drummond wrote a personal thank-you note to Arthur Burrows of the Marconi Wireless Company for their help in organization communications for the inaugural Assembly. Burrow's reply read as such: "It is our confident opinion that wireless will play an important part in creating better understanding between various peoples of the world."[18]

Given the halo of importance surrounding the tools of communication, it is perhaps not surprising that so much of the League's time, energy, and resources accumulated precisely on those questions. Even before the League opened its doors, in 1919, amid a flurry of preparations for the First Assembly, League staff spent a remarkable amount of time searching for a single typewriter that had mysteriously disappeared from the Secretariat. On December 1, a League staff member wrote to the Remington Typewriter Company directly, asking them to kindly report if they ever stumbled across the (presumably) stolen property. The Remington representative responded, clarified the machine's serial number and purchase date, and agreed to keep his eyes open.[19] On its own, of course, the case of the missing typewriter is but a meaningless fragment. Sometimes, though, fragments provide a parallax view of hidden, or less obvious, shades of significance.[20]

What can we discern about the League, and then through the League, about the dynamics of the interwar conjuncture by thinking *with* the missing typewriter? In the first place, there is the fact that in a modern bureaucratic age, the micromanagement of personnel and office supplies simply constituted part and parcel of the workings of power, governance, and governmentality.[21] Jo-Anne Pemberton has argued that the League was, at its core, a global bureaucracy that pursued information as part of its mission to promote the "Western" values of standardization, rationalization, and scientific management.[22] Focusing on these more ritualized aspects of the League's informational work leads us toward analyzing and interpreting *processes* and away from evaluating specific *outcomes*, or the lack there of.[23]

If one spends time reading the League's document trail from the archives to the published reports, a certain pattern of nonresolution does emerge. Memos called for meetings, and meetings called for additional investigative committees, and committees called for conferences, and conferences produced published reports, which often simply explained why a definitive decision on the matter in question remained out of reach. That song and dance recurs in every subject and every section of the League's vast repository of initiatives.[24] However, each of those stanzas contains multifold sediments of meaning, subtexts, and connotations.[25]

There is another point of departure located within the missing typewriter. As media historian Friedrich Kittler reminded us, the typewriter was linked ab initio to industrialized warfare. The Remington Company had made a fortune producing firearms during the American Civil War. Some years after the war ended, the company made up for their loss of business by using the same equipment to produce a new "miraculous writing machine." Giving the timing of the typewriter's emergence, public commentaries celebrated the possibility that the clicking of fingers on keys might eventually put an end to the staccato of artillery fire.[26] However, the birth of the typewriter did not initiate an era of perpetual peace on earth. Rather, the typewriter's appearance marked another episode (in a long history of such episodes) where claims to power rested on a rhetorical juxtaposition of words and weapons. The point is not to "resolve" the binary, but rather to explore how the assertion and reassertion of that binary actually masked the profound connections between crafting narratives and exercising power. After all, Remington supplied both *rifles* and *typewriters* to the Allies during World War I.[27]

Remington's mixed history in the conjoined industries of words and warfare offers an opportunity to think in a different key about the League's informational objectives. On paper, the League's mission to influence world public opinion rested on the apparent neutrality of information. In that perspective, words and knowledge were simply raw materials that various actors or agencies could use to build bridges between diverse peoples and cultures. The interwar moment is certainly full of echoes of that precise faith in the pacific power of global cultural and intellectual exchange.[28] The Belgian author, lawyer, and bibliographer Paul Otlet spent the better part of his adult life trying to build his Mundaneum, which was to serve as a repository of all the world's knowledge.[29] As Alex Wright has argued, in that project, Otlet had conceived of an earlier iteration of the worldwide web, where researchers from anywhere could remotely access millions of books, newspapers, images, and sound recordings.[30]

At first blush, there is a shared mission and a shared set of values in Otlet's Mundaneum and the League's information factory—both seemed to extoll the manifold benefits of open and global information flows. However, just as Remington typewriters emerged from the profits of warfare, the League emerged from the victory of the allied powers in the First World War.[31] We might then consider the extent to which the League's cherished arsenal of informational weapons was truly open and "neutral." For this, we need to step out of the League's records for a brief moment and go back to those of the post–World War I peace settlements.

On February 12, 1919, Walter S. Rogers, communications expert of the American Commission to Negotiate Peace, submitted a memorandum to President Wilson on "Wire and Radio Communications," which outlined "the immediate communication issues present at the Peace Conference." Rogers saw communication as central to the League's capacity to maintain peace. However, Rogers felt that the nations gathered at the Peace Conference should establish communication from a "comprehensive world view point" and suggested that "the important cables of the world be internationalized and put under the control of the League of Nations and that the League undertake the development of cable communication for the general welfare."[32] This suggestion was, however, respectfully declined. Neutrality would result in too great a loss of private profits, and of national public power.

Denying the internationalization of the cable system helps mark the extent to which the League grew from and remained embedded in postwar power structures, which had come to depend increasingly on information networks. If we look closely, we can see not only how the League's "information factory" came to reflect overlapping power-knowledge dynamics, but also, in the words of Marc Flandreau, how "forms of knowing" linked up with "forms of owning."[33] As we will see, the League's production and (uneven) distribution of forms of truth helped to secure both pecuniary and political monopolies on the world stage.[34] In what follows, I look at how and to what ends the League produced symbolic capital for the geopolitical order sealed into place after World War I. The more the League stressed the power of the word to prevent war, however, the more dissenting voices pushed back, not only against the League but also against the word itself. Countervisions and countertruths also circulated into and back out of the League, through the League's ample correspondence, public meetings, and publicity projects. In the end, increasingly totalitarian regimes used those same tools to disavow "talk" and to extoll and justify the use of violence at home and abroad.

Symbolic Capital and the World Picture

Michael Hardt and Antonio Negri have argued that international organizations emerged to provide forms of "symbology" for the elite global control and management of commodities, money, and populations.[35] While I share a similar view, I think of the League's information factory as having produced "symbolic capital" rather than symbology as such. For one, the concept of symbolic capital breaks down more sharply the opposition between information on the one hand and profits, power, and resources on the other. After all, the sources of power and wealth had become more and more immaterial in nature in the information age. Just as advertising generated surplus value by increasing desire, the intangible assets of reputation and credibility had also come to matter increasingly, not only for a state's political legitimacy at home and on the world stage, but also for individuals', corporations', and states' ability to gain access to credit markets.[36] Recent work in the history of sovereign debt regimes and the birth of credit-rating agencies help further demonstrate the ways in which the reputation of states also determined their position on the world stage.[37]

As a *global* center for the production of symbolic capital, part of what the League helped to produce was a series of *representations* of the world itself, which then were linked to specific international divisions of labor, distribution of resources, and balances of power,[38] though such representational strategies long proceeded the interwar moment. In the sixteenth century, ecumenical worldviews vied for preeminence in the scramble for trade routes and "new territories." As Mark Crispin Miller has argued, it was Pope Gregory XV that first coined the term *propaganda* in 1622. Frightened by the spread of Protestantism, the pope created "the office for the propagation of the Faith" (*Congregation de propaganda fide*), to accelerate the church's missionary zeal alongside expanding geopolitical horizons: "They are to take account of and to deal with each and every concern for the spread of the faith throughout the world."[39] It was never just souls at stake but rather the extent to which the number of souls remained tied to securing an expanding portfolio of worldly opportunities and goods.[40]

In his essay "Age of the World Picture," the German philosopher Martin Heidegger argued that other and more secular worldly representation also emerged, which grew from and were sustained by growing empiricisms, including calculations, measurements, and the collecting of all manner of "facts" about the world.[41] As he stated: "There begins that way of being human which means the realm of human capability as a domain given over to measuring and executing, for the purpose of gaining mastery over that which is as a *whole*."[42] The production of each "world picture" also produced the relative position of subjects—and, I would argue, states—in terms of where they stood in reference to the whole. As Heidegger argued: "In such producing, man contends for the position in which he can be that particular being who gives the measure and draws up the guidelines for everything that is."[43] Heidegger implied that whoever produced the world picture also created the hegemonic standards for determining and then demonstrating which peoples or states were greater and which lesser.[44] Competing visions of world order thus came replete with the criteria of inclusion and exclusion, measured in terms of financial, political or cultural, or racial "worthiness."

Taking a cue from Heidegger, the League's information factory appears in some ways to have played a similar role on the world stage to that of world's fairs and colonial exhibitions.[45] As Timothy Mitchell has argued, those nineteenth-century creations also produced world pictures, as experiential microcosms of the entire global order of things. The exhibits put the world on display, with evidence of the "stages" of civilization organized from the behaviors of the most "primitive" peoples, to the accomplishments of the most "advanced." What is more each nation-state attempted to outdo the other, displaying its relative scientific, cultural, and military prowess.[46] I claim that what these exhibitions help us see more clearly is how the techniques of modern power functioned increasingly through the fusion of the strategies of *mise-en-scène* (producing words, images, ideas, facts, and criteria), of *mise-en-valeur* (developing and acquiring material wealth worldwide), and finally of *mise-en-place* (securing political territory, populations, and above all a state's global "position").[47]

Most of the League's work—informational or otherwise—was similarly oriented toward producing symbolic capital for the world picture, which reinforced the political hierarchies, territorial settlements, and reparations arrangements forged in World War I.[48] Even the League's membership criteria had a role to play in guarding this symbolic-as-material order. Questions of who would be allowed to join, and then who could or could not perform certain functions, under what conditions, and (as we will see) in what languages, were just some of the ways that the League produced, distributed, or withheld symbolic capital.[49] What is more, beyond the politics of membership, the League also published all manner of orthodoxy and best practices.[50] Those standards in the fields of finance, social questions, health and hygiene, and labor, then, became part of the narratives of the universal paths to progress and yet, as such, also provided justifications for granting or denying membership, participation, credit, or even statehood. [51]

The question still left unanswered from this perspective is—given that so many states had sophisticated public relations arms in the interwar moment, including world's fairs—why the League emerged at all. Here we might benefit from thinking about the League's emergence the way that economists think about the emergence of the firm.[52] Theorists of the firm argue that if markets worked perfectly, there would be no need for corporations. Thus, they try to discern the nature and kind of "market failures" that lead agents to coalesce and conglomerate their activity under a single roof. Theorists of international organizations (IOs) also sometimes think in this key. Namely, they ask what kinds of "system failures" lead states to outsource some of their diplomatic functions to IOs.[53] The useful point of these lines of thought is not their specific conclusions, but rather their way of asking.[54] For thinking about the "systems" failures of the First World War does offer a different perspective on the League's emergence in general and its truth functions in particular.

My suggestion here is that the League's symbolic role on the world stage grew in part out of the extent to which the violence, destruction, and financial burdens of the First World War created a global *crisis of credibility* for the European-dominated world picture.[55] In this way, the existing mechanisms were insufficient to meet the considerable symbolic capital needs of the partially *discredited* liberal, capitalist, imperial system.[56] If the value of the *word* had increased, it was partially because the value of the *sword* had fallen sharply in the trenches.

Credit, Credibility, and the "Decline of the West"

In 1915, Sigmund Freud spoke of how the trenches had revealed human instincts "in all their nakedness," in contrast to the belle époque's rhetoric of the mannerly march of progress.[57] Suddenly the key insights of psychoanalysis gained more traction, as the war cast light on mankind's darker impulses, confirming the link between the libido and aggression.[58] As Freud implied, those existential crises also had poignant political repercussions. As Oswald

Spengler outlined the eminent *Decline of the West*, many others turned their attention to the nature of the sickness that had caused the war in the first place.[59] Some went so far as to claim that Europe's heart of darkness had been beating steadily in the so-called century of peace before 1914. The blood from the Somme ran backward through time, by ship and by train, via European banks, to King Leopold's Congo.[60] Already Leopold's violence in the Congo had created a credibility crisis for imperialism.[61] The war thus created a fresh opportunity to cast light on a continuity between the violence of colonialism and the barbarism of the trenches.[62]

Throughout the nineteenth and early twentieth centuries, the so-called standards of civilization had long provided leading (Western) industrial and colonial powers forms of valuation for drawing global and local boundaries of inclusion and exclusion. In that nineteenth-century European-dominated world picture, civilization became a measure for granting or denying a range of rights from personal enfranchisement (for individuals), to political sovereignty (for states or would-be states) to market access (for both individuals and states).[63] As the claim went, then, in resorting to savagery, the great powers had discredited their rights to be, in Heidegger's terms: "that particular being who gives the measure and draws up the guidelines for everything that is."[64]

As the measure of "civilization" fell into disrepute, other forms of political unrest took root.[65] As Lenin spoke in 1915: "Socialists must explain to the masses that they have no other road of salvation except the revolutionary overthrow of "their" governments, and that advantage must be taken of these governments' embarrassments in the present war precisely for this purpose."[66] There were other critiques growing beyond Europe as well. Gandhi's Indian nationalism found an opportunity to extend the scope and the *credibility* of its own claims in the postbellum moment.[67] In his *Disillusioned India*, the nationalist activist Dhan Gopal Mukerji declared:

> This non-violent revolution, if it succeeds, may prove an epoch making event in world history. Not only does passive resistance create a purer spiritual atmosphere, it will actually prevent most of the death, wounding and destruction which war involves. The limit is soon reached, where soldiers will refuse to strike or kill the defenseless. India has given many religions to the world. She may now be giving a new method of gaining political freedom without resort to war.[68]

India's nonviolence supposedly rendered it fully "ready" and "worthy," not only for independence, but also to offer an example to the rest of the world of the path of nonviolence.

In light of these alternative orders circulating through the international media, in his study *The Origin, Structure and Working of the League of Nations*, the Australian soldier turned British intelligence agent Charles Howard Ellis described the League's primary function in unequivocal terms. He stated: "In its deepest significance the League is the spearhead in the international field of a movement for recasting civilization."[69] According to Ellis, "recasting civilization" meant proving that the Great War had been a deviation from the values of Western civilization, rather than their natural outcome. He argued that "war is a collapse of civilization, not a means of defending it."[70] Ellis went further in his effort to distance the values of the modern West from the archaic aberration of war. He urged that "war as an institution or method is vastly more anti-social, cruel and stupid than, e.g., ritual cannibalism, trial by ordeal, the duel, witch-burning, the Inquisition, and a host of other dead tyrannies and superstitions."[71] World War I had marked a falling away from those ideals, rather than their organic continuity.[72]

By putting war alongside regressive practices such as "cannibalism," Ellis created a new opportunity to posit the League as the true symbol of "Western civilization" as it was meant to be.[73] Writing ten years after the origin of the League, in an essay entitled "Le Civilisation: Le mot et l'idee," the French historian Lucien Febvre announced that "finally we are confident that such civilization, in which we participate, which we propagate, benefit from and popularize, bestows on us all a certain value, prestige, and dignity."[74] Here Febvre opened the door for thinking once again about *symbolic capital* both within and beyond the League. Restoring the prestige value of something called Western civilization was fundamental to the Europe's claims on a global portfolio of other tangible and intangible assets including its colonies.[75]

This brings us back to the importance of the League declaring itself an organization of the *word*. Once again, Freud provided important nuances, for in the late nineteenth century, he had argued that civilization itself rested on the choice of using *rhetoric* rather than brute force. He stated: "But, as an English writer has wittily remarked, the man who first flung a word of abuse at his enemy instead of a spear was the founder of civilization."[76] Just as Freud linked the use of words to civilization and the use of spears to barbarism, the League's own word/sword binaries rested on a similar premise. In being an institution that abnegated violence, the League helped to restore the prestige value of civilization. Once restored, the League could use the power of the word to recertify the standards of civilization, which would in turn certify the post–World War I world order.[77]

In thinking through the post–World War I settlements, the South African statesmen (and architect of apartheid) Jan Smuts stated: "Europe is being liquidated, and the League of Nations must be the heir to this great estate."[78] Not all Europe was being liquidated; Smuts referred primarily to defeated land empires. In another elision, Smuts did not define what he meant by "liquidation," though, in business parlance, *liquidation* refers to the process wherein an insolvent corporate entity is dissolved and its assets distributed among various claimants. In precisely these terms, a few pages later Smuts declared: "Europe requires a liquidator or trustee of the bankrupt estate, and only a body like the League could adequately perform that gigantic task."[79] It is true that many postwar economies were indebted and financially strained.[80] However, in referring to the bankruptcy of the defeated powers, Smuts referred as much to a decline in their geopolitical credibility as to their insolvency in an economic sense. Their defeat in the war meant a loss to the intangible asset of their status on the international stage, and so a subsequent loss of right to their territorial claims.

There too, the standards of civilization became a useful tool for stripping those powers of their territories and some of their assets.[81] The "barbarism" of these powers toward their colonial or minority populations disqualified them from ruling vast empires. Using this claim to reorder the geopolitical map, then, the victor powers forced a form of chapter 11 bankruptcies on the defeated. As such, the involved territories would be reallocated, and in some cases new indemnities (debts) would be assigned in a series of legal treaties (Brest-Litovsk, Versailles, Saint-Germain-en-Laye, Trianon).[82] We should not forget that states also occupied a market position on the world stage; thus, damaging their credibility served also to divest them of their market share.[83]

Disqualifying certain states from controlling colonies was only one side of the equation. The other side was determining what to do about the relevant territories once liberated.[84] The League of Nations' Permanent Mandate Commission (PMC) took up the task of reallocating those colonies. Here, as Pedersen has so brilliantly demonstrated, the model was not annexation but rather trusteeship. The newly assigned imperial powers would simply manage the territories, until such a time as the territories became ready for self-government.[85] The PMC would then observe and monitor to make sure that each governing power kept the interests of the indigenous populations at heart. In terms of our story, what matters is that the PMC operated as a kind of metaphor for the League's broader role in the international system.

> To those colonies and territories which as a consequence of the late war have ceased to be under the sovereignty of the States which formerly governed them and which are inhabited by peoples not yet able to stand by themselves under the strenuous conditions of the modern world, there should be applied

the principle that the well-being and development of such peoples form a sacred *trust* of civilization and that *securities* for the performance of this *trust* should be embodied in this Covenant.[86]

As with liquidation, the notions of trust and trusteeship also have an economic, as well as a political connotation. Reading the Covenant in this way, it is possible to think of the PMC as a kind of trust fund: the third-party management of a "trust" dedicated to investing in "securities" to increase the value of the civilizational ideal. While the mandates system concerned only those territories directly involved in the territorial resettlement, the purpose of the system was bound up with the goal of restoring the reputation of imperialism as a valid form of governmentality.[87]

Here we can also reconsider Pedersen's claim that a great deal of what the PMC accomplished was informational in nature.[88] It held meetings and gathered statistics and reports produced by the governing powers. It received and reviewed petitions from the colonial populations, also mostly for informational purposes. It also produced knowledge about its work's significance for "guiding" the backward forward. Beyond mere legitimizing discourse, using information to increase the symbolic value of civilization also reinforced the slow, linear timeline to "progress," "development," and then, eventually, to statehood.

From its start then, the PMC certified a supposedly objective set of standards for defining and demarcating the relative developmental position of the various territories.[89] As a way for formalizing (and justifying) the distribution of assignments, every mandate received an alphabetic label, or a grade from A to C, with A as the most civilized and most developed, and C the least.[90] It is perhaps more than coincidental that the grading of the mandates emerged simultaneously with emerging sovereign credit-rating regimes. In the post–World War I period, agencies such as Moody's Investment Services began extending their rating system to nation-states. Those agencies also generated alphabetic criteria that ranked sovereign states by their credit worthiness as such: AAA (minimal risk) with many shades before C, which predicted default with little chance of recovery.[91]

There were other ways that financial and information management remained (at least nominally) intertwined at the League. As the League officials set up the PMC, they also piloted financial rehabilitation schemes and access to capital markets for new and newly restructured states affected by the World War I settlements.[92] The League lent its own credibility for those states deemed sufficiently developed for statehood and yet not "credit worthy" on their own merit.[93] When Ellis described the myriad of ways that the League might help recast civilization, he argued: "A state gains prestige by promptly and loyally fulfilling its obligations as a member of the League."[94] For some smaller states, that meant abiding by a whole range of criteria and being willing to submit to the League's financial and political oversight of their domestic affairs.[95]

At the same time, this set of processes provides additional insight into why, especially European so-called great powers, joined and supported the work of the League. Beyond credibility and prestige, membership at the League also offered forms of reputation laundering, especially for states that had lost credibility through the use of violence either in World War I or in their colonies. It is significant that India occupied a unique position as the only colony to also be an original member of the League.[96] It had secured that place as a concession from Britain amid postwar negotiations. [97] We might ponder the fact that Britain suddenly made a seat at the League for its only colony not only engaged in a *nonviolent* struggle for independence, but whose nationalist leaders had hinted at India's inherent cultural *superiority* of nonviolence. What is more, claims to India's inherent civilizational superiority may have started to ring as dangerously true given the British Empire's massacre of unarmed protestors in Amritsar in 1919.[98] Of course India—the aspiring nation—was not officially represented at the League at all, only India the protectorate of the British Empire.[99] As a discursive proof of that distinction, the British government made a strange demand. The first pages of the printed records of the League's Assembly meetings listed all the participating delegations for each session alphabetically. Keeping up appearances of juridical equality, the members were not ranked, but merely recognized, without reference to who was politically greatest or least among them. Albania stood naturally before Czechoslovakia, Estonia before France, and France before Germany. There was however, one exception to the rule. Set apart with an asterisk, India appeared—*out of order*—indented by a quarter of an inch under Great Britain.[100]

The League's advertising platform meant that something as seemingly inconsequential as the list of delegates had tremendous symbolic significance. British colonial government officials insisted that, just as India was not ready for independent statehood, it should not stand autonomously between Hungary and Lithuania in any of the League's publications. In these ways we can see how the League's informational preoccupations remained tied to producing symbolic capital toward a very specific world picture. Still, to simply use these forms of evidence to assert that the League was a sham, or that it abjectly failed to provide a progressive or inclusive multigovernmental platform, would be to miss other important effects.[101]

Even as the League helped produce symbolic capital for the status quo, it faced a reputational paradox.[102] The League's own credibility depended in part on fulfilling liberalist promises of greater inclusion.[103] As such, the League also created a (semi)public forum, where a plethora of voices could (at least try to) speak their minds, and air their grievances. To those ends, League membership also offered small, new, or economically less powerful states valuable forms of international visibility and credibility that they might not be able to afford otherwise.[104] For example, some Indian nationalists expressed satisfaction that having a presence in Geneva would secure a kind of de facto diplomatic recognition in advance of de jure sovereign status. To the extent that the League provided a global billboard where states and peoples publicly proclaimed or contested their lot, simply *being* there (or deciding not to be there) sent a message.

Perhaps the greatest historical curiosity of the League is the extent to which it generated an intimate space were the global tensions of de jure equality and de facto inequality came into direct contact. For this reason, the means of communication often provided something of a Trojan horse by which other conflicts entered the League. Every tool the League used to produce and hold its world picture static also provided the means by which others suggested edits or alterations to the scene.

The World in a Box of Slides

Of all the League's numerous efforts to produce and certify a certain world picture, among the most evocative is a collection of photographic slides. In 1924, the League's Information Section (under the leadership of Herbert Ames) undertook a project to create a vast series of lantern slides. Since their invention in the nineteenth century, pictorial slide shows had become popular instruments of both entertainment and pedagogy.[105] In 1908, one B. B. Dickinson wrote an article for the *Geographical Teacher* dedicated to praising the merits of this marvelous machine. He stated: "The lanternslide (or photograph) is the only possible way of connecting nature with its representation on a map."[106] The slides allowed geography students to leave the flat and lifeless maps behind and travel the world all while seated at their desks. The League had similar views. For this reason, it dedicated time and resources (even going over budget) to creating slides representing the postwar world and the League's place within it. Once it was complete, the League used the two-hundred-plus slides at its own promotional tours and also made them available for purchase.[107]

Implicit in the use of these slides was the idea that somehow pictures could offer more solid forms of "truth" than could words.[108] If words could slip away from their referents, photographs seemed to offer perfect correspondence between the image and the reality it captured.[109] Of course film was the other visual media par excellence, and the League also worked with and through that art form, especially in the domain of so-called educational cinema.[110] Films too offered a powerful medium for generating "world pictures," capable of convincing or captivating crowds.[111]

There is something about the still and the silent photograph, and so too about the lantern slide project, however, that offers a particularly illuminating view of the League's truth-production machinery. In his treatise on the subject of photographs, *Camera Lucida*, Roland Barthes spoke of that illusion of true reality created through the still image: "By nature, the Photograph ... has something tautological about it; a pipe, here, is always and intractably a pipe."[112] It was that apparently more static, mimetic quality that lingered in the League's plan to use photographs to help produce a *stable* world picture.

There had also been other interwar efforts to capture and represent the whole world through photographs. Between the years 1909 and 1931, the French banker and philanthropist Albert Khan sent photographers on missions all over the world to "capture" the earth's diverse forms of life, including the peoples, landscapes, commercial activities, and architecture.[113] In that visual repository, which appears as a sibling project to Paul Otlet's Mundaneum, Khan compiled an astounding seventy-two thousand colored photographs.[114] There is little doubt that like Otlet, Kahn also had his own *discursive logic*, which framed his efforts to bring the world's diversity to the laps of those who could not travel. However, the League's world picture, had a more explicitly politically motivated objective; it set out to show the *universal* benefits of the world order and orderings that the League hoped to certify and promote.

The slide show opened with the League's own emergence, its origin myths, and their pomp and circumstance. In this way the audiences could participate vicariously in all the dramaturgy of the Paris Peace Conference, seeing the momentous signing of treaties, and portraits of distinguished personalities. Then, the viewers could observe the League's first steps, sit in on the first meetings of the Council and the Assembly, and walk through the various buildings. Later, a series of slides would describe in great detail all the League's additional organs; the International Labor Organization, the Economic and Financial Committee, the Permanent Mandate Commission, and so on and so forth.[115]

From the technical picture of the League's organization, the presentation zoomed outward to the world map—another representational form that invariably laid claim to a specific world picture.[116] In this map, as in that of the fifteenth-century Treaty of Tordesillas, the world appeared divided into two parts. The League's map divided the world between those states that belonged to the League and those states that did not. As a supplement to that geographical set of divisions, there was also a graph demonstrating the precise monetary contributions of each member, a visual aid to illuminate who contributed more and who less.[117] Those slides seemed to recall an earlier statement by Jan Smuts, who pondered how the League should "weight" its members' votes: "If Guatemala counts as one, what value shall be given to the USA? Will it be 5, or 10, or 100, or 1000? Will the valuation proceed on the basis of wealth or population or territory? For if it's population China is first and if it's wealth then it's the USA."[118]

There were also a number of slides dedicated to depicting the organization's various successes. Pictures and graphs denoted the successful resolutions of the Polish-Lithuanian and Aland Islands disputes. Other slides covered the unique situations of Upper Silesia, Danzig, and the Sarre basin and the League's work in those provinces.[119] There were also slides of particularly evocative and historic moments, for example, a picture of an enrobed "King of Ethiopia" presenting gifts of gold and ivory to the future secretary-general Joseph Avenol. Of course, there were inevitably a few disappointments along the way. The Information Section had dearly wanted a picture of a poppy field in Afghanistan to represent the work of the Opium Board. However, given the difficulty of obtaining such a picture, they settled for more pedestrian images of "chemists and druggists at work."[120]

Herbert Ames—a specialist of finance—was particularly eager to illustrate the successes of the reconstruction of Austria and Hungary.[121] In the case of Austria, Ames wanted to find a way to dramatize the League's positive impact on currency stabilizations. Ames asked his staff to find and photograph a small house that would have cost around 14,400 krone in 1913. He then wanted a comparative slide showing the precise amount of bread and cheese that one could have purchased for 14,400 krone during the worst tides of hyperinflation.[122] Despite considerable efforts and a multiday scouting mission, the League functionaries on the spot in Austria never found such a house. In March 1924, one Arthur Pelt wrote to Ames: "I am still trying hard to get a photo of a 14,000 Kr house but I am told by a real estate agent that, in the whole town of Vienna, this small type of cottage is not to be found."[123] After this surprising roadblock (for Ames felt certain he had correctly estimated the cost of pre–World War I Austrian real estate), Pelt proposed a different solution.[124] In a letter to Ames, Pelt wrote: "I suggest, that instead of this photo, we have a lantern slide made of a double chart, the lesser part of which shows the fall of the crown from the Armistice until the League stepped in and the second part should show the stability of the crown since the reconstruction plan is working."[125] Ames was disheartened but accepted this less evocative mode of representation.

Yet another subseries of slides illustrated the topic of the "Greek Refugee Settlement Loan," which had, among other things, helped to subsidize the Greek and Turkish exchange of populations. As article 1 of the Convention concerning the Exchange of Greek and Turkish Populations reads:

> As from the first of May, 1923, there shall take place a compulsory exchange of Turkish nations of the Greek Orthodox religion established in Turkish territory, and of Greek nations of the Moslem religion established in Greek territory. These persons shall not return to live in Turkey or Greece respectively without the authorization of the Turkish Government or of the Greek Government respectively.[126]

The lantern slides focused on the positive outcome of this "compulsory exchange." The text for those slides went as follows: "After the Greek Army evacuated Asia Minor in 1922, about 1,200,000 Greeks which up until then had lived under Turkish rule fled to Greece, suddenly increasing the population of that country by 20%."[127] Evidently this influx of refugees had caused enormous problems for the already strained Greek economy. The text continued: "The Greek government and people were unable to deal satisfactorily with the tremendous problem of establishing this mass of refugees. On their request, the League stepped in and facilitated the floating of a loan of 10,000,000 which was to be spent under the joint control of the League and the Greek Government."[128] Thanks to the League's financial aid, the situation had already been "settled." The inflow of funds had served to create new homes and new livelihoods: "At this moment, in the summer of 1926, about a million of these refugees have settled down as peaceful, hard-working citizens of Greece. Some are living in the towns and working in the industries (tapestry, weaving, etc.), others are fishermen on the Ionian-islands, but the big majority is working on the land as farmers; vine and tobacco growers etc."[129] The pictures then included pacific scenes of "everyday life," with recently resettled Greek peoples happily engaged in their various forms of work. Finally, the text concluded: "Thanks to the League the biggest example of forced emigration known in modern history, which might have been a calamity, has in a few years brought peace and prosperity to the country and people concerned."[130] From the close-ups of personal happiness and productivity, the next slides turned to contributions that had made those story lines possible: London had provided US$7.5 million, New York US$11 million, Athens

US$2.5 million. The surplus revenue that went to the International Financial Committee amounted to US$2,921,586. The value of the land and buildings transferred for settlement by the Greek Government was US$16.4 million.[131]

Hidden beneath (or erased from) this picture were the facts of violence and dispossession that played out during that wave of forced emigration. The recent literature on the subject has described the whole process as tantamount to an act of coordinated "ethnic cleansing."[132] To the extent that the League's world picture produced and secured the positions of peoples and states, it also provides an opportunity to ponder the links between the management of informational public spheres and the techniques of biopower, or, once again, to show forged links between mise-en-scène, mis-en-valeur, and mise-en-place.

Where modern states regulated bodies and questions of life and death within borders, international organizations helped settle questions of *fixity* and *mobility* on the world stage.[133] The year 1919 was a moment when the task of demobilizing appeared fragile precisely to the extent that the war had mobilized bodies across borders, which could transform rapidly into networks of protest. The task of the treaties was not only to redraw national borders, but also to control the movement of bodies, and, then, to remobilize the international flow of capital.[134] Beyond creating formalized criteria of development (ABC, AAA, BBB, CCC) and timelines for achieving it, the League helped discern other questions of position in terms of *movement* or *immobility*. Settling the status of refugees (mise-en-place), regulating human trafficking, negotiating passport regimes, and advocating for free trade—all these questions implied a world order where some people and some goods could move across borders, and oceans, and others needed to remain frozen within them. The luxury of mobility (vertically or horizontally) was also pre-inscribed in the details of the League's slide show.

The Information Section even created different versions of its slide show for different audiences. After seeing the slides on the territorial readjustments after World War I, Pablo de Azcárate of the League's Minorities Section warned Herbert Ames of a potential tender point. He argued that the maps depicting the new borders created at Versailles and the "minority composition" of new states might cause trouble amid European audiences.[135] As a whole, the League was asked to stand guard over the finality of the borders generated after World War I and to make sure that the human bodies designated to each territory remained there, consenting to their newly assigned nationalities. Being on the receiving end of petitions from minority populations in new states (covered in next chapter), Azcárate knew very well how the League's picture of the world might stir up political discord, which might lead to requests for the revision of borders. In light of Azcárate's concern, Ames created an "Anglo-American set" and a "European set," and then promised: "I shall take care that no slides that cause trouble shall be used in the European sets."[136] Through the lantern slides project the League worked to ensure that knowledge would flow in certain directions and not in others.[137] The slide show constituted just one case in a range of the League's publicity and educational campaigns that sought to reach only certain audiences and with certain messages.[138]

Once again, the point here is not the League's failure to achieve its claims of equality or "universality"; rather the point is to reveal the extent to which the League's publicity efforts sought to generate stable truths. Returning to Barthes, *Camera Lucida* posed the following: "It is as if the Photograph always carries its referent with itself, both affected by the same amorous or funereal immobility, at the very heart of the moving world: they are glued together, limb by limb, like the condemned man and the corpse in certain tortures."[139] For those League functionaries working on publicity, the photograph appeared as a powerful tool for creating a stationary "world picture" (limb by limb), which would ensure that the position of some people and places remained "fixed."[140]

Despite the fact that the lantern slide project was geared toward creating representational *stability*, photographs were never straightforward mediums of truth telling.[141] Instead, they were among the media that best served the *arts of illusion*. Lantern slides had long been called *magic lanterns*, as nineteenth-century entertainers would use them to conjure ghosts or spirits or merely to display a series of physical impossibilities.[142] In other words, photographs could equally lead a spectator to question his or her eyes rather than simply believing them.[143] In the ominous year of 1939, the Academie Francaise invited the poet Paul Valery to reflect on photography's impact on literature. While ultimately positive about the marvelous medium, Valery also issued some conceptual caveats: "the more we are tempted to see some underlying connection between the phenomenon called realism and the phenomenon called 'Photography,' the more we must be aware of exploiting a coincidence."[144] In another passage he affirmed: "I might add that photography even makes so bold as to practice an art in which the word has, from time immemorial, specialized; the art of lying."[145]

As Martin Jay has argued, the capacity of photography to serve "mendacity" is less a function of the thing in itself, and more of the "discursive assumptions" at work at the moment of its production and reproduction. The photograph, Jay claimed—with its unique ability to both show and tell—can naturalize or denaturalize, affirm or deny an existing sociopolitical order and its claims to truth.[146] This provides a theoretical point of entry for considering the instances where dramatic contests of assertion and counterassertion took place through the medium of photographs at League.

When fascist Italy invaded the sovereign nation of Ethiopia in 1935, it used the League's public forum to try to legitimatize its actions. Even after explicitly violating the League's principle of national sovereignty, Italy hoped to sway the League (and through the League, the world) to its point of view. To those ends, the Italian delegation brought a wide range of textual and photographic evidence to bear. Among those many files was included photographic proof of Ethiopia as a supposedly barbarous people, unfit for self-rule.[147] Namely, it furnished photographs of Ethiopian practices of slavery as evidence of the African country's unworthiness of full sovereignty.[148] In this battle for evidentiary truth, Italy revived the standards of civilization, but this time as justification for turning a sovereign state into a colony. It also claimed its own resort to violence had been fully justified in response to the need first to tame, and then to civilize the so-called savages. In protest, the Ethiopian delegation responded in kind and in turn. It brought its own counterevidence to the League, photographs depicting the savagery of the Italian conquest, including Italy's use of chemical weapons. Photographs of dead Ethiopian soldiers, with burned and bubbled skinned, provided the arc of the Ethiopian story line and supported its effort to depict Italians as the "real savages."[149]

In the end the League placed (weak) economic sanctions on Italy, and the Italian delegation eventually (publicly, dramatically) withdrew from the League, as a message to the world. To the extent that the League helped generate symbolic capital through specific regimes of truth, there was no way to make those truths hold still. Italy's efforts to challenge its own position on the world stage—in particular its relative lack of colonial possessions compared to the other victors—quickly devolved into a stalemate of different versions of the truth. The League members could not keep the Italian government from using the recently refurbished standards of civilization as justification for violating another of the League's values—the sacrosanctity of sovereignty.

There were thus always subversive possibilities in the League's public pulpit and projectors, even if they were designed to preserve the status quo.[150] At the end of his foreword to de Traz's text, Maurois lingered on one example, where a Chinese delegate stood "voiceless" before his audience of colleagues who failed to take his soft-spoken, awkward orations seriously. However, according to Maurois's account, the operator in charge of the acoustic arrangements in the Assembly simply pressed a button to increase the volume of the microphone. Thereafter, he stated, "the Chinese suddenly acquires by means of an invisible apparatus a marvelously strong voice. The sleepy listeners sit up, in their minds a resuscitated China becomes a menace to Europe."[151] According to Maurois, the Assembly's technical arrangements gave previously inaudible powers a literally amplified platform from which to speak and receive recognition on the world stage. Maurois further asserted that in general the boldness of a delegate's words had to be "inversely proportional to the war budget which the speaker represents."[152] Maurois's anecdote reveals something about the ways in which the League revealed deeper links between power, wealth, and symbolic capital on the world stage.[153] The anecdote also implied that those dispositive acoustics of *amplification* (microphones, radio stations, photographs, typewriters, or the printing press) could either secure or transgress the stability of the order of things.[154] A microphone is not a camera is not a typewriter. And yet, for those who had the right to use the League's public platform, each of these tools became means through which to disseminate different truths (born of differently discursive assumptions) toward different audiences and toward different ends. In the 1930s, critics of the League's wordy and cosmopolitan order—such as Italy—often used those means of communication to promote primordial truths, which were designed to support the outright conquest of an alternative world picture.[155]

On Blood and Semiotics

During the political crises of the 1930s, the League continued to emphasize and promote words and images as vital tools for international cooperation and peace.[156] In 1936, the League held the Inter-governmental Conference for the Adoption of a Convention concerning the Use of Broadcasting in the Cause of Peace.[157] That conference set out to create a series of agreements whereby nations would promise to use the powerful instrument of radio for concord rather than conflict. In the opening speech of that gathering on September 16, 1936, the Norwegian delegate Arnold Raestead, described the perimeters of the work ahead: "Gentlemen, the draft on which you will base your discussions is frankly universalist in tendency." With those universal ambitions in view, Raestead then reminded his colleagues of some potential dangers of the medium under consideration. He stated: "Political broadcasting has enormous potentialities as a means of fomenting international discord."[158]

The precise nature of the radio's power and danger rested with the ways it might slip past borders as an invisible saboteur. Again Raestead stated: "Broadcasts have no material substance, and therefore cannot be stopped at frontiers; they can be directed towards any point in space; the political effects may be extensive and immediate; but they are not easy to foresee, or to control or canalize at need."[159] He then likened radio to other "means of destruction" (presumably chemical weapons, or biological pathogens) that could move through the air and create untold suffering.[160] Just as the League had set out to limit the use of material weapons, it also needed to curtail the use of immaterial ones.[161]

At one level, the League's concern over the political use and misuse of radio appears retrospectively as a futile attempt to curb the growing bond between fascist governments and the media. The Frankfurt school theorists Max Horkheimer and Theodor Adorno provided a compelling case when they stated: "National Socialists knew that broadcasting gave their causes stature as the printing press did to the Reformation. The Fuhrer's metaphysical charisma . . . turned out finally to be merely the omnipresence of his radio addresses; which demonically parodies that of the divine spirit."[162] Yet while their assessment has long occupied a prominent place in the literature on the links between cultures of media and violence, the League's records add additional nuances to those claims of "mass manipulation."

The world picture emanating from the League marked one effort to cover the whole world in specific truth notions, which also implied a certain political and economic hierarchy. But as Raestead's concern with the "invisibility" of radio implies, information weapons were always both powerful and somehow suspect in that they were easy to manipulate and yet difficult to fully control. Thus, to the extent that the League aligned itself so closely with the power of words and data, and slides, resistance against the League's world picture, often began as charges of unreality, or dissimulation.

From cradle to grave the League embodied and reflected this paradox; where controlling images and words as truth provided a means of controlling people and resources, the reality of those images and narratives could always be called into question. This brings us full circle to the typewriter. In 1944, Heidegger criticized that instrument for denigrating the "role of the hand" in writing: "Mechanical writing deprives the hand of its rank in the realm of the written word and degrades the word to a means of communication."[163] But why should the hand constitute a superior form of truth to that of the mechanical keys? Given Heidegger's own problematic relationship with National Socialism, it is worth pondering how and why the post–World War I world picture dissolved into calls for (a violent) return to the real.[164]

Interwar fascisms supposedly offered a world bound by the security of superior blood of one single ethnos or people. A bit of Nazi Propaganda went like this: "National Socialism . . . is exclusively a 'volkic' political doctrine based upon racial principles."[165] That doctrine tried to silence all competing realities, offering instead just one single "totality," which promised its chosen people promised better positions (status and livelihoods), deeper spiritual satisfactions (religion and political theology), and forms of absolute certainty (homogeneity ensured through violence).

Rather than seeing fascism as a local and violent regime cast against the global and peaceful ones born at the League, what we see instead were two universalist paradigms, each vying over the same informational mediums to secure a specific world picture.[166] As the Nazi propagandist Alfred Rosenberg put it in 1930: "Humanity, the universal church, or the sovereign ego, divorced from the bonds of blood, are no longer absolute values for us."[167] Rather he argued: "History and the task of the future no longer signify the struggle of class against class or the conflict between one church dogma and another, but the settlement between blood and blood, race and race, Folk and Folk."[168] The revolution of the German soul, according to Rosenberg, was also a "world revolution" against "racial chaos." We might say that typewriters were taking a back seat once gain to the production of machine guns. But, as we have already seen, it was never so simple. By December 1936, Rosenberg had sold over half a million copies of his book in Germany.[169] As it turns out, the proliferation of words had helped promote, rather than prevent, general rearmament.

Because words were both weapons and forms of symbolic capital, the question of language itself became another front in this battle for eyes, ears, and souls of the world. From its very beginning, language questions threw a wrench in the gears of the League's information factory.

3

On True and False Tongues

> The term Volk [people] is now as customary in spoken and written language as salt at table, everything is spiced with a soupcon of Volk.
> VICTOR KLEMPERER, *The Language of the Third Reich*

Linguistic Disordering and Reordering

A line from the Romanian French poet Tristan Tzara's own *Dada Manifesto*, 1918, went like this: "To impose your ABC is a natural thing—hence deplorable. Everybody does it in the form of crystalbluffmadonna, monetary system, pharmaceutical product, or a bare leg advertising the ardent sterile spring."[1] Tzara's indictment played out on a world stage where not only words but language and the alphabets on which they were based increasingly became a domain of technocratic engineering, with designs to remake societies by altering various grammatical structures. The nature of Tzara's radical poetics, which he offered as a counter to the language-power nexus, was randomization. He even went so far as to write poetry by clipping words from newspapers, putting them in paper bags, shaking the bag, and letting the words fall out in nonorder.[2]

In some ways, the fascist tendency to create neologisms, word reversals, and onomatopoeic slogans mirrored the Dadaist desire to sever words from their meanings, so as to create the world anew. The fascist pursuit of *anomie* was not *a* desire for poetic disorder and indeterminacy, but rather a desire to make language serve only highly specific political ends and actions.[3] Tzara had in mind a form of elegiac resistance: "I write this manifesto to show that people can perform contrary actions together while taking on fresh gulp of air; I am against action; for continuous contradiction, for affirmation too."[4] National Socialism, on the other hand, used linguistic alteration and reform to, in words of Hitler, "abolish the liberalistic concept of the individual and the Marxist concept of humanity and to substitute therefore the folk community, rooted in the soil and bound together by the bond of its common blood."[5]

The Nazi regime was far from the only interwar actor that saw in language reform a crucial political project. Given that language constituted one of the factors that bounded communities together, it also became a domain for consolidating or expanding the fates and fortunes of a people.[6] A diverse number of these reordering projects, which clung to questions of language reform in the interwar years, also passed through the League. Those threads and fragments also provide a glimpse of the different ambitions and values that had come to rest on the concept of language itself as a force of world making, especially in the information age.

Language's Two Faces: Fluid Hegemony, Fixed Identity

In 1924, Clarence Augustus Manning, professor of Slavic studies at Columbia University, described the linguistic dimensions of the inherent and potentially volatile tension between the local and the global.[7] Namely, he argued that language was a central component both of national sovereignty and also of global hegemony. Then, with an eerie foreshadowing of future horrors as yet unseen, Manning stated: "Between these two goals humanity fluctuates and must fluctuate indefinitely before *the final solution* is found for the question raised."[8]

It was not only that language carried the conflict between the local and the global as Manning suggested. There were also other tensions at work. Language served both as a fundamental marker of local identity and also as a tool of communication. On the one hand, it linked household to household in the intimacy of shared dialect. On the other hand, it could move through wires and waves, far afield from hearth and home. Even more importantly, in the information age, language had become an increasingly important tool of both governance and *conquest*.[9] The standardization of national languages had played an important part in the growth and consolidation of modern nation-states, especially in the nineteenth century.[10] Then too, expanding communications networks meant that states also competed to establish more global commercial and imperial spheres of linguistic influence.[11]

In 1915, the French linguist Albert Dauzat had asserted: "It will appear more and more that language is one of the principal factors that favor a people's global expansion."[12] In other words, whosoever determined the dialects, grammars, and vocabularies of first national and then transnational public spheres also in some sense ruled them.[13]

At the League, as with information and images, language questions also became bound up with efforts either to preserve or to contest the reigning world picture. Between 1920 and 1939, an astonishing number of language questions made their way to the League's agenda in a number of different domains. In each case, discussions about the use and even the structures of certain languages invariably summoned deeper conflicts over geopolitical power, position, and prestige. In particular, language became a marker of which states could aspire to global hegemony, and which would remain confined to a more localized sphere of influence.

At the first and most obvious level, just as the League extolled the values of international conversation, it also institutionalized French and English as the *only* acceptable official languages at the League.[14] Five years before the League opened its doors, Dauzat had proposed that French and English share the global public sphere, creating a linguistic "entente cordial" that would ruin the aspirations of "pan-Germanism."[15] In some way, the League's Anglo-French language policy helped bring Dauzat's ambition into fruition. However, there were also deeper, explicitly territorial dimensions to that linguistic alliance.

At the Paris Peace Conference, the Committee of New States undertook the massive project of deconstructing the defeated land empires and redistributing their territory and primarily on ethno-linguistic lines. Leon Dominion, a US consultant on territorial questions for the Paris Peace Conference, stated: "Greater possibilities of enduring peace exist whenever the delimitation of new frontiers is undertaken with a view to segregating linguistic areas within separate national borders."[16] And indeed, on the maps left behind by the Peace Conference, the words "LINGUISTIC BORDER" labeled thickly drawn lines crisscrossing Europe.[17] In between those lines appeared the names of states—some new, some revised—that corresponded to these puzzle pieces.[18] In this way, the impossible ideal of one people/one territory became a template for redrawing frontiers amid the ethnically and linguistically diverse populations of the dissolved empires.[19]

Because Europe's new boundaries could not actually accommodate the diverse demographic reality, other statutes had to be devised. Thus, on the maps, within new borders, there were little patches of color identifying islands of minorities that had been cut off from a larger ethno-linguistic unit or were too minor to warrant their own.[20] Thus, the architects of this new order declared that the surest way to prevent future interstate conflict was to assure that those islands of national minorities would retain the right to preserve their own national consciousness without persecution. Decision makers worried that such persecution could lead to either cries for self-determination or irredentist appeals across borders.[21] For this reason, the League of Nations would be tasked with ensuring that new states preserve their minorities' "right to nationality," which included the use of their language in education, commerce, worship, the press, and the courts.[22] As we will see, those Minority

Treaties also created another mechanism for political oversight and intervention into that potentially important and contentious region.

However, as it was with communication technologies, wherever language helped seal the post-Versailles world order into place, it also provided the means of challenging that order. Various actors and agents also mobilized language questions to contest and call into question the underlying power structures over which the League stood guard. For one, there were efforts to have more "official" languages included at the League. However, of greatest interest here is that power politics surrounding language questions led to a whole range of efforts to modify the world picture by reworking the structure, the vocabularies, and even the alphabets of language more broadly.

In that frame, some advocated the use of an artificial language, created and engineered to provide a "neutral" lingua franca for the global public sphere. On the other hand, there were also efforts to improve, modernize, or reform certain national languages as a first step to making them more user friendly for international speakers. However, by the 1930s, language debates and proposals took a darker turn. In an echo of the quest for more concrete and more totalizing forms of "truth" and "reality," some states began extolling the need for the "purity" and "authenticity" of certain languages. Purified mother tongues would first provide a defense against the "impurity" of immigrant dialects and the "inauthenticity" of artificial languages. In many cases these efforts to reform and purify national tongues foreshadowed acts of violence both at "home" and then "abroad." The "purified" German tongue did not remain tucked within the reduced borders of the post–World War I German state but rather would expand, in step with the sword, to reunite and provide living space for a geographically expansive linguistically singular Volk.

Before 1933, however, there were ample discussions already taking place about which languages could aspire to global lingua status, and which would have to endure a more localized fate.

Rewording the Map

At the Paris Peace Conference, a little-known author by the name of Albert William Alderson had been peddling his linguistic plan for world peace. Alderson's pamphlet asserted: "If you want peace you cannot have polyglotism."[23] Alderson suggested that the project of international governance had inherited the curse of Babel. God had scattered the earth's people and confused their tongues precisely at the point where they had cooperated to exceed their limits, to be like God, to have dominion over the earth and the heavens. So how could a world separated by the proliferation of local languages come together again as a single unified human community? Alderson claimed that war would end only when the earth's people once again all spoke a single tongue. To speed up that eventuality, one nation—presumably Britain—would have to use the threat of the sword to force its language on the rest.[24]

There were, however, also other and less violent "total" solutions circulating in the corridors of Versailles.[25] Advocates of invented international auxiliary languages (with names such as Esperanto, Volapük, Ido, Parlamento, Occidental, and Cosmoglotta) had come to appeal to peacemakers to consider the merits of their novel grammars.[26] The speakers of those created tongues also believed that linguistic disunity threatened the project of global peace, which depended on mutual understanding. However, rather than eradicating the rich diversity of mother tongues, all the world's people might instead learn a second, invented tongue.[27] In each case, those languages had flexible vocabularies and used simple grammatical rules so that populations could learn them easily.

There were also much older projects in this frame. As Sheldon Pollock has explored, there were also medieval and early modern variants of idealized cosmopolitan linguistic communities. Sanskrit and Latin, imbued with ecumenical resonances, also sought to tie and to bind speakers and believers alike into forms of kinship within and across regions.[28]

The very fact that communications technologies allowed words to travel at greater distances and more quickly gave new impetus to international languages, which proliferated in the nineteenth century. Before World War I, such artificial languages had gained only limited traction.[29] However, support for an international language germinated in the trenches.[30] For if language could shape reality, and if violent conflict was imbedded in national languages, then (the argument went) international vocabularies might create the immaterial scaffolding to support a permanent cease-fire.[31]

As soon as the League opened its doors in 1920, the Secretariat found itself on the receiving end of hundreds of proposals suggesting the use of an international auxiliary language. Many of those appeals began the same way and followed the same line of argument. The supplicant would first state that the world had grown smaller, pulled together via railways, telegraphs, telephones, and radio. They would then emphasize that the war had proved that a smaller world did not necessarily constitute a more peaceful one, and nations therefore needed new tools to strengthen international understanding. While the creation of a world political organization marked a positive start, the multiplicity of languages weakened the power of discussion, conciliation, and publicity to prevent conflict. What is more, national languages carried the seeds of conflict into the machinery of peacemaking. International-language advocate Montague C. Butler made such a case in a letter to the secretary-general: "On every hand we hear such phrases as 'international cooperation,' 'workers of the world unite,' 'brotherhood of man,' 'League of Nations,' nevertheless the advocates of these ideals are apt to forget the first step is the removal of the language barrier which largely prevents their realization."[32]

By 1920, it was true that the question of official languages was already creating trouble within the global talking shop. During the inaugural Assembly, eighteen delegations proposed that the League consider adding Spanish as an official language alongside French and English.[33] As it turns out, 36 percent of the Assembly came from Spanish-speaking nations, and the delegates thus argued that such significant statistical weight merited serious consideration.[34] In the end, however, a specially appointed committee decided that the dual language system would remain in place. As a concession, the committee agreed to let delegates give speeches in their own tongue, so long as they paid the costs of interpretation.[35]

In that same Assembly, emboldened by the rancor surrounding Spanish, the South African delegate Robert Cecil brought forward a resolution concerning the international language Esperanto. The resolution proposed that the League should at least encourage (if not actively endorse) the teaching of Esperanto in the world's schoolrooms.[36] Of all the international-language schemes, Esperanto gained the most popular institutional support in the postwar period. In the story of its growth and evolution, Esperanto had moved in parallel with the politics of nineteenth-century Europe, back and forth in cycles of national conflict and international expansion.[37] The language's creator, Dr. Ledger Ludwik Zamenhof, was born in 1859 into a Jewish family in Polish Bialystok, a city whose population spoke Russian, Polish, German, and Yiddish.[38] In that context, Zamenhof began studying international languages in hope that they might create a sense of community across linguistic divides. After considerable research, Zamenhof decided to create his own language, Esperanto meaning "one who hopes" in 1887.[39]

By the early twentieth century, Esperanto had gained a small but growing following of international supporters. In 1908, the newly founded Universal Esperanto Association (UEA) attracted members from all over the world. In 1918, the UEA outlined a campaign to encourage the League of Nations to recommend that all its member states include Esperanto as part of national curricula alongside national tongues. After all, the language accomplished what the League promised: a harmonization of nationalism and internationalism. People could continue to use their mother tongues around their own dinner tables, and then reach for Esperanto in the international domain of commerce, travel, or diplomacy.[40] With that, the UEA made a considerable effort to pique the interest of the League and eventually succeeded.[41]

As soon as the proposal in favor of Esperanto hit the Assembly floor, however, it immediately met opposition. The French minister Gabriel Hanotaux fumed at the thought that the League would deny a *real* language such as Spanish and then waste time contemplating the merits of some *fabricated* tongue.[42] Hanotaux also admitted that he feared that Esperanto might damage the international prestige of French.[43] Nevertheless, the Assembly still requested that the Secretariat open an inquiry into the use of Esperanto around the world, especially in the domains of education, commerce, and science.[44]

In 1921, the Secretariat embarked on a fact-finding mission. To those ends, the under-secretary-general, Inazō Nitobe, attended the World Esperanto Congress taking place in Prague that year. Nitobe was not immune to the conference's inspirational tone, and he returned from Prague convinced that Esperanto might help level the international playing field, especially for Asian people struggling to acquire Western languages.[45] What is more, Nitobe saw wisdom in the warning that national languages carried the seeds of war and misunderstanding. He stated: "The towers of Babel are multiplying, making worse than ever intercommunication and intercommunion among the nations of the earth."[46]

In the end, however, Nitobe put his own personal reactions aside and advised the League to avoid any official endorsement of the artificial language.[47] It was too early in the League's life for the organization to risk entangling its fate with any untested movement.[48] However, Nitobe still argued that the League should at least continue to investigate the question. To those ends, the Secretariat sent queries to ministries of education, scientific societies, chambers of commerce, and organizations as varied as the International Association of Poultry Instructors and Investigators and the International Ice Hockey League.[49] According to the report based on those voluminous results, numerous international bodies were in fact actively using Esperanto in 1922.[50] Even more surprisingly, several governments, such as those of Albania, Bulgaria, Japan, China, and Russia, were already experimenting with or at least considering teaching Esperanto in some schools.[51]

When the Secretariat presented its findings in 1922, a heated debate ensued.[52] The Brazilian delegate Raul de Rio Branco fumed that the work of the League must be based on the existence of different nationalities. Later, Rio Branco went so far as to publish a pamphlet outlining the reasons why Esperanto posed a threat to nationality, to the League's legitimacy, and to capitalism itself. There, he stated: "In the hands of that subversive party and its subaltern clients, a universal language would eventually be the language of an anti-national army."⁵³ Though Esperantists claimed that they had no intention of replacing national languages, many feared that once in the hands of any radical party, Esperanto would usher in the withering away of states and market structures.

Despite a tendency to link Esperanto to international communism, the Italian communist Antonio Gramsci had actually criticized the language on opposite grounds.⁵⁴ He denounced it as an elite cosmopolitan creation, the language of the "bourgeois who travels for business or pleasure, of nomads more than of stable productive citizens."⁵⁵ In truth, there was as much evidence to support Gramsci's perceived link between Esperanto and capitalist interests as there was to support the link between Esperanto and communists. Despite the French government's negative position on the issue, the Paris Chamber of Commerce introduced Esperanto courses into its commercial schools during the 1920s. The Italian Chamber of Commerce in Switzerland organized an international conference in support of Esperanto and published the proceedings in 1923.⁵⁶ Those proceedings, which took place entirely in Esperanto, argued that language barriers tended to reinforce trade barriers. Thus, Esperanto might help restore a world of mobile goods and capital.

Gramsci and Rio Branco thus found some common but improbable ground: they both feared that Esperanto undermined the ability of language to serve a specific relationship between politics and the economy. There was indeed some evidence that many Esperantists expressed a strong commitment to loosen the ties binding language and a certain kind of "official" politics. One revealing case study along these lines involves the unique role that the Swiss linguist and avid Esperantist Edmond Privat played in promoting the language at the League. Privat was president of the Universal Esperanto Association and author of Esperanto texts and histories.⁵⁷ He had also served as a French-English interpreter for the first two Assemblies and anonymously authored and edited the reports on Esperanto. In addition to his pro-Esperanto leanings, Privat had a long history of supporting the independence of small and colonial nations. He had attended the Paris Peace Conference to advocate for the independence of Poland, was a supporter of Indian nationalism, and was a close friend as well as, later, biographer of Gandhi.⁵⁸ Privat believed very strongly in Esperanto's ability to alter the international field in a way that would help disadvantaged states and nationalities.

Because his role at the League prevented him from advocating for Esperanto in the Assembly, in 1921 Privat made an arrangement with League delegate Prince Arfa ed-Dowleh. If the Persian delegation hoped to eventually gain a Council seat as a counterweight to European interests at the League, it needed a larger representation. At the time, the Persian government simply did not have the funds to commit to participation in the League. So Privat agreed to serve on the Persian delegation without payment, on the condition that he could use his position to promote Esperanto whenever the question arose.[59] The Persian government agreed and retained Privat free of charge until 1927.

The British Foreign Office found this arrangement a troubling sign of the ways in which Esperanto might create backchannels for undermining traditional power structures. A confidential memo that circulated to the cabinet in March 1923 called Privat an "Esperanto Maniac" and deemed him wholly unqualified to represent Persia's interests at the League.[60] Above all, the British Foreign Office was concerned that foreign delegates would be able to influence the position that small states took at the League. Privat, they argued, had been able to use his position to give the impression that Persia had more interest in the question of Esperanto than it actually did. However, beyond Esperanto, the memo betrayed a deeper fear of how "internationalism" in all its forms might undermine British interests at the League and beyond.[61] Thus, the cabinet resolved to use its weight at the League to encourage states to choose their *own nationals* as delegates. Along these lines, the cabinet asked the British Robert Cecil—another supporter of Esperanto—to leave the South African delegation and join the British one.[62] The case of Privat reveals the extent to which Esperanto appeared to undermine the so-called *natural* basis of power.

Despite Privat's efforts, the League had already started cooling on the issue by the end of 1922. The Third Assembly adopted a resolution to transfer the question over to the International Committee on Intellectual Cooperation (ICIC).[63] The ICIC considered the matter but in August 1923 issued a statement suggesting that the League should concentrate on promoting the classical study of foreign languages.[64] In a broader sense, ICIC reacted against Esperanto's reputation of being a tool for outsiders seeking a place at the insiders' table. The ICIC stated their distrust of the artificial language in the following terms: "The Committee is not convinced of the need for direct communication between uneducated or imperfectly educated individuals in different countries."[65] Rather than merely rejecting Esperanto, however, the ICIC asserted that it would consider endorsing efforts to revive Latin as an international language, as a way of renewing a global republic of letters. After that blow, Esperanto disappeared from the League's agenda. From 1923 onward, every plea that arrived at the Secretariat in favor of Esperanto or any other international language received a polite but dismissive reply.[66]

The League's consideration and then rejection of Esperanto brings back into focus the extent to which achieving a monopoly on *the symbolic realm* (or symbolic capital) constituted a central preoccupation of both national and international political institutions. In terms of the geopolitical world picture, Esperanto's promise of linguistic universality based on political neutrality was precisely what made it appear as such a threat.[67] To the extent that a state's relation to and presence in the "world" constituted a form of symbolic capital, the immaterial asset of language was valuable indeed.

At the League, the global symbolic community—the world picture—also came into being through the rituals of using the official languages. All others had *to pay* (in time, money, or both) for acquisition, translation, and interpretation. But the League also had to make sure that certain powers did not try to rewrite or relabel the world map. In the same moment that the League denied the use of a universal language, it was also mediating conflicts between and within newly drawn linguistic borders.

In the 1920s, the German linguist and scholar Karl Vossler warned that the attempt to make political borders coincide with linguistic ones had been a terrible mistake. He asserted that language was flexible, constantly in motion. It was perfectly natural, Vossler argued, for a man to speak "Czech with his maid, Hungarian with his coachman, French with his mistress, Italian with his master, English with his governess, and . . . German with his family." Political borders, on the other hand, were not flexible and could "be changed only in jerks." Thus, tying frontiers to language would mean either that the borders would have to become more flexible and accommodating or that they would constantly have to be reconfigured, perhaps violently.[68] It was as if Vossler had seen the writing on the walls.

Minor Tongues

In *Philosophical Investigations*, the Austrian philosopher Ludwig Wittgenstein described language in terms of an intimate, historically layered locality:

> Our language can be seen as an ancient city: a maze of little streets and squares, of old and new houses, and of houses with additions from various periods; and this surrounded by a multitude of new boroughs with straight regular streets and uniform houses.[69]

He proposed that language worked as a bridge between past and present as well as between the self and society, with each individual hearth linked to the broader city via grammar's regular streets. Of course, Wittgenstein also developed a second point about the relation between language and thought, his most famous quip: "The limits of my language mean the limits of my world."[70] The *limits* imposed by Wittgenstein were those of logic, and he was concerned with how the structure of a language constituted a range of conceptual constraints. We cannot think, the reasoning goes, beyond the confines of the grammars we inherit. Yet, given the philosopher's own trajectory via the First World War and the interwar moment, we can read his words even against their own intentions. Read differently, Wittgenstein depicted language both as realm of retreat and also as a realm of confinement. One could always rest in the warmth of the dialect of mother tongue, walk down the familiar streets of one's native lettered city. Yet, to the extent that the public (either national or global) also offered a domain of power and opportunity, language could provide an impassible border. The "limits of one language," indeed also signified the limits of one's access to the world.

On the one hand, the League's Minority System was designed to ensure that the national minorities in the newly created or revised states would be able to enjoy the comfort of their mother tongues not only privately, but also publicly. The treaties supposedly safeguarded the ability of designated subpopulations to receive an education, worship their gods, and conduct their business in their own language. Any infraction on the part of the ruling government gave the minority in question the right to petition the League of Nations, which would then consider all the provided evidence.[71]

However, the Minority System also became a symbolic stage where language became a modality for reinforcing *confinement* and limiting certain forms of *worldly access* to people and states. The irony of the League's petition system, however, was that it was primarily for "informational purposes," and petitioners themselves rarely heard anything about the fate of their appeals.[72] For a petition to even make it to the Council for consideration, it had to meet stringent criteria to be deemed "receivable."[73] Even if a petition met those criteria, the main point of the system was to then confront the accused state with the claims and give them a chance to respond before the eyes and ears of the watching and listening world. Rarely, the Council would authorize an onsite investigation into the complaints. However, such an investigation was undertaken not to correct the abuse, but rather to gather additional information for discussion.[74] Eventually, details of the whole affair would be published in the *Official Journal of the League of Nations*. The only punishment a violating state received was bad publicity.

While the petitions moved through the gears and cogs of the League's information system, the relevant officials had to weigh in on the legitimacy of the claims. Sometimes, the members of the Minority Section turned themselves into makeshift linguistics or anthropologists. In 1925, the Minorities Section received a petition from a group of Jewish minorities in Poland, requesting to use their language in public schools. Article 10 of the Polish Minority Treaty ensured that a portion of public funds would go toward Jewish schools. However, the treaty did not designate the language of instruction. Norwegian diplomat and Minority Section member Eric Colban sought some clarity from his colleagues. He asked: "Are the Jews thus free to choose if they use Polish, Hebrew or Yiddish?"[75] The response Colban received strongly asserted that Hebrew was absolutely out of the question; after all, the movement for the revival of Hebrew (unlike the revival of Latin?) "was artificial and illegitimate."[76]

The revival of Modern Hebrew had taken place within roughly the same time span as Esperanto. Ya'akov Abrimovitch had initiated the process of reforming ancient Hebrew initially for writing purposes. Eliezer Ben-Yehuda (1858–1922) further engineered and promoted the full reform and revival of Hebrew as a spoken language. In 1879, Ben-Yehuda wrote *A Serious Question*, concerning the necessity of reviving the Hebrew language as a way of restoring the nation of Israel. Ben-Yehuda reacted against the rising tide of European nationalism, which had increasingly targeted Jewish communities, either demanding assimilation or forcing expulsion. Zamenhof had originally been an active Zionist; however, he began to distance himself from the movement at a time when it began explicitly drawing a link between the revival of Hebrew and the demand for a national home in Palestine. As Ilan Stavans has asserted, Ben-Yehuda was convinced that Hebrew could continue to live as the language of the Jewish community only if and when the Jews had their own territorial nation-state.[77] Where Zionists dreamed of writing its place name on the map, Zamenhof wanted to create a language so that itinerates and globe-trotters could greet each other on common ground.

In dealing with the question of Hebrew language instruction for Jewish children in Polish schools, the League also evoked images of the map of the world, showing spaces where an "illegitimate language" could take root and spaces where it could not. In fact, the text of the agreement in the British Mandate for Palestine promised that English, Hebrew, and Arabic would function in absolute equality as the official languages for administrative and official purposes.[78] However, the heart of Europe was a different story. The Minority Section memo on Jewish schools continued: "If Zionists in Palestine want to practice political archeology that's their business but we will not encourage claiming nationality on artificial lines in Europe."[79] In short, Europe was a place where *real* languages legitimized *real* political projects. Of course, in truth, Hebrew was not much less an artifact of invention than, say, modern Italian, which after 1871 was also used first to standardize the language and then to secure a unified territory. However, language constituted a domain where politics sought to affirm the *reality* of the measures used for determining the practices of possession and dispossession. In the end, the League decided the petition did not merit further review. They argued that Jewish children in Poland could already use Yiddish in schools, and that should suffice.[80]

There were also a number of cases where the League consulted experts of language and ethnography to review a minority claim. Between 1925 and 1927, for example, the Secretariat helped run an investigation into the "true" ethnicity of Macedonia. The goal was to determine if Macedonians could be considered a *national minority* with special rights in Yugoslavia or not.[81] The Bulgarian government claimed that Macedonians were ethnically Bulgarian and thus accused Yugoslavia of failing to meet the terms of the Minority Treaty in providing those peoples with sufficient "cultural autonomy."[82] The Yugoslavian government claimed not only that the Bulgarian government used the Macedonians to stir up irredentist sentiment, but that the Macedonians were ethnically just as Serb as they were Bulgarian. For its part, the Yugoslavian government even cited the work of French linguist Antoine Meillet, who had apparently proclaimed "the inhabitants of Macedonia are not Bulgarian; neither their language, their customs, their memories of the past, their national consciousness, nor anything which distinguishes them as a people is Bulgarian."[83]

Under the guise of getting to the bottom of the *reality* of language questions, these procedures took up tremendous time and resources. Rather than seeking a true resolution of the issues, the main goal was in fact to simply bring them before the world public. The question is, *why*? In one sense, the Minority Treaties afforded the League a point of observation into the domestic affairs of region that had long been a tinderbox in European politics. Just as the Peace Treaty gave national self-determination to those European nations, they issued a series of legal qualifications. Here, the "Standards of Civilization" came back into play. The Minority Treaties applied only to those powers deemed insufficiently developed or too inherently politically unstable to handle heterogeneity in their domestic affairs. Thus, the League would monitor these states until they were deemed to have developed sufficient civil societies (and economies) to stand alone.[84] There was an implicit echo in the logic of the mandates and minority systems to "produce" categories for determining the "position" of places within the hierarchy of the world frame.[85] Where the C mandates were those deemed least capable of self-determination, the Minority Treaties created imaginary A+ mandates in Europe. As further evidence of the link, in 1932, Iraq gained its juridical independence by agreeing to a Minority Treaty, so the League could supervise Iraq's treatment of its Kurdish and Assyrian populations.[86] At a Council meeting on May 19, 1932, the members drafted the following resolution for Iraq to sign: "Iraqi nationals, irrespective of race, language or religion, form part, on a footing of equality, of the body of the state." On July 13, 1932, Iraq submitted its minority declarations, which guaranteed protection for non-Moslem populations and for the use of the Kurdish language.[87] With these guarantees in place, Iraq progressed from an A mandate to an A+ minority power.

There are more resonances still between the two systems, even outside of the League. For when mouthpieces of the British Empire explained why India was not yet ready to govern itself, one of the most prominent and often repeated reasons for postponement was that of the so-called communal problem.[88] Namely, colonial officials declared that the nature of the tensions between the Hindu majority and the Muslim minority were too ancient, too deeply rooted, too volatile, and thus stymied the necessary stability for building a modern state.[89] Echoing the Crown's rhetoric, the British academic C. A. Macartney claimed that Britain was the only thing standing in the way of communal violence in India. He stated: "In the Indian situation today there are quite two distinct conflicts. There is the conflict of the native against the Englishman and that of the Hindu against the Mahomedan. ... The presence of the English in India is postponing the true clash between the native races."[90]

Unlike the mandates system that marked a clear "ABC" ladder toward independence, to the extent that the "A+" was imaginary, the Minority Treaties never specified when, how, or if a designated state might hope to be free of some form of international supervision.[91] With every minority complaint, the League garnered further evidence that new or revised states lacked civil societies healthy enough to fully and justly govern their own affairs.[92] Again and again, the League advertised the continuing difference in *status* between those states subject to Minority Treaties and those not. As one final variable, the League's financial restructuring programs in those regions often appealed to evidence garnered in the social and political domains to justify the continued need for financial oversight.[93]

Perhaps unsurprisingly, these measures that publicized a permanent gap in status among major and minor sovereigns soon became points of public contention. In 1925, during the Sixth Assembly, the Polish, Lithuanian, and Romanian delegations proposed universalizing the Minority Treaties. After all, a frank look at the linguistic and ethnic map of the world would reveal that all states contained minority populations.[94] In response, however, just as the League had determined the "reality" and "unreality" of certain languages, the discussion turned to what constituted a "real" minority for international legal purposes.

When the discussion came to the Assembly floor, delegation after delegation insisted that they did not have minorities, at least in the sense defined in the peace settlements. Rather, their states had civil societies sufficiently practiced to handle diversity without threatening national unity.[95] Paul Hymans of Belgium urged his eastern European colleagues to drop the issue altogether. He argued that to generalize such a treaty would cause *fictional* minorities to rise up all over the world and cry for rights.[96] On the other hand, the minorities "protected" under the peace settlements were "real," organic cuttings unavoidably separated from their original root systems.[97]

Where "real" minorities became a measure of a lesser status in the world of states, however, acts of erasure and rewriting followed. After Germany entered the League in 1926, it did not have to sign a Minority Treaty. What is more, the German delegation used the Minority System to protest the treatment of "German nationals" within the states created at its territorial expense.[98] In response to these additional dynamics, the Minority Treaty states began asserting that they too were without minorities; they did not have a minority problem.

In 1928, the League of Nations Association of Yugoslavia confidently asserted, "There are no Jugoslav minorities in the Jugoslav state. Is Picardy a national minority in France, or Lombardy in Italy, Hanover in Germany?"[99] Those little islands of distinct ethnicities and tongues had become an obstacle to fuller forms of sovereignty on the world stage. It is therefore perhaps unsurprising that, in the early 1930s, violence against "national minorities" increased rather than decreased under the international public eye. What is more, in a fusion of words and violence, tactics of erasing *bodies* proliferated alongside additional efforts at revising or reforming language itself.

From A to Z: Acts of Revision, Acts of Erasure

After the ICIC rejected Esperanto, it entertained one final project of language universalization.[100] In 1929, during the Eleventh Assembly, in an echo of its support for the revival of Latin, the ICIC supported a proposal by Lin-Yu Yang and Dr. Aikitu Tanakadate, which recommended "to all countries the universal adoption of Roman characters." The proposal suggested that nations using ideographs or other non-Roman-based scripts should work to create an alphabetic equivalent for use in international correspondence. The memo asserted that "the unification of writing will facilitate the acquisition of language and consequently will promote mutual understanding among different nations and races."[101]

Before bringing the question before the League, in 1928, Tanakadate had written a pamphlet in support of the romanji, or romanization, movement in Japan. According to that little tract, the Latin alphabet would allow Japan to communicate more easily with the West. In particular, Tanakadate articulated an anxiety that Japan remained a second-class citizen in the international political community and invested romanji with the ability to make Japan more competitive and thus more prominent.

Nitobe, by then convinced of Esperanto's insufficiencies, also supported the romanji movement. He went so far as to argue that Latin characters would help Japan begin to "think in terms of the West." Modernizing the Japanese language, he felt, would provide an invaluable route for modernizing Japan itself. Nitobe had frequently expressed admiration for the "courage" of the Bulgarian government, which had struck three "unnecessary" letters from its alphabet in 1921. According to Nitobe, this simplification better equipped Bulgaria to educate its citizens and modernize its institutions. In a similar strain, Nitobe concluded that, rather than adopt Esperanto, Japan needed to focus on reforming its own script as a way to simultaneously preserve and Westernize Japanese national culture. With so much "catch up" to accomplish, Nitobe believed that "the intellectual resources of Japan ought not be squandered on acquiring or retaining . . . complicated symbols."[102] Reforming the alphabet would—among other things—allow greater numbers of Japanese people to acquire literacy rates on par with the West.

Those "complicated symbols" in question were the kanji, or Chinese, characters. Tanakadate's tract went so far as to claim that in modernizing its alphabet Japan would also be able to rid itself of vestiges of a Chinese legacy.[103] Tanakadate made an implicit argument that Chinese characters had *dominated* the Japanese language for too long. Casting off the scripts was a way of reversing that domination. In the end, the romanji movement never took hold. However, only four years later, Japan invaded Manchuria. While perhaps not causal, efforts to revise the word often came as a prequel or a cosign of other more material modes of altering the world. At every turn language appeared as a domain for altering a nation's fortunes.

The League's proposal on universal characters had referred to the "success story" of Mustafa Kemal's rapid Latinization of the Turkish alphabet. After the dissolution of the Ottoman Empire at the end of the war, Kemal (Ataturk) emerged as the leader of the Turkish nationalist movement. In 1928, Kemal mandated the adoption of an alphabet based on Latin sources rather than on Arabic script. Kemal intended for the new alphabet to sever the link between modern Turkey and the Ottoman Muslim past recorded in the Arabic script. Thus, not only did the Turkish government rapidly set up an alphabet committee to effect the changes; it subsequently undertook a mass literacy campaign that mobilized educators in every corner of the state to teach the literate the new alphabet and the illiterate to read.[104] In Kemal's view, these newly educated citizens would contribute to Turkey's scientific and industrial uplift, while the Latin alphabet would ensure a closer and easier correspondence with the international community.

It took the ICIC committee until 1934 to publish its full findings on the question. The ICIC commissioned Otto Jespersen, a Danish linguist, to write the report.[105] In his comments published in *L'adoption universelle des caractères latins*, Jespersen asserted that a Latin/Roman-based alphabet was the only script eligible for universalization, precisely because it was the one used "in the countries of greatest importance to the world."[106] In the end, however, Jespersen argued that language reform was ultimately a national rather than an international question.[107] And, indeed, the report contained evidence that the time for "universal" language projects had passed. The report cited the fact that, when the League first started investigation, Latinization had found some support in Russia. Yet, by the time the report was being drafted, Stalin had curtailed all Latinization projects and had mandated the use of both the Russian language and the Cyrillic script. Furthermore, when questioned about the possibility of adopting Latin characters, the World Zionist Organization responded to the ICIC that it considered such a measure as "an act of profanation and destructions towards the spirit of race."[108]

Even in Turkey, things had changed. By 1930, Kemal had asserted that it was time for another wave of language reform, namely, efforts to purge the Turkish language from all foreign influences.[109] To those ends, the special committee assigned to language questions set about searching for Turkish equivalents for all borrowed words. Where none were available, they created neologisms. As Geoffrey Lewis has stated, this effort was a "catastrophic success."[110] The Turkish vocabulary transformed to such an extent that citizens found themselves groping for words that no longer existed in the official sense. As the rapid and traumatic purge of the language began creating internal confusion and division, an act of linguistic legerdemain intervened. Ataturk's linguists proposed the "Sun Theory of Language," which claimed that all languages had derived from Turkish, the original tongue of Babel before the curse was cast. Thus, ridding the Turkish language of outside influence became redundant, since all those words were derivative at the outset.[111] The Turkish case demonstrates the local-global tensions embedded in the politics. While language continued to determine a state's place in the world, it also increasingly provided a symbolic front for guarding the "purity" of the nation.

In 1921, the linguist and international auxiliary language advocate Edward

Sapir had set out to sever what he considered the sentimental tendency to conflate race and language. As he put it, "that a group of languages need not in the least correspond to a racial group or culture is easily demonstrated. We may even show intercrosses with racial and culture lines. In the United States there are several millions of negroes who know no other language. It is their mother-tongue, the formal vesture of their inmost thoughts and sentiments. It is much their property, as 'inalienably "theirs"' as the King of England's."[112] By the 1930s, however, critiques of the ethereality of signs became linked to calls to reunite language and race.

In an echo of Heidegger's critique of the typewriter, in 1937, J. R. Firth stated: "We live in an age of 'phones'—gramophones, telephones, microphones, and goodness knows how many other 'phones.' Excellent as all these things are, we must not become so obsessed with the technique of reproducing disembodied voices that we regard speech as being mainly an affair of frequencies, amplitudes, decibels and standard vowel resonances."[113] Firth hoped to remind his fellows that language still remained fundamentally "material": "speech is the outcome of flesh and blood, a bond between kith and kin."[114] In this way, efforts to purify language by expunging foreign elements often corresponded to efforts to erase other, foreign elements from the body politic. National language reforms and the persecution of "minorities" increased together in the 1930s, from Bulgaria to Iraq.[115]

In 1933, after the fall of Weimar and during the Fourteenth Assembly, Herr Von Keller stood before the League and argued that the Jews in Germany were not a national minority, and that the Jewish question was altogether separate from the minority question. Like all serious global powers, Germany had no minorities. However, after 1934 the National Socialist government also undertook extensive language alteration and reforms. First, the Nazi government also set out to "purge" the language of foreign words; even *hertzian waves* had to be renamed, erasing any traces of their Jewish discoverer Heinrich Hertz.[116] In a similar frame, Esperantists of every ethnicity were singled out as enemies of the state, for (the claim went) Esperanto was in fact a Jewish language.[117] In *Mein Kampf*, Hitler stated that "as long as the Jew has not become the master of other peoples, he must speak their languages whether he likes it or not, but as soon as they become his slaves, they would all have to learn a universal language (Esperanto for instance) so that by this additional means the Jews could more easily dominate them."[118] Zamenhof's remaining family died in a Polish concentration camp.[119]

Purging foreign elements from the German language constituted only one side of the coin. Shortly after taking power, the National Socialists also started to reengineer the German language, altering vocabularies, generating buzzwords and neologisms. As W. J. Dodd has argued, as soon as 1933, a number of dictionaries and glossaries emerged that were dedicated to recording these radical lexical changes. Among the most famous was that of Heinz Paechter, a German Jewish exile who, after 1940, worked at Columbia University's Institute for Social Research as well as the American Office of Strategic Services (OSS).[120] The opening chapter of Paechter's dictionary laid out the threat embedded in the reduction of all speech to mere slogans: "it transforms the categories of Nazi thought into the folklore of the community which uses these symbols."[121] While rooted in National Socialism and the German language, Paechter spoke more generally of all totalitarian language projects. "The language that is spoken in totalitarian countries conveys the climate of the totalitarian mind. It is more than a vehicle of communication. It is a vehicle of command, which helps shape the pattern of the social structure and its ritual."[122]

Between 1933 and 1945 the German Jewish philologist Victor Klemperer (who survived owing solely to his marriage to a German woman) also kept a notebook of the linguistic changes taking place through the state's propaganda machine. He later published that notebook under the title *Language of the Third Reich: LTI; Lingua Tertii Imperii*. Among his many observations, Klemperer focused on the government's tendency to create a new vocabulary of superlatives. Among the words that supposedly threatened the nation was the word *Welt* (world). Klemperer stated: "'Juden und Bolschewisten' [Jews and Bolsheviks], entities whose ranks do not in the least outnumber Germans, are transformed into massive 'Weltfeinde' [World-enemies]."[123] Here then we hear the strange contradiction. On the one hand, the "purified" German tongue provided the bases of its organic political community. However, since German speakers (and the enemies of the Reich) stretched across the whole world, so did the quest for *living space* for the German people. Nitzan Lebovic has demonstrated the underlying concept of *Lebensphilosophie* (philosophy of life) underwrote the principle of clearing a vast territorial expanse for the self-realization of the Volk.[124] The first step to those ends was to move outward to reunite all those islands of "native Germans" under one territorial umbrella. One by one, the linguistic borders fell. From there, the Reich would move steadily outward, to occupy more of Europe and then to restore the lost colonies.[125]

The case of National Socialism's urge to expand its hegemonic claims by expanding its linguistic presence on the world stage, however, was not without parallels. Other and ostensibly democratic regimes also attempted to wrap the whole world picture in a single sign system. When the Thirtieth Esperanto Congress convened in London and asked for official political support, the

British government responded: "It is undesirable to support organizations which have as their object the encouragement of artificial languages when we are seeking to secure the adoption of English as the second language in all foreign countries."[126] To further those aims, however, the British government supported the use and diffusion of another international auxiliary language, namely, Basic English. In 1930, C. K. Ogden invented this boiled down version—850 words—of English to use for international communication.

Basic English had the same rationale as Esperanto, as Ogden's book *Debabelization* stated: "The absence of a common medium of communication is the chief obstacle to understanding and therefore, the underlying cause of war."[127] Unlike the neutralist aims of Esperanto, however, Ogden created the language based on the "natural ascendancy" of English and the desire that it should spread throughout the world. Winston Churchill strongly advocated the language and even included the merits of Basic in a speech he gave at Harvard in September 1943 on the Anglo-American model for a peaceful postwar world order. He saw the spread of English as crucial to that order, for "such plans offer far better prizes than taking away other people's provinces, or lands, or grinding them down in exploitation."[128] For that reason, the British government provided considerable financial backing for Ogden's Orthological Institute, which created textbooks and Basic English translations of other works.[129] Evidently that language—and not just Soviet or Nazi language games—had been one of the real-world inspirations behind Orwell's Newspeak.[130]

Language, however, was only one signifier of power and position running through the cables and wires. Another was money. In Hugo Ball's first *Dadaist Manifesto*, he perceived a link between the two sign systems. He stated: "A line of poetry is a chance to get rid of all the filth that clings to this accursed language, as if put there by stockbroker's hands, hands worn smooth by coins."[131] Over ten years later, during the final plenary session of the League's International Conference for the Suppression of Counterfeit Currency, the Albanian delegate made some closing remarks. At the time, Albania did not have a national mint or printing press, and it lacked its own national system of money.[132] Still, on April 20, 1929, Stavro Stavri offered a closing tribute to a distant Ur-hero: "I must offer a tribute to the inventor of the alphabet, first because he discovered a means of rendering human thought immortal and, secondly, because, by his classification of the letters, he has, in this convention, accorded my country the place of honour."[133] If only in alphabetic terms, and if only for a moment, those who had been last were now first.

It is to this conference, and the question of money in general, that we now turn our gaze.

4

Fabricating Currencies:
Paper, Gold, and Other Facsimiles

> We have slipped unawares out of the economic field into the field of psychology.
> SIGMUND FREUD, *The Future of an Illusion*

Mercurial Mediums

Like language, money constituted yet another tool through which specific "world pictures" were both forged and contested. The same mechanisms that made it possible to sever language from territory, and to some extent from reality—the telegraph, the telephone, the printing press—also made more apparent the breach between money and its value. When Ferdinand de Saussure explained the relation between language and the material world, he also reached for an economic analogy: "For instance, it is not the metal in a piece of money that fixes its value. . . . Its value will vary according to the amount stamped upon it and according to its use inside or outside a political boundary."[1] Just as the link between objects and their names was arbitrary and only semistable, so too was the link between currencies and their worth. Moreover, it was not inherently the weight, amount, or physical nature of gold or silver that gave money its value, but rather something far less tangible—the consensus of a community of users.

Many others have cited resonances between the nature of language and that of money.[2] The primary point here, however, is not to validate the analogy, but rather to suggest that where it rings true, it is because similar historical dynamics pressed down on both.[3] Like language, currencies reflected the boundaries of a given community, as well as its place, presence, and prestige on the global stage. Also like language, money questions were always linked to questions of either crossing or defending national borders. Thinking about parallels between money and language moves against the grain of a contemporary literature that juxtaposes the seemingly fixed materiality of the gold standard and the supposed immateriality of fiat and floating systems of the 1970s.[4] As with realism and idealism, or the word and the sword, the juxtaposition between "metal" and "fiat" money itself needs to historicized and contextualized. As we will see, interwar money polices and theories often responded either explicitly or implicitly to the dangers posed by an increasingly intangible financial system.

In 1919, the American economist Irving Fisher bemoaned that the war had exacerbated monetary instability: "Inflation in various forms, such as paper-money inflation and bank-credit inflation among the countries at war, and gold inflation among other countries, has everywhere caused a depreciation of monetary units."[5] As a way of making sense of this depreciation, Fisher, like Saussure, pointed to the rupture between money's nominal (perceived) value and its real (purchasing power) value. The numbers on the face of bills stayed the same, yet they did not stretch as far as they once did. Fisher argued: "The truth is, the purchasing power of the dollar and other monetary units has always been and, until some radical remedy is applied, always will be unstable."[6] On its own, money was a hopelessly mercurial medium. Most dangerously, high-velocity cross-border transactions and periodic banking crises posed a threat because popular faith in the legitimacy of political orders could rise and fall with the value of currencies. The question was how to create solid and stable national currencies without sacrificing a certain fluidity of international exchange.[7]

Once again, the League's records reveal how money matters stood at the center of other philosophical and political struggles to define, produce, or control the *real* and the *solid*. The organization was among the liveliest interwar centers of activity for thought and policy experiments in, among other things, every dimension of money.[8] Especially under the auspices of its Economic and Financial Organization, the League served as home base for an international cadre of experts dedicated to caulking the gap between monetary forms and values. From its very beginning, the League tackled issues of inflation, currency stabilization and reform, and, most importantly for our purposes, the question of *counterfeiting*.

In each of these efforts, until after the Great Depression, the League reasserted the importance of reintroducing the supposedly sturdier foundations of a revamped international gold standard.[9] By 1935, however, the League operated in a world where gold had lost its symbolic thrall over the public consciousness and policy makers were again experimenting with other anchors.[10] As a correlate of this transformation, the very fact that the League's archives reveal Irving Fisher's involvement in the eugenics movement points to the necessity of pondering the fuller range of values embedded in the question of monetary value.[11] Once again, as people began to lose faith in "international standards," or in the "solidity" of gold, many turned to supposedly more stable because more primordial anchors. Those tensions emerged most clearly within the postwar debate on inflation, the perceived dangers of paper currency, and the fault lines within the promises of gold.

Paper Sins and Golden Redemptions

Of all the evils identified as being born of the trenches, the printing of money to cover wartime expenses appeared particularly insidious. Just as violence first garnered support from citizens and then faded into distrust and war weariness, the same waning of faith occurred with regards to irredeemable paper currency. The diatribes were legion. A choir of critics bemoaned how the printing of money during the war had pushed society onto unsteady economic foundations, far from the "solid" virtues of a metal standard. What is more, those who rejected inconvertible paper often sighted the *flimsiness* and *sinfulness* of money, beyond the reach of redemption. Along those lines, one postwar American academic, C. C. Arbuthnot, claimed: "The war can be fought without inflation of the currency by the government or banks, just as the navy can fight without a ration of rum."[12] Fiat paper money thus was a vice rather than a necessity, and the consequences of its adoption were as severe and numerous as the "broken bodies" and "shattered minds" stumbling off the battlefields.[13]

Curiously, during World War I printing money was the acceptable norm. Part of that support echoed in a context in which the phrase "scraps of paper" had taken on layered significance. Legendarily, when the German Kaiser invaded Belgium, he referred to the treaty protecting Belgian's neutrality as merely a "scrap of paper." The idea that deeply held supposedly civilized values of law and contract could be reduced to little more than paper became a frequently cited trope in various contexts. Considerable allied propaganda was dedicated to showing liberal values were weightier than paper, and worth the spilling of blood to protect.[14] At the same time, economic reinterpretations of the rallying cry also came to the fore. For example, in *The Coming Scrap of Paper* (1915), the British author Edward W. Edsall spoke out in favor of paper currencies. He argued that the state of emergency of 1914 had merely allowed the public to see the limits of gold. The problem was one of a temporal disconnect. The war's needs were urgent, and yet as he stated: "Gold could not be obtained at a moment's notice. It has to be dug from the bowls of the earth."[15] Thus, governments had to devise another solution: "Therefore it was necessary to resort to something that was immediately available—viz. paper—and this was impressed and invested with the dignity and function of gold."[16] Along similar lines, a 1918 Roscoe "Fatty" Arbuckle fund-raising film titled *Scraps of Paper* also turned the phrase to illuminate allied economic strategy. The film showed the portly Arbuckle waltzing into the office of the German Kaiser and reminding him of his own quip "a mere scrap of paper." Subsequently, the film shows the Kaiser being defeated by new scraps of paper, buried alive under a deluge of allied war bonds as "mighty as bombs."[17]

Once again, the interwar moment was but one episode in a much older series of debates about how money might best hold or store value.[18] As David Fox and Wolfgang Ernst have argued, money underwent a multicentury process "of dematerialization," through the emergence of "bank money, paper money, and currencies de-linked from any substratum in precious metals."[19] And yet, rather than a linear trajectory from metal to fiat, monetary thought and policy continued to return to the question of how to ensure real and stable value. The form here was as much a part of the debate as the function. As state-issued paper money came into use—along with the credit and debt structures of modern nation-states and their standing armies in the sixteenth and seventeenth centuries—so did distrust of the flimsy fabrications of the printing press.[20]

After World War I, the idea of the weightlessness of paper money and other financial instruments once again began to haunt efforts to reassert and reestablish political control. Fatty Arbuckle's triumphant flood of paper suddenly seemed a dangerous weapon that might turn into friendly fire, defeating the governments that had made use of them. The reasons for this shift were manifold. The fresh demonization of paper currency had a great deal to do with the contexts and politics of uncertainty surrounding peace and reconstruction efforts. And too, in a moment of revolt and outright revolution, the link between economic instability and political malcontent came to the fore.

One of the most famous interwar quotes along these lines was: "The best way to destroy the capitalist system is to debauch the currency." The origins of this often-quoted remark remained long in question: it seems to have first appeared in John Maynard Keynes's *Economic Consequences of the Peace*, where Keynes attributed it to Vladimir Lenin, though no such statement appears in any of Lenin's writings.[21] Even if the statement is falsely attributed, however, putting those words in Lenin's mouth allowed Keynes both to tell a cautionary tale and also to point the way forward. "Lenin was certainly right," Keynes insisted, "there is no subtler, no surer means of overturning the existing basis of society than to debauch the currency."[22] In many ways, *debase* would have been a more straightforward word to describe the phenomenon. In 1919, Keynes was still a mostly classical quantity theorist who correlated the money supply and the price level, or inflation.[23] *Debasement* would have thus been a more literal description, denoting the loss of value as a result of oversupply. *Debauch,* or *debauchery,* on the other hand, summoned insinuations of perversion and a broader destruction of values beyond pecuniary value.

Intentionally referring to paper inflation in the language of vice and virtue, Keynes warned that monetary debauchery caused currencies to fluctuate wildly from moment to moment, breaking down stable relations between debtors and creditors.[24] Unhinged from all natural anchors, economic life would become little more than "a gamble and a lottery." Most devastating of all: "The sight of this arbitrary rearrangement of riches strikes not only at security, but at confidence in the equity of the existing distribution of wealth."[25] Of course there were countless postwar malcontents ready to question the "existing distribution" of wealth and the power structures that held it in place. In this precise context, Keynes was aware that the bursting of any speculative bubble—including one born of the oversupply of money—could open a door to political revolution. And Keynes was no revolutionary.[26] However, while the critique of monetary debauchery was an antispeculative and prostability statement, Keynes did not say that the arbitrary rearrangement of riches per se was the problem. Rather, it was the sight or public awareness of that arbitrary rearrangement that posed the greatest threat to stability. The question of course is why such a revelation of *arbitrariness* was so dangerous, and, more pointedly, what part money played in exposing or concealing such a revelation.

The League of Nations' immediate postwar economic priorities offer some insight into these questions. The cypher rests in the efforts the League made toward economic restoration, as well as to the restoration of certain economic narratives. That is to say, League experts at least initially followed and promoted lines of argument meant to move the world economy forward by reviving some elements of a classical liberal past.[27] And yet, as with any renaissance, the *classical* elements in question were also as much the work of construction as of reconstruction. Examining the conditions of their production provide clues as to why it became so important to insist on the reality of a sound, so-called natural economic order, as against some unsound, "unnatural" one. Moreover, the tension between paper and gold offered a touchstone to which the debates about how best to secure a stable economic *reality* frequently returned.

After World War I, over the course of several publications, Swedish economists Gustav Cassel, member of the Economic and Financial Committee, offered the international equivalent of a State of the Union address.[28] In *The World's Monetary Problems,* he cited the underpinnings of the world's inflationary woes as consisting of the sum of a precipitous rise in prices, a decrease in commodities, and a sharp increase in the money supply.[29] According to Cassel, inflation was a sign of disease at the very root of the system, which had grown of artificiality, excess, and all manner of unnatural appetites. First, Cassel decried the "artificial creation of purchasing power" that had let governments spend beyond their "real" capacity. He also denounced "a falsification of the money market by too low a rate of interest." Finally, he claimed that the first two sins had been made possible by a third: none other than "an arbitrary supply of legal tender."[30] With regards to the increase in the money supply, he too cited the egregious overprinting of inconvertible currency to fund the war effort. Yet, for Cassel, the form of this artificial purchasing power mattered little, whether "bank-notes, other notes, or book credits in the banks."[31] What mattered was that the war's production had taken place disconnected from any steady and firm economic reality. Thus, the war had been not just a human tragedy, but a poorly financed and thus economic tragedy as well. Specifically, he criticized the fact that states had covered war expenses not by the virtuous means of savings and taxation, nor even by borrowing and lending alone, but also by acts of pure invention. Namely, they had resorted to the false idols of fiat banknotes dumped into circulation in order to sustain issues of war bonds, along with manipulations of the interest rate.

Thus, in this logic, inconvertible paper notes formed just one of many modern financial instruments that appeared as the monetary equivalent of yellow journalism. To their orthodox critics, such tools were little more than sensationalist fictions posturing as truth in order to make a profit. And yet, holding to what we know of the tight relation between the press and ruling powers, any attempt to draw distinctions between *truth* and *fiction* in money matters also implied promotion of a certain worldview. In a mirror image of political efforts to own or control the press, policy assertions of monetary truths were very much fragile inventions in need of constant upkeep.[32]

From its start, the League was tasked with supporting such tending. Cassel, in speaking for the League in the early 1920s, was one among many who set out to prescribe what it would take to return the world to its natural equilibrium, or what he dubbed "stable conditions in money matters."[33] He insisted that the most urgent task was to encourage the eradication of any "arbitrary measures" that would make the money supply "artificially easy."[34] The origin of the problem was clear, and Cassel explained it in frank terms. Namely, he cited the widespread adoption of paper money "without any definite relation to gold or the paper of other countries."[35] The solution was relatively simple, as he stated: "It seems pretty sure that most countries look forward to the restoration of a gold standard . . . as the real rescue from the hopeless muddle of the present paper-money systems,"[36] though he admitted that prewar parities remained out of reach.

As Zara Steiner and others have argued, the primary theme of postwar policy making in Europe was the call to return to the prewar world.[37] Thus, at the Brussels Financial conference in 1920, and then again at the Genoa conference of 1922, the League imagined restoring conditions of free trade as isomorphic to the workings of an international gold standard.[38] The subsequent promotion of gold as a solution to the sins of monetary debauchery continued to juxtapose the so-called real and natural qualities of a metal standard as opposed to the artificiality of unredeemable paper. What is more, appeals to gold's superior qualities also referenced its successful historical precedence as proof of concept.

In a sense, the League helped paint a newly romanticized picture of how the pre-1914 gold standard had operated.[39] In their vision, gold was an automatic system, to which national money was anchored, and an international balance of payments took place via cross-border shipments of metal. Further, central banks of participating states cooperated according to certain "rules of the game," and in so doing supported free trade and exchange rate stability.[40] Central banks should take heed of gold inflows and outflows in order to fine-tune their monetary policy. Such was the orthodox view of the prewar monetary system that appeared again and again in the League's policy recommendations. Yet, despite the appeal of this picture, the gold standard had never in reality operated so smoothly. In fact, the nineteenth century gold standard of the 1920s was, as Eichengreen and Flandreau have argued, little more a "mythical beast."[41] Convertibility suspensions were common enough to be considered the rule rather than the exception.[42] The same could be said about myths that emerged during the interwar and persisted beyond regarding allegedly high levels of pre–World War I central bank cooperation. Indeed, there is ample evidence to suggest that, before the war, central banks did not readily cooperate.[43] The question to pursue is thus not only how but also why this myth of prewar economic instability emerged within the interwar crisis.

This is not myth building pure and simple, but, as we saw with language, the reinvention of traditions supported a certain ordering of the world picture within and between states.[44] The conditions through which a modified gold standard remerged in the 1920s constituted a reframing of the symbolic status of gold amid nineteenth-century dematerializations.[45] Walking back through the range of social and political meanings that gold acquired before the war sheds some light on how those meanings were picked up and transformed after 1914. In particular, there were new resonances around the rhetorical conflict between paper and gold that grew in the three-way lovers' quarrel between information systems, state building, and financial capitalism.

All That Was Solid; or, The Melting of Gold

In his treatise dedicated to understanding the place and meaning of money in modern life, the German social theorist Georg Simmel evoked the surge of electrical currents and impulses. He stated: "Thus, money is involved in the general development which in every domain of life and in every sense strives to dissolve substance into free-floating process."[46] Indeed, money's forms and meanings were transforming as a result of new modes of banking and finance also supported by communication technologies. By 1872, telecommunications companies were inventing and extending the art of wire money transfer. The Western Union Company, for example, had begun transferring sums between several hundred towns—a network capacity that only grew with time. In Europe, branch banking systems were expanding, which further facilitated the geographical stretching of more rapid transactions. In comparison to such advances, metallic money was tedious.[47]

What is more, metallic currency forms, with their erratic supply left to the vicissitudes of mineral exploration and discovery, were also perceived as inadequate to meet the needs of industrializing states, expanding empires, and the business cycle. Within this context, the American monetary theorist and adviser Charles Conant articulated money's dematerialization. In 1899, Conant stated: "Credit has taken the place of money to a large extent in the larger transactions of commerce."[48] In this way, credit was like steam—a largely invisible, but crucial component both of national economies and of the international financial system.[49] The forms of credit he identified as particularly important were paper banknotes and "other banking credits," which had "largely substituted for metallic money in exchanges."[50]

There was still, however, a widely held belief in the exorable link between money and precious metal. In order to make way for more flexible monetary instruments, pure metal currency had to be discredited.[51] To those ends, Conant stated: "Metallic money is the natural medium of exchange in a community where confidence is lacking or credit is undeveloped."[52] Thus, using a civilizing logic, Conant implied that metal currency, like a primarily agricultural base, denoted an earlier stage of development. It was a tool for so-called backward places that lacked robust political and financial institutions.[53] Well before Conant, the primitivism of metal, especially gold, had already gained momentum. In the US gold rush of 1848, for example, often racially inflected popular images of spectators painted (frequently immigrant) fortune seekers as greedy, ravenous, and uncivilized. Later, Freud would link coveting gold to a regressive block, a symbol of the unconscious inability to move beyond the anal phase of development.[54] You could hear that logic foreshadowed in Conant's words, where "gold buggery" marked a primitive form; by contrast supposedly civilized nations dealt in credit forms of money, such as paper linked flexibly to gold.

Following this thread, the spread of gold as a standard, as opposed to the spread of its use as money, marked a victory for paper currency.[55] The irony is that the gold standard provided a *symbolically tangible* rather than fully tangible anchor. The mere image of metal was a kind of symbolic capital that states produced to help garner public confidence in paper notes, giro transfers, and bank deposits.[56] It also created a more, instead of less, active role for the state itself in monetary matters.[57] Standardized territorial currencies had been a phenomenon of the nineteenth century with both a political and a technological component. For centuries, and in most territories, a multitude of privately issued paper currencies and government-controlled metallic coins, both foreign and domestic, had coexisted.[58] New methods of printing and minting meant that for the first time governments could produce more standardized currencies in mass quantities.[59] Currency production became another joint in the connection between state and nation building projects and "print capitalism."[60] To return to the language metaphor, as states relied on print technologies to overcome multiple dialects and standardize one single national tongue, heterogeneous monetary forms also gave way to standardized currencies.[61] It is particularly significant that national currencies appeared in the aftermath of efforts at unification in Europe, or, in the case of the United States, after the violent divisions of the Civil War.[62] Thus, these currencies were also tools for reinforcing the power and legitimacy of states.[63] Still, new monetary regimes also formed a tender spot, a bruise, vulnerable to the pressures of political critique.

There was also a historical antecedent for the interwar fear of paper, and those suspicions and doubts were deeply connected to the print nature of money itself. As with the mass reproduction of books, photographs, and art, the printing of banknotes made it very difficult for the public to discern "true" and "authentic" images and information from fakes.[64] Indeed some critics perceived in the "fabricated" and so untrustworthiness of paper currency a reflection of the modern state's tendency for falsehood and prevarication. While those were longer-term dynamics, the nineteenth century saw a range of nascent strategies to authenticate and naturalize both currency and, via the currency, the state itself. For one, the later part of the nineteenth century witnessed in many states a strengthening of counterfeit laws. Of course, this grew in part because the same technology that allowed states to print more standardized currencies also enabled more sophisticated forgeries. Yet there was something subtler at work in anticounterfeit measures than simply protecting national currency in an economic sense. In the United States after 1865, statutes not only protected the newly unified national currency from forgery but also delegitimized Confederate money as well as the multitude of privately issued circulating currencies.[65] By using the law to identify fakes and frauds, states could hide the fraught and fragile production process by which their own currencies had become truth to begin with.

Counterfeit laws afforded states one tool for naturalizing and *rendering authentic* printed standardized national currency. There were other strategies as well. For example, Herbert Spencer provided a natural justification for states' use of the printing press. Borrowing an old metaphor, he said that if states are a body politic then money is the "blood in its veins." Spencer then soothed those who worried about the inflationary possibilities of printing money, calmly assuring his readers that more complex societies, as bigger bodies, simply required more blood. The printing of money was thus connected to the primordial authority, and so authenticity, of statehood, in contrast to charlatans printing illegitimate notes.[66]

Naturalizing the state's printing capacity in this way was still not enough to secure full confidence in the newly standardized legal tender. Given the nature of fractional banking and speculative finance, periodic financial crisis still created panic about the ephemerality of account balances. In that context, there were also questions about the extent that paper currency would hold its worth under shaky financial conditions. For these very reasons, the allure of metal continued to hold powerful appeal. All the more dangerously, those who criticized could always attack the unreliability of paper instruments. Marx spoke of metal as solid and therefore trustworthy because at least it was real, at least it was located in the earth, and at least its excavation was a product of labor.[67] What is more, he was convinced that the system would never be able to escape its metallic anchor. In the third volume of *Capital*, Marx stated:

> With the development of the credit system, capitalist production continually strives to overcome the metal barrier which is simultaneously a material and imaginative barrier of wealth and its movement, but again and again it breaks its back on this barrier.[68]

Marx saw in metal's duality one of capitalisms flawed internal contradictions. As Conant had highlighted, in terms of national economies, pure metal coin was no longer practicable. Thus, gold as a standard, rather than a money object, emerged, permitting states the financial flexibility to expand and intervene, while simultaneously retaining public confidence in the "certainty" of metal. In short, it both accommodated increasingly immaterial forms of finance as it also provided a semblance of a tangible anchor. In its very nature, the gold standard confirmed Simmel's assertion that money's symbolic importance had begun to "overshadow its significance as a substance."[69] Gold's symbolic appeal won out against a number of other competing theoretical paradigms and standards, each of which more closely mirrored the way modern money worked in practice.

In the domain of economic thought, several monetary theories emerged that sought to understand money as distinct from any metallic reference. Both Henry Dunning Macleod in the late nineteenth century and Harold Mitchell-Innis in the early twentieth began theorizing money's inherent value as linked to credit or debt rather than metal.[70] Additionally, the fin de siècle moment saw the explicit articulation of pure state or chartal theories of money. Georg Friedrich Knapp's *State Theory of Money* proposed that it was the state, and only the state, that gave money its real value. As he famously stated: "The soul of currency is not in the material of the pieces, but in the legal ordinances which regulate their use."[71]

Beyond chartal theories and their turn-of-the-century popularity, other thinkers had sought to stabilize money more explicitly with information. Even earlier than state and credit theories, William Stanley Jevons, for example, had begun working on a standard that would make use of the world of financial information to fix the value of money. In what came to be known in shorthand as "gazette standard," he proposed a standard linked to the prices of key goods.[72] Immediately, however, this raised the hackles of some prominent sages in the world of economics and finance. Economist and editor of the *Economist* Walter Bagehot fiercely pushed back against Jevons's proposal: "he [Jevons] thinks that it can put out to mankind a far better theoretical standard of value than gold or silver." And yet, aghast, Bagehot outlined his objections to that system: "When asked 'what is a pound' you cannot tell the people, 'the pound is a list of such and such articles.'" Bagehot went on to say that relating money to an abstract standard required a stable chord, linking one to the other, which would never be found in some inconvertible currency-based abstract information.[73] Thus he argued that the civilized world needed "precious metals as a standard of value like our forefathers."[74] We might assume that Bagehot found a gazette standard problematic because it would alert the public to the inherently constructed nature of modern markets. Perhaps too, even subconsciously, it threatened to reveal the extent to which information stood at the heart of wealth and power. As editor of the

Economist, Bagehot was very much part of the machine that used the press to paint the financial world in a certain light. The gold standard was thus offered as a primary color used for painting a particular world picture.

We can think of the standardization of state currencies, the rise of central banks, and the international gold standard partly as political efforts to bolster and solidify national economies amid immaterial international financial fluxes and flows.[75] Yet equally important was how gold's symbolic power functioned internationally. Scholars have found that modernizing states adopted it one after the other, not necessarily because it offered a superior standard, but because of its prestige dimension.[76] Indeed, just as states painted pure metal as regressive, the gold standard was the ultimate symbol of progress—a benchmark of civilization and being civilized.[77] International gold shipments did take place, and there were real mechanical features at work. However, there were also significant prestige dimensions of its use, which included some important privileges.[78] In that context so-called money doctoring, or providing monetary expertise on the virtues of gold, subsequently offered developed states a window and point of intervention into the affairs of less developed economies. As great power states advised lesser powers to stabilize on gold through expiatory deflation, they were a kind of forerunner of structural adjustment programs.[79] They also foreshadowed the interwar League stabilization plans. And yet never did those advising industrial states practice golden orthodoxies as faithfully as they preached them. For, the absolute constraints of gold were too binding.

We can thus see how the nineteenth-century gold standard worked as a powerful symbol that gave the appearance of natural-seeming solidity and virtue to certain political and economic orders both nationally and internationally.[80] Here then we acquire a way of pondering why the interwar period sought to restore a gold standard system that never was. In short, we can consider that gold's symbolic features, its mythologies, were always its most powerful attributes. Further insights appear along those lines when we consider how the interwar myth making about a nineteenth-century gold standard went hand in hand with an equally powerful myth of nineteenth-century peace.

Critical observers meeting in peace congresses during the war emphasized that the First World War was very much the natural outcome of interimperial competition growing on volatile neural network of (competitive) financial capitalism and the history of the decimation of indigenous people.[81] Yet, in the immediate postwar moment, the narrative that emerged especially in the victor states was that both the violence of the war and the paper used to finance it were unnatural deviations from nineteenth-century liberal ideas.

To glorify gold as an anchor of peace and stability was in part to deny the ways in which nineteenth-century liberalism flourished nationally and internationally (once again) as entwined with imperial violence and exclusionary politics.[82] To call for its restoration, then, was to call in some sense for the exclusionary privileges of that system. In the interwar moment, states facing war-weary citizens and subjects and so political revolt both at home and in the empire needed new sources of solid and natural credibility. They needed to justify national and international divisions of power and resources as well, and yet needed the confidence of their constituencies to forge stability and reconstruction. Thus, they reached for the solidity of golden anchors as one prong of restabilization.

Before continuing to follow this thread, there is another question to pose. Why might it have been that so many publics accepted inconvertible paper during the Great War only to demonize it after? As a partial answer, I want to cite what I call the *empirics of violence*, or that a state's use of violence offers a solution when other forms of a state's legitimacy are breaking down. During World War I, the nature of violence had suddenly given states enough solid credibility that societies were willing to accept the weight of paper instruments. Paper was justified with duty to country, and backed with blood. Recall that public outcries against the printing of paper currency emerged at roughly the same time that support for World War I itself was on the wane.

We can also perceive something of a correlation between the insistence on gold and patterns of violence: under the nineteenth-century gold standard, there had been violence at the margins or the periphery of industrialized nations. That is, the extent of the violence was either hidden from the view of the majority of the population in the West, or somehow justified by the terms of manifest destinies and civilizing missions.[83] During the war, however, violence moved to the center of industrialized states and involved those whole societies.

In a sense then, gold was necessary to secure public confidence during a time of so-called peace and commercial and imperial expansion. That is not to suggest that the compulsion for gold constituted some completely self-conscious ruse, whereby elites merely lulled the masses to sleep. Rather, the difficulty of the postwar moment, the loss and confusion, also simply heightened the nostalgic lure of supposedly simpler times and deeper truths. Even the sagest of experts could not always discern the worldviews embedded in their economic insights. We can, however, bring some of those more latent worldviews to light, by rereading the claims in favor of the creation of a gold exchange standard over any of the proposed alternatives.

Phantom Currencies: The Gold Exchange Standard and Its Hierarchies

As in the nineteenth century, gold was not the only proposed solution for returning the world to sounder economic foundations after 1918. Just as proponents of the idea of an international language hoped to reduce both friction and unfair advantage in international communication, advocates of a single currency, a world unit of account, felt certain it would summon a more equitable world economy.[84] At the Brussels conference, the delegates discussed suggestions for an international currency unit.[85] Afterward, many advocates of those schemes also approached the League both to discuss the possibility of a single currency for the world, and also to provide a more international unit for the League's accounts.

In 1919, René de Saussure—scholar, "resident of Bern," brother of the famous linguist, and devotee of Esperanto—wrote to the League about the question of an international currency. He appealed in particular to Nitobe, Inazō, the very League official who had taken such an interest in Esperanto. René de Saussure proposed the use of the international florin, which was a tabular currency based on the international metric system and equal to approximately 2.48 gold francs. He spoke in particular of the ease of creating a "purement fictive" (purely fictive) standard, and of its merits. The suggestion followed on the back of a recent publication, in which he argued that the study of the structures of actual languages could serve as a template for the design of artificial ones.[86] He too saw language and money as domains where the power of creation and invention could provide tools for building a world far better than the natural one.

Unsurprisingly, the League rejected this proposal and others, instead adopting the gold Swiss franc as a unit of account. As the report on this question indicated: "The accounts of the League are kept in League of Nations gold francs representing a given amount of gold and contributions of Member States are legally payable either in gold at Geneva or in currency."[87] Even this gold franc was simply another variant of an imaginary currency: it was nothing more than the gold franc of the Latin Union between France, Italy, Belgium, and Switzerland that had been suggested during the international monetary conference of 1867 as a universal currency and a tool to promote global peace.[88] At that time (1920), with the franc now an inconvertible paper currency, and the same situation prevailing for Belgium and Italy, this ghost of the past existed only in its Swiss incarnation. The question then was not really between real currencies and imagined ones, but rather more about a choice to naturalize one currency by pointing to the artificiality of the other.

The League also rejected more broadly the idea of an international currency unit for facilitating international trade. As Cassel argued: "If we analyze the different schemes put forward in favor of a new international standard, we shall almost invariably find that they involve the creating of new masses of paper currency." And thus, "ultimately then, such schemes unveil themselves as a policy of continuing on a world-wide scale, the process of inflation hitherto carried on as a national concern."[89] Reasons for denying existence to an international currency standard were once again the fact that it would push the world toward a paper currency. In truth, the gold exchange standard that was proposed at that point and endorsed at the Genoa conference in 1922 was even more of a paper standard than its nineteenth-century counterpart. It proposed to allow states to hold in their reserves—instead of gold—paper currencies in the shape of "bills of exchange"—private paper debts originating in the finance of international trade. The condition was that they should be denominated in a currency that was by contrast convertible into gold (thus the expression gold *exchange* standard). These bills would be "as good as gold," and their substitution to gold bullion in central bank reserves would reduce worldwide competition for physical gold. As if by magic, the gold exchange standard invented an international gold supply that was not constrained by the materiality of gold in vaults. Just as the nineteenth-century gold standard justified itself by pointing to the risk that insufficient gold output would induce deflationary pressure motivating calls for monetary management, the interwar standard justified this key currency system by highlighting the risk and scarcity of the world's gold supplies.[90]

Thus, to some extent, the symbol of gold elided both the inherent paperness of the exchange standard system and its inherent inequalities. For the description of this new exchange standard did not include any hint of its actual relation to geopolitical rifts and disparities. Closer reflection, however, reveals the extent to which it was very much a political mechanism that decided which states would hold gold and which would hold "key currencies." In general, the victor powers or more advanced economies held gold, while the defeated or less developed held reserve currencies. Of course, the economists rationalized this system as meeting the demands of the postwar economy.

At one level, most European states were in this same boat, for, as one League publication asserted, "the problem of post-war reconstruction, in a physical sense, is essentially a problem of accumulating physical capital at a more rapid rate than is normally achieved in peace-time," and this had "explained" the choice of the gold exchange standard.[91] And yet some states had fewer ores, or less capacity to attract gold. For one, beyond the fact that reparations heavily weighed on the external accounts of only some countries, the postwar order had also been reorganized in order to shrink the market size of the defeated powers. New states had to kick-start new economies in many cases without the necessary financial or political infrastructure. Again Cassel spoke of the irony of this difficult dilemma: "The principle of nationality has been applied with a stress quite incompatible with modern economic conditions, requiring a large home market and a wide area for the free movement of international trade."[92]

Many new or revised states thus solved their budgetary deficits with the printing press. Hyperinflation was primarily a disease of the defeated (Germany), or, at the least, the states born of defeat (Austria and Hungary).[93] Once again, the horrors and traumas of floods of anchorless, meaningless paper appeared as a specter.[94] It was in this context that the League's role as an interwar "money doctor" took on new significance. And in fact, it was in that moment that the term "money doctoring" came into use to describe the practice of monetary advisement as it had played out under the classical gold standard.[95] In the 1920s, these new states needed credit to stabilize, and yet their instability made them poor candidates for sovereign loans. The League thus served as a financial mediator, working with governments and financiers to secure loans for these governments facing high inflation. However, these loans included the condition that the new states accept the proposed gold exchange standard and the creation of central banks that would operate within the strict budgetary guidelines set by the terms of the loan.[96]

Just as with the Minority Treaties, the League loans included a laundry list of "best practices," and the League's role was to observe and intervene into the states' internal economic affairs.[97] However, once again, the terms of aid often constrained states' rate of development. As in the case of a Latin alphabet, or levels of literacy, or treatment of minorities, "gold" operated as an ever-moving qualifier of civilization. The system's double bind for select states was a matter not just of national prestige, time, and labor, but also of financial solvency. Economic stability was also a criterion by which these states were supposed to prove they were capable of greater autonomy. And yet the terms of those loans also tied their hands.[98]

The rhetoric of the universality of the gold exchange standard system hid, or at least elided, the implications of the fact that the very states plagued with hyperinflation were also the "reserve currency" states. Thus, in a sense their financial solvency was yet again even more bound to the fates and fortunes of the powers whose currencies operated as reserves. While central management and thus convertibility suspensions were more possible in gold-holding states, they were less possible for those holding currencies as reserve. The irony, too, was that charges of paper sins of hyperinflation naturalized the normal inflation, the ongoing printing, and then imperfect convertibility that existed everywhere, in every state, well after the return in many states to "gold." Here again, the product was that of symbolic capital: the *idea* of gold provided an anchor for political credibility above all else. Still it also offered a double bind of uneven constraints and opportunities. For one, it provided more flexibility for those who took up gold willingly than for those who were compelled onto gold.

In the end, the decline of the interwar gold exchange standard was as much about the decline in its power as a credible symbol as it was any technical fault in the system itself. Its loss of credibility came in part through the slow and steady efforts of those most constrained by the system. Within this power struggle, the League was tasked with bolstering and stabilizing the international monetary order. Here then we return to a familiar pattern, where the promotion of gold and efforts against counterfeit came together to provide touchstones for public confidence in the truth of the currency.

False Uttering: *L'Affaire des Faux Billets*

On June 5, 1926, French prime minister and minister of foreign affairs Aristide Briand wrote a careful but impassioned letter to the secretary-general of the League of Nations. Briand wrote this letter only a few days before he stumbled on his own economic and monetary policies. For the French franc had been battered in international markets and was itself on the verge of hyperinflation.[99] Despite the difficulty of France's own situation, Briand's letter focused on another matter: the problem of counterfeiting. In particular, he hoped that the League would take up the question and launch an international initiative dedicated to addressing this "inherently international" question. As he stated: "Though such crimes deal a blow in the first instance at the financial strength of the country whose currency is counterfeited, they are also capable, as a direct consequence, of disturbing international public order."[100]

While counterfeiting had indeed been a fairly widespread problem in postwar Europe, Briand approached the League because of a specific set of circumstances: after the discovery of a Hungarian ring that had been counterfeiting one-thousand-franc bills. In French, *l'affaire des faux billets* created a highly publicized scandal and a great deal of panic within the French government, not only for the threat it posed to the franc, but also because it summoned deeper fears about central European efforts to reverse the terms of the peace settlements.[101]

Indeed, the context of the Hungarian counterfeiting ring was embedded in the postwar order, in which, after signing the Treaty of Trianon in France in 1921, Hungary found itself with a considerable loss of both territory and population, and landlocked. Afterward, many Hungarians held France directly responsible for the punitive bluntness with which the treaty carved up the former Austro-Hungarian Empire. The precise details of the story varied quite a bit from publication to publication.[102] However, most agreed that the plot was hatched among a cadre of right-wing would-be royalists who hoped to return the Archduke Albrecht to the throne. The group needed money, which at the time was both scarce and also difficult to raise; they decided to fund their contemplated coup by printing francs.

It may seem strange to counterfeit a currency that was looming on the brink of hyperinflation and thus a steep loss in value. However, the counterfeiters had an extramonetary logic to their choices. As one publication quoted: "France, whose will had deprived Hungary of two-thirds of her former territory through the peace treaty of Trianon, was to be paid out partly by a further inflation of the French currency."[103] Thus, beyond reasons of profit, the Hungarian counterfeiters hoped precisely to make France pay, not just in money, but also in further exposing the inherent weakness and the paper-ness of the franc.[104] Despite the real crises of the franc, the public relations surrounding the French economy avoided the parallel between France's monetary situation and hyperinflation in the defeated territories. The subtle distinction between normal inflation and abnormal inflation was long repeated at the League. For example, in a retrospective of the 1920s, a League publication claimed that hyperinflation in Germany had resulted in part from Germany's ideological failure to accept the quantity theory of money.[105]

In the specific case of Hungary, the counterfeiters worked against the conditions imposed as a result of the League's stabilization loan, including the requirement that Hungary eliminate thousands of government positions.[106] Even before the implementation of those programs, the election of the League's commissioner-general for the supervision of Hungary's financial reconstruction generated resistance. When the news broke that the League had appointed the American Jeremiah Smith to the job, the prime minister, Istvan Bethlen, apparently first insisted on verifying that Smith was not Jewish (he was not).[107] However, as the League's proscribed austerity measures played out, those unpopular programs became tangled with rampant anti-Semitism and xenophobia. In the background of the counterfeit plot was a rumor mill that blamed Hungary's woes on a contrived conflation of French thievery and "Jewish" international finance.[108]

Behind the slanderous conspiracy theories, counterfeit efforts grew within and pressed on the double standards at work in the interwar moment. Within an echo of the claim that France (great powers) had no "minorities" came another form of doublespeak. Despite the real crises of the franc, the public relations surrounding the French economy avoided the parallel between France's monetary situation and those instances of hyperinflation in the defeated territories. What is more, in crisis, France was permitted to direct its own economy; Hungary had to accept external supervision. That is not to say that the League's efforts were altogether negative or ill conceived, but rather that they emerged to protect the world order enshrined in the peace treaties. As a case in point, the French government later used the discovery of the plot to argue (unsuccessfully) that the League should prolong its financial oversight of Hungary beyond the proposed termination date of 1926.[109]

While France discovered and dismantled the counterfeit plot before those false bills entered circulation, the affair still reverberated in French policy circles.[110] The French delegation's efforts to draw attention to the problem of counterfeiting might then be read as a counterpart to its efforts to increase its gold reserves from 7 to 27 percent between 1927 and 1932.[111] The point here is not—as is the usual question—whether France caused the Great Depression through its hoarding of gold. Rather, the point is that anticounterfeit measures on the one hand, and the advertising of its "golden security" on the other, constituted two sides of a broader effort to renew confidence in the franc, and thus in France.[112]

What better way, then, to advertise the solidity of the paper franc than to draw international public attention to the illegitimacy of counterfeit? Briand's letter was read aloud at the fourth meeting during the fortieth session of the Council on June 10, 1926. At that session, the French rapporteur Joseph Paul-Boncour explained why his government wanted the League to take up the question of "internationalizing the methods of suppressing the counterfeiting of currency."[113] Furthermore, he stated: "The manufacture internationally of counterfeit currency was no longer a matter concerning only the national sovereignty of a given country, but directly concerned, materially and morally, the whole international community."[114]

Upon Briand's request, the Council created the Mixed Committee to begin an initial investigation into the state of international counterfeiting, and to prepare the groundwork for an international conference, which eventually took place in 1929. In the meantime, the Mixed Committee held meetings at Geneva from June 23 to June 28, and again from October 10 to October 13, 1927, during which time they collected comments on the state of counterfeiting from the central banks of various countries. They also cooperated with the International Criminal Police Commission, which was created to halt the upsurge in counterfeit after the armistice in the early 1920s.[115]

As a result of this request, the League played a part in the emergence of stronger international cooperation on matters of crime and policing.[116] And yet, despite the criminal and legal rationale, drawing attention to the matter of counterfeit seemed to be every bit as important as actually halting counterfeit. As the Czech rapporteur Edvard Beneš described: "The political and psychological effects of such a circumstance were even more serious than the material loss involved."[117] The extent to which money's symbolic dimensions overshadowed all else can be found in the gap between statistical charts and the narrative given to those statistics. The statistics on how the mechanical features of the gold exchange standard impacted monetary stability were indeed rather light.[118] Similarly, the actual nature and extent of, and monetary loss caused by, counterfeiting rings were neither precise nor definitive. According to official figures collected at the League (which included a caveat regarding the difficulty of arriving at definitive numbers), between 1924 and 1927 authorities around the world had confiscated the equivalent of three million dollars' worth of counterfeit notes and coins. Indeed, for a world total this was not a terribly dramatic dent. Yet there was widespread support for holding an international conference on the issues. The report of the Mixed Committee stated (echoing Beneš): "Far more important than the figure itself is the latent danger of this evil, which attacks the very roots of the world economy."[119] The nature of that evil was the negative effect that counterfeit might have on general "confidence."

Along those lines, the report further described the heart of the concern: "Counterfeiting endangers, not only the property rights of individuals, but also the monetary sovereignty of the State and those economic relations which depend intimately for their development on complete confidence in the security of the currency."[120] After all, confidence, the invisible lifeblood of impersonal modern market economies, was a fragile thing—difficult to secure and sustain.[121] Moreover, confidence in the legal tender went two ways, wherein a loss of faith in money could undermine public trust in the state, and vice versa. Thus, as the report stated: "The counterfeiting of currency strikes a blow not only at the public order of the State where the offence is committed, or at the credit of the State whose currency has been forged, but to undermine public confidence in the medium of exchange, as presented by the currency, thus hindering international economic cooperation."[122]

The real trouble was that of the technologically produced difficulty of distinguishing between authentic and inauthentic. As the draft convention on counterfeit prepared in 1927 stated: "The criminal law should include and punish with adequate penalties any fraudulent making or . . . *uttering* of currency."[123] Of course, in English, the verb *to utter* simply means to speak or to articulate, but as an adjective, *utter* can also mean total, complete, or absolute, as in *utter ruin* or *utter despair*. The third and least common definition of the word refers to putting money into circulation. And indeed, in uniting all the connotations of *utter*—speaking, totality, and circulating money—legal tender emerges as a statement that seeks to be absolute. A *false uttering* then becomes a counterstatement, or a lie that threatens the truth claims of the official currency.[124] Like hyperinflation, false utterings could also draw attention to the fact that both ostensibly legitimate and illegitimate currencies were increasingly creatures of the printing press. In short, they threatened the print and informational nature of modern money. And, indeed, it could be difficult to draw lines between legitimate and illegitimate monetary forms: it was said that the Bank of France not only studied the Hungarian counterfeiters' techniques but also adopted those methods of manufacturing banknote paper.[125]

This underscores the dangerous extent to which the authenticity and credibility of state currency remained vulnerable to disclosure and exposure. The worry was twofold. At a deeper level, if people could not tell the difference between the original and the reproduction, they might lose faith in the solidity of the real. On the other hand, if they could not tell the difference between the fake and the real, they might use the fake money as if it were real, and thus there would be an artificial increase in the money supply. This increase might summon hyperinflation, revealing the breach between money and its worth.

Figures such as Irving Fisher and other advocates of the tabular standard claimed to be able to eliminate such risks. In 1928, Fisher explained more fully the breach he had identified long before between "nominal" and "real" by coining a new term: the "money illusion." He defined this phenomenon as "the failure to perceive that the dollar, or any other unit of money, expands or shrinks in value."[126] He explained that even gold was not a sufficient remedy against fluctuating value, since its value also fluctuated. So Fisher suggested that a more scientific remedy had to be found. For now, what matters is that most of the text was devoted to outlining the necessity of puncturing the money illusion, and thereby removing the delusional speck from the public eye. Yet Fisher admitted that to puncture the money illusion might be to rupture the essence of what secured the public's confidence in the currency, though he remained optimistic that a scientifically stabilized tabular standard would be so steady that eventually it would also engender the public's confidence, and so based on fundamentals that it would even be impervious to counterfeit.

Yet Fisher had a blind spot: he failed to see money as a symbol and a tool of both private and state power, and not just a neutral medium or a potential mirror for a fixed or fixable reality. Perhaps this was (partially) his own *genetic bias*, his own assumption of the fixed difference between the solid interested world of flesh and the neutral world of finance. Money was a mere servant of the interests of the ethnos.

Freud tended to share with Fischer a binary way of understanding "illusion" and "reality." In his *The Future of an Illusion*, Freud also tacked illusions as a mode of faith that kept people from accepting or dealing with the real. Quoting from the English edition that appeared the same year as Fisher's book, Freud stated: "What is characteristic of illusions is that they are derived from human wishes." And yet Freud perceived a parallel that Fischer missed. As an illustration, Freud stated: "One may describe as an illusion the assertion made by certain nationalists that the Indo-Germanic race is the only one capable of civilization."[127]

Despite their differences, Fisher and Freud still each endowed science (in some way and to some degree) with the ability to dispel illusion. Yet, as Freud also highlighted, claims of superior (racial) forms of "reality" also promised to dispel "illusions." Thus, there were many technological, political, and even spiritual dynamics standing in the way of some easy reunion between the "nominal" and the "real."

In terms of designing monetary policy, most authorities hoped to maintain the money illusion rather than puncture it. Those illusions served political purposes.

In this way, the League's counterfeit conference defined the primary problem in the following way: "Counterfeiting strikes a blow at public confidence in that instrument of exchange that currency represents in abstracto."[128] The conference proceedings portrayed deep concerns about what the "artificial" threatened to reveal about "real" currency. Namely, it threatened to expose the fact that the value of money was a fundamentally variable and illusory phenomenon to begin with.

In this frame, to the extent that money stood as a symbol of national power, one leitmotif that emerged during the conference was the threat internationalism posed to the value and solidity of national currency. Whereas in the nineteenth century tackling the problem of counterfeit had been primarily a national issue, at the League participants emphasized the extent to which not just money, but also confidence had become deeply international concerns. To the extent that information and financial systems stretched the question of confidence across borders, then greater weight fell on the question of how to stabilize not just currency but also faith in the currency.[129]

At the conference's opening session on April 9, 1929, at 11:00 a.m., the presiding president, the Czech delegate Vilém Pospíšil, again painted the picture of a world of increased monetary interdependences: "Technical progress and the evolution of human activities are constantly extending the scope and intensity of these (monetary) relations; their development is accompanied by a simultaneous increase in currency exchange between countries in which, particularly since the war, increasing use has been made of paper money—apart of course, from the various methods of compensation."[130] The argument was that the growth of this international (information) economy had made it more difficult to discern and protect the trust in "national" monies. Once again, the proceedings of the conference articulated the concern: "The more extensive use of banknotes, the facility with which the currency of one country can be changed in other countries, the difficulty for the public of testing the genuineness of foreign currency are circumstances which have encouraged criminals to greater boldness, and lead them to extend their sphere of action and to creation organizations with ramifications in a number of states." What is more, the participants imagined darkly clad conspirators lurking behind every corner: "these gangs of forgers find accomplices in every country who are ready to assist them in obtaining the means of committing the offence and at the same time to enable them to escape prosecution and punishment."[131]

For precisely these reasons, Vespasian Pella of Romania stated: "It was very important to realize that nowadays the counterfeiting of currency might constitute a new form of terrorism." To those ends he drew a striking juxtaposition, claiming that the effects of violent terrorism "had very ephemeral, or at any rate, limited results." However, counterfeiting a nation's currency could "strike at the whole political and social organization of a given country" and so have "profound and lasting consequences."[132] These profound and lasting consequences included, once again, the extent to which counterfeiting might expose deeper contradictions within capitalism. In one discussion, the Japanese delegation asked if a counterfeiter could be held liable to punishment if he counterfeited without the intent to profit. The Belgian representative Paul Servais responded that this was a dangerous road to go down: "the only instance which he could imagine the hypothesis raised by the Japanese delegate arising would be of the person manufacturing the note came out of a dance-hall, saw a poor man and gave him the thousand Franc note, he had the indirect advantage of appearing charitable, and had therefore an indirect profit."[133]

In fact the scene that Servais described echoed one in the poem "Counterfeit Money," by the French poet Charles Baudelaire. In that text, Baudelaire described his companion giving a "generous" contribution to a beggar. However, when Baudelaire praised his companion, the friend admitted, the coin had been a counterfeit one.[134] Servais had brought that story to suggest that these matters of intent and their relevance for prosecuting the crime of counterfeiting were best left to judges. However, held side by side with Baudelaire's poem we can see an emerging set of mentalities, whereby counterfeit had the ability to expose, in Keynes's words, sight of the "arbitrary" distribution of wealth. While the poem marked a kind of cruel joke against a pauper it also raised another question: if in some way all money was *created*, why should some have more than others?

Anther frequently repeated theme in those proceedings was the role that trust might have to play in the question of counterfeiting. Some delegates spoke out for the "safety" of older, more isolated ways of living, buying, and selling. The delegate from New Zealand explained that New Zealand had very few problems of counterfeiting currency, and the idea that someone could convert bills from one to the other, was, to his mind unlikely, for "persons who have such in their possession have the greatest difficulty in disposing of it until their bone fide have been well established."[135] In other words, New Zealand did such a good job of keeping immigrants out that the country's natural suspicion of *strangers* rendered the country less susceptible to fakery or trickery. Here too we hear a growing discourse that tied the evils of fakes and untrustworthiness to questions of immigration and xenophobic desires to decide who belonged and who did not.

As the conference closed, it had been able to ratify a number of signatures but had very little effect on the alternation of domestic laws. Of more interest is the fact that, despite a push to have a similar conference on securities and bills of exchange, that effort found little support.[136] It was the symbolic effect of counterfeit, not its economic effect, that actually posed the greatest danger. In the end, despite intentions of international cooperation, the League had provided a platform where nations either advertised or became more resolute in the need to demonstrate the "truth" of their own currencies. It also seemed to heighten their respective sense of danger regarding how the global informational sphere posed a threat to the appearance of solidity and authenticity of their own paper currencies.

Of course, by the time the conference was ending, global recession was already heating up, which began to undermine the sense that gold was compatible with the survival of statehood. In particular, there grew a fear that the global immaterial risks ran straight through the gold standard.[137] As Ragnar

Nurkse, who worked for the League, later explained: "Each country sought to protect its domestic credit system from the influence of fluctuations originating outside. When the precepts of the gold standard ran counter to the requirements of domestic monetary stability, it was the latter that usually prevailed." Individual countries became more and more anxious to escape the rigors of the worldwide cycle of booms and slumps. Gold and exchange reserves thus came to be used as cushions, buffers, or insulators, instead of acting as transmitters.[138] At first what happened was a scramble for gold; later, one by one, country after country left gold altogether.[139] As the public mood shifted away from gold, theories also changed. Some states begam claiming that rather than a "natural anchor" gold had been a mere conspiracy, an act of trickery on the part of an "international" (read bolshevist or Jewish) elite.Ô

The Illusionists; or, How Gold Became "Artificial"

Sensing that states were getting ready to shed their gold commitments, the League instituted the Gold Delegation to investigate the matter. The body was called into being in 1929 to look specifically at the "fluctuations in the purchasing power of gold" and its economic impact.[140] Shortly after the League created the delegation, the Depression shifted the nature of its investigation. More generally, as a critique of gold emerged in the early part of the recession, and as states ostensibly sought to free themselves from the constraints of gold, many experts cited "insufficient" global gold stock for keeping up with monetary demands. Yet on this matter the delegation uncovered a range of mixed statistics, none of which conclusively proved or denied such a material lack or abundance of gold.[141] What seemed to truly be under investigation in the world at large was the geopolitical system, of which the gold exchange standard had become a symbol.

In 1932, the collectively authored "Report of the Gold Delegation" offered a lengthy review of the principal benefits and some of the difficulties of the gold exchange standard. It admitted that the gold exchange standard had to some extent transferred the crisis from financial centers (sterling) to those who held the "key currencies" that were suddenly spiraling downward. What is more, they also admitted that the paper reserve system had in fact created some inflationary (overprinting) pressure. Nonetheless, they reaffirmed the basic soundness of the idea, and offered some solutions for its resuscitation. Namely, they suggested that reserve currencies be chosen more carefully for their potential stability, and, secondly, that the system should be facilitated through a Bank for International Settlements. Again demonstrating the supposed link between gold and peace, the report further stated: "Further, we believe that it would do much to establish complete confidence in the system were an international understanding reached that the reserves which countries hold abroad for the maintenance of their currency should not be subject to seizure or confiscation in time of war."[142] However, a deep shift was at work. By 1934, the League began accepting paper Swiss francs rather than gold Swiss francs for its member contributions. Once strong supporters of the gold standard had by 1935 become not only defectors, but vocal opponents. Even Keynes likened faith in gold to faith in God.[143] Perhaps more surprisingly, one member of the League's delegation expressed a strong minority opinion against gold: Gustav Cassel.

Since the 1920s, Cassel had undergone a veritable revolution in his mindset. In his *The Downfall of the Gold Standard*, Cassel point by point dismantled the myth of gold as he had helped to first articulate it in 1918. He started by denying that the gold standard was such an "old and venerable institution."[144] To the contrary, he proposed that "the short time it existed sufficed to expose the inherent weakness of the system," discrediting the idea that it had ever worked automatically, smoothly, or efficiently.[145] He also stated that, in general, it had served to strengthen states rather than international bonds.[146] He asserted: "Thus the pre-war gold-standard system never attained those results which were constantly proclaimed, and generally believed, to represent its principal merits."[147]

While fifteen years earlier Cassel had described unanchored paper as illusory and unnatural, in 1936 he turned the same critique against gold. He explained that the gold "hoarding" of the early Depression had in fact resulted from what he described as an "artificial" position given to gold.[148] He argued: "The artificial demand for gold that is fostered by the gold-standard system always has a tendency to strengthen protectionism."[149] Moreover, he explained why states held gold so dear, despite its faults: "The principal merit of the gold standard is commonly held to be that it offers the possessor of currency 'something tangible' into which he may convert his money." To those ends he exposed the fact that it had been a long time since citizens could actually transform notes into gold. Thus, he implored: "It is not time, in the face of these facts, to weed text-books of the traditional representation of gold reserve as a 'cover' for the note circulation or as 'something tangible' behind it?"[150]

In his chapter aptly called "The Illusion of a Return to Gold," Cassell definitively asserted: "Gold has failed, both as a means of payment and a standard of value."[151] Punctuating his disbelief that gold had ever really been a tangible or secure truth, Cassel added: "Whatever may be said of Dr. Schacht's monetary policy and his way of managing the German currency under the Nazi regime he must at any rate be credited with the great merit of having unmasked, once for all, the humbug of 'strengthening' a currency by means of borrowed gold reserves."[152] As Cassel was writing, many states already abandoned gold, and some were also steadily preparing for the possibility of war—that other "tangible" touchstone for a national economy.

Barbarous Relics and Degenerate Art

In Munich in 1937, the Nazi party staged an art exhibit to extol the virtues of great, traditional classical German art, which supposedly expressed the values and purity of the Volk. As a counterexample, the same exhibit also displayed some 650 examples of "degenerative" modern art. These were supposedly distorted, unfaithful, monstrous depictions of the influences of cosmopolitanism, Jewry, and communism.[153] These later paintings were hung alongside placards that listed the outrageous amounts of money the art would have cost under Weimar hyperinflation. In one swoop, the Nazi party under Hitler drew a line between the destructive "fictions" of the previous regimes and the supposedly more solid truths of National Socialism. There is an irony in this juxtaposition. After all, the Weimar Republic had eventually stabilized the currency with the introduction of the Rentenmark, backed by land.[154] National Socialism, however, went even deeper into paper tides.

Nazi economic policy was shaped by what was called the *Wehrwirtschaft* theory.[155] It grew from the idea that every aspect of the economy should be integrated into the military machine. And yet, rather than any one discernable monetary policy, the Nazi regime played fast and loose with the printing press. In equal parts, the party used printed monetary forms and propaganda to highlight the illegitimacy of its "enemies" and the "naturalness" and trustworthiness of the Volk. Alongside a range of strategies, including printing money and controlling prices, the Nazi government also consistently counterfeited foreign bills as an act of war.[156] In 1940, the Nazis dropped what looked like American dollar bills onto the streets of Paris. Yet, inside those bills was a message about the "evils" of the "Jewish dollar" and "Jewish international finance."[157]

Here, then, was the heart of a shift, again through paper, back to the certainties of state-sanctioned violence. In that context, the American fascist sympathizer Ezra Pound also set out to explain why a strong state was all the solidity that paper money needed.[158] Pound had been influenced by the social credit theories of C. H. Douglas, which combined a credit money system with centralized guarantees for stable incomes prices determined by the rate of consumption.¹⁵⁹ The idea was that consumers and their needs could drive and create the terms of prosperity—money need not be tied to any a specific anchor at all.

In his essay *What Is Money For*, Pound stated: "Money is a general sort of ticket which is its only difference from a railway or a theatre ticket." This theme of the truth effects of theater remained an important leitmotif throughout Pound's career. In "The Promised Land," he had uttered: "Truth is not untrue'd by reason our of our failing to fix it on paper. Certain objects are communicable to a man or a woman only with 'proper lighting,' they are perceptible in our own minds only with proper 'lighting,' fitfully and by instants."¹⁶⁰ In some sense, Pound thought that merely adjusting the lighting might solve the world's monetary problems.

First he claimed that a money ticket became a problem or would start to "wobble," as he called it, only under a corrupt system. Virtuous states were the only possible means of establishing, in his words, a "JUST and HONEST currency."¹⁶¹ In chartal-cum-social credit theories, Pound did away with the implications of Saussure's insight and Fisher's fear. He proposed a once-and-for-all solution to that ever-fluctuating relation between money and value. As he stated: "SOVEREIGNTY inheres in the right to ISSUE money (tickets) and to determine the value thereof." The state simply set the value of the currency and ensured that all citizens (at least all those deemed worthy) could have the things they needed. In this view, the goal was to show precisely that the old order of distribution had been arbitrary. Pound suggested that states created tickets to provide three square meals for all the members of community and in fact praised Hitler and Mussolini for proving it was possible. Pound claimed that a state saying it couldn't build a road because it lacked the money was like saying, "It cannot build roads because it has no kilometers." Money and prosperity could be made and distributed; it could be given and withheld at will.

According to Pound, the success of fascism rested on the fact that it had allowed state money based on national wealth to replace, in his words, "GOLD manipulated by international usurers." Where the blood and the soil created the basis for a stable printed money ticket, international usury—with all its anti-Semitic connotations—had apparently been to blame for the previous poverty of many states and people. To those ends, Pound directly quoted Hitler, saying: "The struggle against international finance and loan capital has become the most important point in the National Socialist program."

Despite his belief that strong states might print tickets, Pound indicated that not all print mechanisms could be trusted. One should avoid, for example, taking as truth anything that poured out of "Jewspapers" or the mouths of professors. According to Pound, this world of international news and finance, preaching loans and gold, had been peddling its wares "via the corrupt League of Nations (frontage and face wash for the worse international corruption at Basel)."[162] Thus, in seeking to break the constraints of the international system, of which the gold standard was a key component, the pendulum of monetary symbols had swung back away from metal. It swung in the direction of an open use of the printing press based on the certainty of race, and too of violence. In a symbolically violent summation, Pound asserted: "USURY is the cancer of the world, which only the surgeon's knife of fascism can cut out of the life of the nations."

On his deathbed, after he had fled Austria and Nazi occupation, and despite all his reservations about the symbols of gold, a cancer-stricken Freud gave three Austrian gold coins to his personal physician as a dying gift.[163] Perhaps it was an act of nostalgia, a gesture toward things more solid, more enduring than flesh. After all, Freud's own flesh was plagued by cancer on the one hand and "the knife of fascism" on the other. Some years earlier, in 1928, perhaps in a moment of prescience, the League had placed a sample of the currencies of all the member states in a time capsule. They then placed the time capsule under the cornerstone of the foundation of the new Palais des Nations.[164]

When the building opened its doors in 1938, the picture of the world preserved beneath the League already read like an obituary. Two years before, however, a young Jewish intellectual walked into the old Assembly hall, took out a gun and shot himself in front of the eyes of the world, or so he thought. It is on his story—and the question of so-called false news—that our story will end.

5

Fiat Lux?
False News and Hidden Flesh

> We brought you truth, and in our mouth it sounded a lie. . . . We brought you the promise of the future, but our tongue stammered and barked.
> ARTHUR KOESTLER, *Darkness at Noon*

Let There Be Light

In 1936, a little over a year after the passage of the Nuremburg Laws in Germany, a dramatic episode took place on the League's public stage. On the afternoon of July 3, during the sixteenth session of the Assembly, a Czech journalist, poet, and filmmaker by the name of Stefan Lux walked onto floor, took out a gun, and shot himself, not in the head, but in the heart. With this strategic choice, Lux lived long enough to observe the reactions of those standing around him.

By poetic coincidence, in Latin, *Lux* means light.[1] What is more, *Fiat Lux*, or "let there be light," was the very first phrase that Gutenberg printed on his revolutionary machine.[2] The phrase itself came from Genesis 1:3, as God set out to create the world from the dark formless void: "God said, 'Let there be light'; and there was light." In that frame, Gutenberg had linked the printed word to the defeat of darkness via the widest possible dissemination of scriptural truth and revelation. It was also in a spirit of *shedding light* via the printed word that Stephen Lux took his life on the Assembly floor. Lux had become increasingly pained as many journalists and world leaders had been failing to report on or even fully accept the nature and extent of the Nazi threat.[3] In an act that Émile Durkheim might have labeled an *altruistic suicide*, Lux used his own body and his own death in an attempt to illuminate the real nature of the political malignancy that was threatening the world.[4] According to his final correspondence, Lux hoped that his demonstration would motivate first public censure of and then coordinated action against Germany.[5]

In taking his life at the League specifically, Lux seemed to believe that the whole "civilized" world not only would be watching but also would receive the *true* meaning of his message. On July 4, 1936, the *New York Times* recounted an employee's testimony at the hotel where Lux had been staying on the evening of July 2: "'Last night he paid his bill at the pension where he had been staying and settled all his other obligations. He told the pension proprietor to watch for an important development today connected with himself. The proprietor took this as a joke. 'Are you then going to be elected president of the Czechoslovak Republic?' he asked. 'No,' replied Mr. Lux seriously, 'but this development will be sensational.'"[6]

In the end, however, Lux's death did not have as much of an impact as he had hoped. The event received a flurry of press coverage initially, but the attention soon faded.[7] For its part, the League administration tried to minimize any damage the incident might cause to the League's reputation. Thus, Lux's story is conspicuously absent from the printed proceedings of the 1936 Assembly, and the archival material on the event is remarkably meager.[8]

The sparse archival preservation of Lux's mission is all the more interesting given its precise timing. For several years beforehand, the League of Nations had been studying the role of the press and broadcasting in maintaining world peace. Those inquiries spent time, among other things, parsing out the importance of *truth* and the dangers of so-called *false news*.[9] The question of false news had also been reverberating on the world stage beyond the League and had become a buzzword within a set of forces that pushed Lux to his death in the first place. The defamatory moniker "the lying press" existed before the rise of National Socialism but found new life in that regime and took hold in other (even ostensibly democratic) states.[10] However, that label quickly became a political weapon designed to question the truth of any opposing political position or point of view.[11] As with counterfeit currency, or Esperanto, key politicians decried false news or "the lying press" in order to naturalize and garner support for their own programs, along with, increasingly, their pogroms. Such claims also resounded within a broader tendency: efforts to criticize, limit, restrict, or outright abolish the workings of a free press.[12]

By moving between Lux's story and the League's Conference on False News, we can also look more closely at the relationship between interwar media, competing claims of "true" and "false," and the rise of state-sanctioned violence. As we will see, despite a putative commitment to the truth, often "facts" that threatened the stability of a certain "world picture," got modified or even redacted. What is more, even the ideal of truth telling had to contend with the dynamics of unstable and endlessly malleable webs of signs and signals. Of greatest interest here is discerning what the League's and the media's treatment of the facts of Lux's suicide might reveal about how information systems helped to facilitate and justify violence on a much greater scale.[13]

Before turning to the details of Lux's story, however, I want to spend some time with another interwar character, namely the Jewish German man of letters Walter Benjamin. As it happens, Benjamin also took his own life, in 1940, while fleeing the Gestapo.[14] After lucky breaks, narrow escapes, and a harrowing journey through a mountain passage in the Pyrenees, Benjamin's fate fell into the hands of border control agents. He and his party happened to arrive at the exit point between France and Spain just as the legal window for emigration was closing. Rather than wait for a resolution, Benjamin took a deadly dose of morphine.[15] Before his tragic end, however, Benjamin had long theorized how the rise of information systems had silenced rather than *illuminated* human experiences. He had been a subtle prophet of how media flattened or exaggerated stories in ways that actually fed the abstracting and dehumanizing logic of mass annihilations. Thus, here, Benjamin's insights offer an interpretive framework for understanding how and to what ends the League and the press "spun" the details of Lux's life and death.[16]

Death Comes for the Storyteller

In the very same year that Lux made his final journey to Geneva, Benjamin sketched a portrait, outlining the characteristics of an artisan in danger of extinction. This essay, "The Storyteller: Reflections on the Works of Nicolai Leskov," first appeared in a journal entitled (of all things) *Orient und Okzident*. Later, Benjamin's friend Hannah Arendt republished that essay, along with a number of others, under the title *Illuminations*.[17] For Benjamin, the figure of the storyteller embodied something sacred, a link to the heart of the human condition increasingly at risk in the modern world. In the capitalist mechanical age, which was also the age of mass media, the art and craft of telling a story had, in Benjamin's words, "already become something remote from us and [was] moving further and further away."[18] To Benjamin's mind, storytelling had become a rare occurrence just at the moment when words and images could multiply and travel as never before.[19] In his words: "Every morning brings us news from across the globe, and yet we are poor in noteworthy stories."[20] What is more, if stories were disappearing, it was partly because they were being crowded out by information. Again, Benjamin claimed: "If the art of storytelling has become rare, the dissemination of information has played a decisive role in this state of affairs."[21]

For Benjamin, one problem with contemporary information was that its primary purpose was to certify, verify, and make a (usually narrow) statement of some kind. As he asserted in consternation, "nowadays no event comes to us without already being shot through with explanation."[22] There was a reason for this urge to "explain" or summarize. Both the news and mass-market fictions competed for the attention of hurried consumers, tapping their feet or sitting on the edge of their seats, waiting for the punch line, the bottom line, or the titillating exposé.[23] Every headline, every scandal, every sensational plot, however ostensibly different in form or content, arrived in a form reducible to a single headline or buzzword. Perhaps the most dangerous element of the rise of information was the way in which all new information or any set of facts could simply reinforce the reductionism of clichés.[24]

By contrast, the goal of storytelling was not to explain and certainly not to summarize.[25] Benjamin argued: "It does not aim to convey the pure 'in itself' or gist of a thing, like information or a report."[26] Even here, Benjamin was not calling for the abandonment of accuracy or facts as such. In fact, he claimed that in a story "the most extraordinary things, marvelous things, are related with the greatest *accuracy* [my emphasis] but the psychological connections among the events are not forced on the reader[;] it is left up to him to interpret things the way he understand them, and thus the narrative achieves an amplitude that information lacks."[27] The important point is that this "amplitude" constituted another form of truth, beyond political, journalistic, or even scientific truth: what he called "the epic side of truth," whose primary function was to generate wisdom.[28]

If we think about epics as a genre, we might get closer to the truth forms Benjamin had in mind. On the one hand epics grew out of oral traditions, thus while they might be told and retold, each teller would tell the tale with his or her own inflections. In this way, the story remained alive because continually in motion. More importantly, epics usually moved back and forth between the events of the hero's journey and thick descriptions of the environment: the quivering of a single leaf, the whiter light of the morning as opposed to golden light of afternoon, jars and jars of wine and olive oil laid by in the cellar, and the texture of woolen blankets. Those seemingly ordinary details not only enriched each twist of fate but also provided a vehicle for the exploration of patterns of meaning and significance.[29] This was important for Benjamin because somehow the "mundane" was at the very root of the human experience. He stated: "Boredom is the dream bird that hatches the egg of experience. A rustling in the leaves drives him away."[30] Thus the truth-as-wisdom available in stories (whether fictional or fact based) required time and patience to fully unfold.

There was also something else. Benjamin asserted that unlike the report or even the "popular novel," which usually concerned "one hero, one odyssey, or one battle," the epic was usually highly layered, dedicated instead to describing "many diffuse occurrences."[31] Decades later, perhaps taking her cue from Benjamin's work, when Hannah Arendt explored the relationship between truth and politics, she also referenced the nature of epics. Arendt asserted that to some extent a truth teller (or a storyteller) had to abandon the goal of producing a policy-relevant "lesson" for the higher goal of gaining insight. In Homer's epics, Arendt perceived a fertile path toward what she called "the disinterred pursuit of truth." She stated: "I think it can be traced to the moment when Homer chose to sing the deeds of the Trojans no less than those of the Achaeans, and to praise the glory of Hector, the foe and the defeated man, no less than the glory of Achilles, the hero of his kinfolk. This had happened no where before[;] no other civilization, however, splendid, had been able to look with equal eyes upon friend and foe."[32] Policy needed stories with a single voice. However, in epics, multiple perspectives—even conflicting ones—could coexist. The point was not the "definitive account," but the question of the meanings ascribed to the events by different perspectives.

Thus from Benjamin to Ardent, the epic offered an alternative model to truth telling, with special emphasis on the textures of human life itself. According to Benjamin, those forms of truth were dying out, threatened by a variety of reductionisms. First, there was a reductionism of "objectivity" that led authors to seek distance from their experienced humanity. Epic truth, or wisdom, by contrast, required an author to remain completely connected to his or her own human life. Benjamin stated: "Thus, traces of the storyteller cling to a story the way the handprints of the potter cling to a clay vessel."[33] Here the handprint did not connote the register of forensic science or the writing of autobiography. Rather, Benjamin implied that the storyteller should remain deeply anchored in the cycles of human life, including his or her own.[34] From here Benjamin made a rather radical assertion: "Death is the sanction for everything that the storyteller can tell. He has borrowed his authority from death. In other words, his stories refer back to natural history."[35] Staying anchored to the reality of death, according to Benjamin, endowed storytellers with the ability to tell the truths most needed, those harder-earned truths of *insight* and *perspective*. Remaining close to death, its specificity, its rituals, its losses, was how the human community remained connected to the value and the meaning of human life.

If contending with one's imminent mortality was so important for the storyteller, one would think that the violence of the First World War would have led to an increase in stories. However, as far as Benjamin was concerned, that had not been the case. Benjamin claimed: "Wasn't it noticeable at the end of the war that men who returned from that battlefield had grown silent—not richer but poorer in communicable experience? What poured out in the flood of war books ten years later was anything but experience that can be shared orally.[36] For one, the scope and scale of the war had made it difficult to even grasp the nature of its experiences. Benjamin stated: "Beginning with the First World War, a process became apparent which continues to this day. For never has experience been more thoroughly belied than strategic experience was belied by tactical warfare, economic experience by inflation, bodily experience by mechanical warfare, moral experience by those in power. A generation that had gone to school on horse drawn street cars now stood under the open sky in a landscape where nothing remained unchanged but the clouds and, beneath those clouds, in a force field of destructive torrents and explosions, the tiny, fragile, human body."[37]

Benjamin offered insight into how transformations in the modern relationship to the facts of death and dying had actually helped to make that world of trenches and mechanically produced mass deaths feasible. The modern forces that had produced so much violence had first banished the sight of dying, "further and further out of the perceptual world of living."[38] Benjamin articulated those transformations as such: "In the course of modern times, dying has been pushed further and further from the perceptual world of the living. It used to be there was not a single house, hardly a single room, in which someone had not once died. Today people live in rooms that have never been touched by death—dry dwellers of eternity; and when their end approaches, they are stowed away in sanatoria or hospitals by their heirs."[39]

A twin problem to that of "objective distance" was the parallel distance that had grown between people and their relationship to death. Benjamin also seemed to believe that information itself had helped both to flatten life and to sanitize death. It is perhaps not a coincidence that the removal of the sight of dying that Benjamin described also happened in tandem with the rise of obituaries. In this new format, the *death announcement*, a life appeared as a report, *or a summary* of key events and accomplishments, and intimacy as a list of the next of kin.[40] As a kind of virtual parallel to the sanatorium, the media could report on dying, or narrate dying, without shedding light on the meaning or experience of death. In an analogous insight, war reporting and many war memoires also in a sense managed to sanitize the sights, sounds, and smells of the trenches. Human bodies transformed into mere information, they became little more than a series of images, tangled limbs in battlefields, and rows of graves. What is more, those more gruesome descriptions and photographs mingled with those of pretty faces, dapper gentlemen, and advertisements for department stores.

Later, Horkheimer and Adorno expressed a parallel critique of information: "The most intimate reactions of human beings have become so entirely reified, even to themselves, that the idea of anything peculiar to them survives only in the extreme abstract[;] personality means hardly more than dazzling white teeth and freedom from body odor and emotions."[41] The consequence of this process—perceived in Benjamin and described in Horkheimer and Adorno—was that wherever life and especially death appeared as mere information, violence had become all the more possible and on a greater scale. For if dying was a mere abstraction, so too might be killing. If a life could be reduced to a stereotype, or a report, it was all the easier to erase.

This is why, for Benjamin, the stakes of storytelling were so high. Storytelling could restore value to life, in its embrace of the particular, by remaining close to the shared reality of death. That is why storytellers could come into being only through the radical acceptance of their own mortality. As Benjamin phrased it: "Yet characteristically, it is not only a man's knowledge or wisdom, but above all his real life—and this is the stuff that stories are made of—which first assumes transmissible form at the moment of his death."[42] It was through the acceptance of his transience that a storyteller took on the role, not of a policy adviser, but of a teacher: "He has counsel—not for a few situations, as the proverb does, but for many, like the sage."[43] This third truth, epic truth, was neither scientific nor journalistic so as to "inform," nor political so as to incite action. It was truth as the act and art of listening and reflecting on the meanings of events and people.

However, even true storytellers still depended on the presence of willing listeners, ears capable of discerning the epic and *human* forms of truth they were trying to relay. As it was, in a world of information, circuits of words and images could cast a shadow over the figure of a man—a fragile human body—as he tried to bring the sight of death before the eyes of the world. And so we turn to the story of what became of Stefan Lux's story.

In Media Res

It was not until the 1980s that someone set out again to write the history of Lux's suicide.[44] That someone was the journalist Betty Sargent, who had been an international news correspondent in Geneva in the 1930s. Sargent arrived shortly after Lux's death, yet strangely, by her own account, no one had ever spoken to her of the event. As Sargent reported her essay first published in 1989 (and later reprinted in 2001): "My interest in Lux is relatively recent, for although I served almost five years in Geneva as a correspondent for American and British newspapers—beginning in 1937, less than six months after Lux's suicide—I never heard his name mentioned there during that time."[45] It was only five decades later, when Sergeant returned to the archives of the *Manchester Guardian*, that the journalist first encountered Lux's name.[46] From there, she went looking for answers. After half a century of silence,

Sargent wanted to "set the record straight" about what she called "a tragic instance of a lost opportunity in history."[47]

As Sargent retold it, the whole affair took place in the already tense Assembly session. On that July day, delegates gathered to discuss the recent string of events threatening world peace—the departure of Germany from the League, the Italian invasion of Ethiopia, and internecine conflict in Spain. It was amid that chorus of apprehensive voices that Lux fired the gun into his chest.[48] After an ambulance came and transported Lux to the hospital, doctors discovered that Lux already had another bullet lodged in his lungs, a souvenir that had been with him since fighting for the Austro-Hungarian Empire in the First World War.[49] Despite the physicians' efforts, Lux died at nine o'clock that evening.

Evidently, Lux wanted the contents of his briefcase delivered to Joseph Avenol, who served as the acting secretary-general of the League from 1933 until 1940. Sargent also relayed that League officials informed the press that Lux's briefcase had contained a letter addressed to Secretary-General Avenol as well as five other letters addressed to Anthony Eden, King Edward VIII, the *Manchester Guardian*, *The Times* of London, and Geneva journalist Paul du Bochet.[50] When the press pushed the League about the contents of Lux's letters, they gave a parsimonious statement. The *New York Times* reported "the letter to Mr. Avenol said in effect that he [Lux] intended to kill himself publicly at this last meeting of the Assembly to draw attention to the plight of the Jews in Germany. The other letters are supposed to be of the same purport."[51]

In the following days, international newspapers renarrated this version of Lux's story with subtle differences. While some papers affirmed that Lux's final letters were found in his briefcase, others claimed he had been carrying the letters in his pocket, while still others asserted that Lux set the letters directly on the podium.[52] There were also several different versions of Lux's final cry in the Assembly. The *New York Times* claimed that he uttered: "C'est le dernier coup" (This is the last blow).[53] The *Chicago Daily Tribune*, the *Washington Post*, and *Jewish Exponent* described Lux's final words as such: "This is the end, it is all over."[54] The *Journal de Genève* maintained that Lux cried out: "C'est la dernière victime" (This is the last victim).[55] The *Israelitisches Wochenblatt*, on the other hand, reported the following: "With his last strength, he cried: 'C'est ma dernière', he could not go further."[56]

Despite variances in the details, the press tended to cite Lux's motives in the same key. The headline in the *Philadelphia Inquirer* read: "League in Turmoil as Czech Ends Life: shoots self to Protest Nazi Anti-Semitism; Reform discussed."[57] Paper after paper gave the same explanation: "Stefan Lux . . . died at 9 p.m. After declaring that he wanted to protest against the treatment of Jews in Germany and to draw attention to their suffering" [*sic*].⁵⁸ And again: "His gesture, a letter explained, was for the purpose of calling attention of the world to the plight of Jews in Germany[.] Mr. Lex [their spelling error] is himself a Jew, native of Vienna, and a naturalized Czechoslovakian."⁵⁹ And again: "Lux wished to draw attention to the plight of his fellow Jews in the Third Reich."⁶⁰ Some even put an extended commentary along these lines right in Lux's mouth. The *Los Angeles Times* reported this scene: "As Lux slid to the floor after shooting himself he gasped to a colleague: 'I want to die as a public protest to the way Germany is treating Jews. I am not sorry. My mind is lucid.'"⁶¹ The *Chicago Daily Tribune* also gave this same account with a slight rephrasing: "'I want to die as a public protest to the way Germany is treating the Jews,' he gasped as he fell to the floor. 'I am not sorry. My mind is completely lucid.'"⁶²

This version of Lux's statement and motives endured well into the twenty-first century. As recently as 2002, Costa-Garvas's film *Amen* opened with the Lux episode. In the very first frames, we see a man walking through the Palais des Nations, making his way to the Assembly. Once there, the man distributes some pamphlets to the delegates seated in the front of the Assembly. Once the security guards are called, the man then hurriedly throws the remaining pamphlets into the crowd before speaking out: "My name is Stefan Lux. I am Jewish. The Jews are being persecuted in Germany, and the world doesn't care. I see no other way to reach people's hearts."⁶³ With that, Lux points the gun to his own heart and pulls the trigger. Costa-Garvas chose this scene as an echo to the film's primary theme, namely, the travails of a German SS officer who tries to inform the pope about the reality of the death camps. Lux served to reinforce the broader point, once again, about the difficulties of transmitting messages and the tragedy of disregarded testimonies.

Even if we acknowledge that Lux's death marked a "missed opportunity" to alter the course of history, the more difficult question is why and how Lux's efforts got distilled as "noise." Answering that question requires looking again at Lux's own testimony, the motivations he offered, and tracking what it was that his audience actually received and understood of his message.

At one level, it is perfectly correct that Lux died to protest the Nazi persecution of the Jews. It is certainly not a coincidence that Lux chose the moment that League conference convened to clarify the legal status of Jewish refugees from Germany.⁶⁴ What is more, as Sargent reveals, Lux had spent the better part of his life before his symbolic death fighting anti-Semitic stereotypes. He had been born in fin de siècle Hungry to Jewish parents, studied drama in Vienna, and by 1911 had moved to Berlin to pursue acting and writing. Lux also wrote some volumes of poetry under the pen name Peter

Strumbursh.⁶⁵ There are no traces (at least that I could find) of why Lux chose to write his poetry specifically under a pen name, especially given his lifelong attraction for the limelight.

After serving in the war, Lux helped to found the Social Film Society in Berlin.⁶⁶ There, Sargent reports, Lux served as the artistic direct for the society's premiere film, entitled *Justice*. The film starred Rudolph Schildkraut and portrayed the forced expulsions that the Jewish people faced over the centuries. According to Sargent, the film was scheduled to premiere in March 1920, yet after the Kapp Putsch, the financial backers withdrew their funds, and *Justice* never made its public debut.⁶⁷ In 1920, Rudolph Schildkraut immigrated to the United States, where he had established a Jewish theater in New York, and later he secured some significant roles in Hollywood films such as Cecil B. DeMille's famous *King of Kings*.⁶⁸ Forty years later, in Hollywood, Schildkraut died of a heart attack.⁶⁹ Stefan Lux, on the other hand, had stayed behind in Europe, with its rapidly multiplying landmines.

In the 1920s and early 1930s, Lux went from job to job, working for various film companies and writing for the leftist German paper *Die Weltbühne* (The world stage).⁷⁰ That journal seemed to move in a fate line parallel to that of Lux himself. Before the war, the journal operated under the name *Die Schaubühne* and had been dedicated strictly to theater. After the war, the journal changed its name and content, becoming a forum for social and political criticism more broadly.⁷¹ Then, in 1933, the Nazi regime banned the journal, though its editors continued to print it in exile.⁷² Just at the moment that *Die Weltbühne* went into exile, so did Lux. Fearing for his life, he took his wife and son back to his birthplace, which was then located within the revised borders of Czechoslovakia, rather than in Hungary. Lux's landlord in Berlin had seized the family's belongings, thus the family arrived in Czechoslovakia with only a few belongings in a suitcase. Fortunately, Lux was able to find work as a photojournalist for the *Prager Press*. Three years later, Lux used those press credentials to gain entry to the League of Nations.⁷³

Seen as one among a throng of "homeless intellectuals," there is little doubt that Lux conceived of his protest as a symbolic act in the fight against National Socialism in particular and anti-Semitism in general. And yet, on July 6, 1936, Lux's personal friend Dr. Arthur Heller, representative of the capital city council in Prague, wrote to the League in the staccato of telegraphic type: "Lux did not die for the Jews but for the humanitarian ideal and Last Not Least for the League of Nations stop I hope that this heroic action will not remain without effect."⁷⁴ A closer look at the contents of the letters in Lux's briefcase seem to confirm that Heller had reason to be frustrated with how the press had been representing Lux's motivations.

Lux's letter to Avenol, written in German, still exists in the League archives. Perhaps significantly, given the politics of language at the League, the secretariat never had the letter translated to French or English. In that note, dated July 2, Lux began by apologizing to Avenol for writing in German and expressed deep regret that his lack of linguistic abilities had prevented him from writing in French. He also apologized for any inconvenience, embarrassment, or discomfort that his death might cause to the League. Lux then begged for understanding, although he was convinced that his death's positive impact would more than outweigh any possible negatives. Lux then assured Avenol that Paul du Bochet—the journalist from the *Journal de Genève* who had helped secure Lux's press accreditations—had no foreknowledge of the suicide.

Finally, Lux made his request: "You will find, Mr. Secretary General, enclosed in this communication, five letters, sealed and addressed. I humbly dare to entrust these letters to *you* [Lux emphasized Avenol's trustworthiness], Mr. Secretary General." Lux then asked Avenol to "kindly ensure" that the letters would "reach their addressees in the shortest and most expedient way."[75] While the letters did reach the press correspondents in question, no single paper published them in full. As for the letters to the British politicians, the Secretariat sent them to the British Foreign Office in Geneva, who then sent them back to the authorities in Geneva.[76] Sargent finally tracked down a copy of Lux's letter to Anthony Eden in the Swiss federal archives in Bern.[77] That letter addressed more explicitly what precisely Lux hoped to accomplish with his public death, a concerted effort at disambiguation. He wanted to shed light on the dangers lurking on the world stage.

Lux began his letter to Anthony Eden with an expression of his right, as a "dead man," to be heard. He then continued: "Permit me then, Sir Eden, to pass over all the details concerning my insignificant person . . . and permit me to begin *in media res*. What I have to say is important like life, and serious, like death."[78] Starting in the middle (in media res, the starting point of most great epics), Lux moved directly to the question of the dangers on the world stage. He begged Eden to solve the Italian Ethiopian dispute quickly, for there was one fact that mattered more than all the rest: "The German government, that group of men guiding the fate of the once great German people arbitrarily and without any restraint, this group consists without exception of real criminals."[79]

In pointing to the criminality of National Socialism, Lux also claimed another right endowed by death, the right to call things by their "proper names."[80] The right of naming remained connected through the inexorable bond between truth and life, as in *Fiat Lux*. In that vein, Lux exclaimed: "I do not whisper, Sir Eden, I shout it out: in Germany, you are dealing with criminals. The German partners with whom you negotiate, discuss, and exchange memoranda, are criminals." He then spoke more strongly still: "And I don't use this word as an oratorical phrase.... No, these are mentally and psychologically inferior, petty criminals and thugs, marked almost without exception with signs of moral insanity; most of them, in addition, have criminal records or a dark past that shies from the light.... These are the attested facts, Sir Eden, that can be easily documented a hundredfold."[81]

Yet despite the existence of such empirical evidence, the League and the leaders of the world's sovereign nations were not engaging baldly or boldly with the "attested facts." They were, to varying degrees within each state, cooperating, negotiating, and compromising with Hitler's regime.[82] In light of those diplomatic strategies, Lux urged: "Sir Eden, I beg you with my last strength; face up to the facts, abandon this fatal apathy, don't get caught up in trivial formalities."[83] In short, Lux pleaded with Eden to lean in and listen: "As a human being you must understand the speech of another human being and you must act humanly."[84] Lux ended by restating his hope: "I passionately wish to believe that a miracle will take place and that the death of a barely known minor writer, one 'unknown solider of life,' may spread some truth and clarity."[85]

These subtleties of Lux's message never fully penetrated the force field of public opinion. On July 6, the Zurich-based *Israelitisches Wochenblatt* requested a copy of Lux's letters, but the Secretariat responded that the League had no plans to make them publicly available.[86] We can imagine a number of reasons why League officials might have been reticent to report on the fuller story. First, the League was occupied with minimizing reverberations of a scandal. Along those lines, the Secretariat immediately launched an investigation to ensure that Lux had followed all the League procedure in securing press access. Lux's credentials from the *Prager Press* are among the few the documents that remain in the archives, and they appear to provide proof that the League had followed its due diligence.[87] In a related key, the Secretariat also conducted an extensive study of how Lux was able to penetrate the Assembly floor from the press gallery, and the League then used those results to produce stricter security protocols. With those efforts made and in place, as far as the Secretariat was concerned, the episode was over.[88]

The simple desire to minimize the event's reputational costs, however, does not answer the question of why the League reported erroneously that Lux *explicitly* declared his death an effort to draw attention to the plight of the Jews in Germany. Pondering this misrepresentation leads in a different direction. After all, the supposedly trustworthy hands into which Lux placed the contents of his final message were those of Joseph Avenol. Lux could not have known that in a few years' time, roughly as Walter Benjamin was running away from France, Avenol would be running toward it. In August 1940, Avenol resigned from the League and left Geneva for France, where he then offered his services to the Vichy regime. To his dismay, however, and perhaps because of his former affiliation with the League, Avenol never managed to secure such a position. So, in 1943, the former secretary-general was forced to flee back into exile in Switzerland. Despite his personal political disappointments, Avenol's "unproblematic" heritage made it possible for him to cross the border again, mostly unhunted and completely unharmed.[89]

These dimensions of Avenol's own story line cast a different light on the fact that the League's press statement focused so singularly on Lux's *Jewishness*. Once armed with these motivations for Lux's death, the press evoked a series of stereotypes ranging from the flagrant to the subtle. On one end of the spectrum, some periodicals declared that Lux was a "deranged refugee." As Sargent discovered in her research, a Nuremburg tabloid run by the Nazi lackey Julious Streicher titled *Der Stürmer* printed a caricature of the suicide with the following caption: "In the League of Nations Kosher blood flew; A Jew Shot himself as a gesture yesterday. He announced to the outside world: the League of Nations has been shot."[90] As Christian Goeschel pointed out in his study *Suicide in Nazi Germany*, this was not the only time that Streicher used print space to address the symbolic suicide of a German Jew. In 1933, Fritz Rosenfelder, a businessman from Stuttgart, shot himself after being expelled from his beloved local gymnastics association. An anti-Nazi pamphlet later printed his suicide note: "My dear friends! Herewith my final farewell! . . . I depart without hatred or resentment. . . . How much I would have preferred to sacrifice my life to my Fatherland! Don't mourn—but try to enlighten and to help the truth become victorious."[91] When Streicher saw the pamphlet, he published a rebuttal. After quoting some of Rosenfelder's text, he stated that "if *the Jew* [my emphasis] Fritz Rosenfelder wanted to contribute to a change of the attitude of Germans toward *the Jews*, he died in vain. On the contrary, we . . . would not mind if his racial comrades sent their regards in the same way." In this way, Streicher asserted, through suicide, the Jewish question might be "solved in a simple and peaceful manner."[92]

Once again, we see the act of naming as an act of invention: "the Jew Fritz Rosenfeld." With this utterance, every other detail of Rosenfeld's life, including the circumstances of his choice of death, suddenly became insignificant. In a similar frame, the titular assignment "Stefan Lux the Jew" cast a long shadow. Here we see the workings of a process that Horkheimer and Adorno would explore in 1944: "Once things have gone so far, the mere word Jew appears like the bloody grimace whose image—skull and mangled cross in one—is unfurled on the swastika; the fact that someone is called a Jew acts as a provocation to set about him until he resembles that image."[93] Thus whatever the intended content of Lux's message to the world, his every word, and even his death, became shrouded in the stereotype of his *Jewishness*.

The same pattern of reducing Lux's to his Jewishness also took place in less expected, less overt ways. Even in more neutral publications, slowly Stefan Lux came to resemble the label assigned to him, "Stefan Lux the Jew." In one *New York Times* article, "Suicide Shot Rings at League Session," the author began with the sadness of the event: "Tragedy in concrete form intruded itself into this gathering of the League of Nations today." From there, the author provided a litany details of Lux's biography, including his age, his nationality, the fact that he had been driven from Nazi Germany, and the name of the paper he had been working for when he took his life. Then, suddenly, the report continued: "He had a wife and a 12-year old son and was far from penniless."[94] *Far from penniless?* Whence or from whom did the reporter get this piece of information? And what was the rationale for including it, especially given ample evidence to the contrary? As the *Israelitisches Wochenblatt für die Schweiz* reported on July 10, 1936: "Since his flight to Czechoslovakia in 1933, he [Lux] lived in Prague with his wife and child and they lived in very modest conditions. He supported his livelihood with fees from newspapers for which he wrote. . . . His wife needed to borrow money to make the journey to Geneva. By the time she arrived, she found that he [Lux] had already died."[95]

The *New York Times* was not the only periodical to raise questions of finance, even if obliquely. While the fact was not directly related to Lux's finances, for some reason the *Chicago Daily Tribune* chose to draw attention to the fact that the whole incident had played out in the "10,000,000 palace," in Geneva.[96] Perhaps the authors were not (or perhaps they were) conscious of the ways in which their references to finance could echo inside the long tradition of economically inflected anti-Semitism.[97] In subtle ways, referencing the cost of the League building resummoned, if only implicitly, those postwar caricatures that depicted the League as conspiratorial Jewish bankers set on world domination.[98]

At the other end of the spectrum, even those who hoped to revere and honor Lux equally absorbed his message into their own logics and ambitions. The *Israelitisches Wochenblatt für die Schweiz*, for example, printed an extended obituary for Lux. After giving a richly detailed account of Lux's life, the author then declared "the sacrificial death of Stephan Lux is a Maccabees deed."[99] With this labeling, once again, Lux's act became immersed in story lines outside of himself. The reference came from a tale of the seven

Maccabees martyrs, as told in several of the Books of the Maccabees.[100] This set of scriptures—which are canonical for the Jewish, Catholic, and Eastern Orthodox faiths, but deuterocanonical for Protestants—tell the revolt story of Judas Maccabeus and his followers against the Greek Seleucid Empire in the second century BCE. While there are a number of slightly different narrations and interpretations, all versions tell the triumph of Maccabeus in pushing back pagan laws and restoring Israel to the Jewish people by way of securing adherence to holy law and right practice.[101]

Of course, in situating Lux within the "Maccabees" tradition, it is important that the Maccabees revolt began with acts of martyrdom. Several testaments focus on the story wherein King Antiochus Epiphanes of Syria brought seven devout brothers to trial, along with their mother, Solomonia. The brothers were each given the chance to save themselves by breaking Jewish law (either by eating pork or by worshiping an idol). Each refused, and each was tortured to death in turn. When all her children had died this righteous death, in some accounts Solomonia simply raised her hands in prayer and then died herself; in others, she committed suicide.[102] It was supposedly this martyrdom that inspired the forces of Judea to take arms against the pagan invaders.[103]

In calling Lux's suicide a "Maccabees deed," the author of the *Israelitisches Wochenblatt für die Schweiz* may have been consciously folding Lux's act into the struggle of the Jewish community not only for its survival, but also for the practice of Jewish law, and perhaps too, the cause of Jewish political sovereignty. While it is clear that Lux fought anti-Semitism, he was nonpracticing and appears not to have been an active participant of the Zionist movement. But perhaps there were other connotations at work—after all, the author of Lux's obituary never fully specified what he meant by "Maccabees deed."

As Philippe Ariès reminds us in his magisterial study of attitudes toward death, the word *macabre* and the French word for corpse, *macchabée*, both have their roots in the book of Maccabees: "It is not surprising that around the fourteenth century the dead body—the word cadaver was seldom used—was given the name of the holy Maccabees. The Maccabees had long been honored as patron saints of the dead because they were believed, rightly or wrongly, to be the origination of the prayers of intercession for the dead."[104] Ariès reminds us it was only later that the term *macabre* took on notions of "horrible" or "gruesome." Originally, the famous "dance of the macabre" had a different meaning: "the moral purpose was to remind the viewer both of the uncertainty of the hour of death and of the equality of all people in the face of death."[105] In this precise sense we can perhaps think of Lux's death as a "Maccabees deed," an act designed to reinforce death as the great leveler, a point of absolute human equality. For it was, after all the "universal" principles of justice and the "standards of civilization"—which the League claimed to uphold—that Lux was asking the world to defend.

To the credit of the *Israelitisches Wochenblatt für die Schweiz*, the obituary article also allowed various interpretations of Lux's life and death to coexist and do so in multiple languages. Another line stated: "We, who bow down in awe from this readiness to sacrifice, receive more motivation not to grow weary for the fight for justice, the highest aim of humankind: each of us should fight in our place for this aim."[106] What is more, the article printed a statement that Lux's wife made: "Before her departure, she told a journalist . . . that she suspected that Stephan Lux, who was always thinking about himself last, intended to state a political demonstration with his action, a suicide in the name of Europe in order to remind the League of Nations of his duties."[107]

In that same piece, we also get a glimpse of Lux's burial in the Jewish cemetery of Veyrier, which turns out to stretch across the Franco-Swiss border.[108] There is a legend that the cemetery itself provided a secret mode of escape in the most dangerous days of the Second World War. For under the guise of funeral rights, the mourners could furtively cross the border. As such, it also became of focal point of further anti-Semitism.[109] In 1936, though, standing on that transnational piece of earth and surrounded by walls, several people came to speak at Lux's graveside. Monsieur Levy-Wallisch, president of the Israelite Community of Geneva spoke: "I want to welcome, in the name of the Israelite Community of Geneva, in this peaceful resting place, the funerary remains of a martyr.[110] The journalist Robert Dell—Betty Sargent's close colleague and the president of the International Association of Journalists Accredited to the League of Nations—also spoke at Lux's graveside. Dell came as one of the designated recipients of Lux's letters, to reiterate the fact that Lux had sacrificed his life for the human community.[111] He also reminded those gathered to mourn that journalist Stefan Lux knew and saw clearly the threat the Nazi Germany posed against the right to speak and think freely.[112] Dell saw Lux as one among many victims of the growing persecution directed more generally against "intelligence and the liberal professions."[113]

In 1934, Dell had also published a character study of National Socialism in order to expose that government's real nature and intentions. In his *Germany Unmasked*, Dell devoted time to exposing the way that the Nazi government was systematically attacking the free press. "The press that Hitler and Goebbels have destroyed included papers with a world-wide reputation as the Frankfurter Zeitung. . . . He [Hitler] sneers at the Jewish German Press for being '*anstandig*,' for repudiating violence and brutality and relying on intellectual methods, for advocating peace and trying to diminish national hatreds.... The once great papers of Germany are dying."[114]

In 1932, when National Socialism was just a party in Germany, and not yet *the ruling party*, the League had turned its attention to the perturbing prevalence and influence of so-called false news.

The Way, the Truth, the Lie

In *Mein Kampf*, Hitler linked the League of Nations and the "lying press" together, as if two strands of a single phenomenon. There he stated: "Was it not the German Press that understood how to make all the nonsensical talk about 'Western democracy' palatable to our people, until an exuberant public was eventually prepared to entrust its future to the League of Nations?" He then continued: "The function of the so-called liberal Press was to dig the grave for the German people and REICH.... To them the spreading of falsehood is as much a vital necessity as the mouse is to a cat. Their sole task is... preparing the nation to become the slaves of international finance and its masters, the Jews."[115]

It is not as if National Socialism was the only interwar combine of voices that presented their political enemies and the press as coconspirators of *dissimulation*. To the contrary, that party was one exceptionally abhorrent choir among a multitude, each echoing gradations of similar sentiments ranging from the moderate to the more radical. Because the League stood on the authority of *world public opinion*, and perhaps because it too had been accused of promulgating the "lying press," it also tried to help define the line between true and false, news and propaganda. Between 1931 and 1936, the League undertook a number of inquiries into the troubles that false or inaccurate news could create for the cause of international peace and stability.

In 1931, for instance, the precise question entered the League as a discussion in *The Collaboration of the Press in the Organization of Peace*, which fell under the general rubric of "moral disarmament" and was published a year later in a publication of the same title.[116] All the normal League procedures unfurled, as the question passed back and forth between the Council, the Assembly, and special committees until it reached the Information Section, which produced the requisite summaries. The first extended discussion on the problem of falsity, came in the course of a special committee charged with drafting a "General Convention to Improve the Means of Preventing War." During those committee meetings, the affiliated delegations discussed the growing problem of political propaganda in general as well as "tendentious or inaccurate information" in particular. Some members of the committee even went so far as to suggest that given the ease with which untruth could travel, the League might support efforts toward the coordinated standardization of antipropaganda laws. The language of that proposed draft convention read as such: "The High Contracting Parties undertake to endeavor, so far as their national laws permit, to suppress all verbal or written propaganda designed to prevent a peaceful settlement of the crisis."[117]

Because the question of any form of overt censorship would inevitably be contentious, the matter went to the Council. On September 29, 1931, the Council commissioned an inquiry into the "question of inaccurate news which may disturb the maintenance of peace and good understanding between the peoples."[118] To those ends, the Secretariat sent a questionnaire on the subject to a large number of journalists and press associations, asking for their feedback. The Council also requested that the Secretariat keep abreast of the outcomes of the Conference of the Directors of Press Bureaus taking place in Copenhagen in 1932.[119]

To those ends, Secretariat sent a circular letter to sixty-four countries and over 130 press organizations. The inquiry extended over several months as the responses trickled in. In 1932, the Secretariat presented a selected summary of the replies, including the results of the Copenhagen conference.[120] Evidently, the Copenhagen conference had produced two different proposals for how to deal with the question of false news. On the one hand, the conference concluded: "It further seems undeniable that free, prompt and abundant information is one of the most active remedies against inaccurate news."[121] Here then they posited a kind of "quantity theory" of truth, where the accurate would simply overtake the inaccurate. Yet, while it shied away from direct controls on the press, the conference did support an initiative to set up a "Court of Honor" at the Hague, as a method for sousing out and trying journalists known to have spread "false or tendentious news."[122]

Many of the responses to the League's inquiry seemed to contain a similar mixture of sentiments, namely, a desire to avoid direct censorship, yet a willingness to nonetheless entertain other means of controlling or monitoring overt forms of *prevarication*. The response of the International Federation of Journalists, June 8, 1932, began by rejecting censorship of any kind. And yet they also stood vehemently against "the deliberate distortion of news, or any other dishonest practice, such as the forging or fabrication of documents." Stephan Valot, the designated representative of that association, stated: "No one realizes better than journalist themselves the importance of getting rid of journalists of dubious character." To those ends, he suggested that his own organization would provide a system of vetting, and he encouraged the

League to help insist that all working journalists should apply for an International Federation of Journalists card.[123]

The question of the links between "false news" and the character of journalist appeared in other responses as well. Ermanno Amicucci, representative of the Fascist National Syndicate of Journalists, stated, "the problem of finding means for preventing the spread of false or tendentious news likely to disturb the maintenance of peace and good relations between nations would appear to be difficult, if not impossible, to solve, since the very delegation which raises the question states that it will never agree to any restriction being imposed on the freedom of the Press, even if the only alternative is to endure the evils of freedom."[124] Amicucci continued to argue that there were only two ways of preventing the spread of false or tendentious news—either by a state monopoly or by preventative censorship. Both ways inevitably involved restrictions on the freedom of the press. Obviously, he concluded, false news would continue to be a problem wherever a so-called free press operated. He then asked the question of how to "clarify" and "purify" what he called "the sources and the channels of the distribution of news." In the end, Amicucci concluded "the only way to obtain practical results [was] that adopted in Italy, where journalistic work is entrusted under suitable laws to persons of recognized honesty, education and sense of responsibility." With this Amicucci revealed the reigning procedure in Italy, namely that if any journalist failed in his duties, "he may not continue to exercise a profession for which he has shown himself to be morally unfitted or without the necessary political sense of responsibility." Then in a final statement, Amicucci clarified: "In other words, the adventurer and the ignoramus must not be allowed to engage in the profession of journalism merely out of regard for the fetish of liberty."

Analyzing the range of responses that League received, most of the letters simply extolled the virtues of *truth* and disavowed the evils of *falsity*. Even where those took a distance from the promises of censorship, very few went so far as to problematize the political subtexts of "false news." In the interwar moment, the French (and Jewish) historian Marc Bloch had a different, more subtle take on the deep problems and paradoxes of so-called false news. Bloch—who would die as part of the French Resistance in World War II—shifted the question away from the reasons of the production of false news, to that of its reception.[125] He argued: "The error reproduces itself, grows, and ultimately survives only on one condition—that it finds a favorable cultural soup in the society where it is spreading. Through it, people express all their unconscious prejudices, hatreds, fears and strong emotions."[126] In other words, people had a tendency to believe any story that confirmed their preexisting beliefs.

There was, in that League report, one voice that tackled the question in a vein similar to that of Bloch. That figure was Clarence Streit, who happened to be Robert Dell's predecessor at the International Association of Journalist Accredited to the League of Nations and was also the *New York Times* correspondent in Geneva. Streit began his response to the League with a by-now familiar expression: "The Press since it began—*fiat lux* were the first words ever printed—has unrelentingly fought false news." Just as a doctor vows to do no harm, Streit suggested that any journalists worthy of his credentials sought to avoid falsehood and reveal the truth. He then launched into a series of contextual qualifications, asking those reading his words to consider all the weight of history and circumstances that rested in these terms "true" and "false." First of all, he explained, "every item we write must, before it reaches the reader, go through many machines and the hands and mentalities of many men unknown to each other, often speaking different languages."[127] Beyond this vast machine of information flows that passed across borders and time zones, Streit also pointed to the difficulties lurking in the fact that journalists had to rely on "human sources." Those human sources were often susceptible to the lure of human interests, interests that might try to prevent the publication of certain truths, and push for the publication of deliberate fabrications.[128] In these ways, he affirmed "the gatherers and the writers of news are exposed to the risk of what we report being more or less distorted or falsified by being cut down after it reaches the home office through the exigencies of space, time, editorial or publishing policy, outside influence, etc."[129]

Even if one could control for these challenges, there was also the question of readers and readership. Streit reminded his readers that even when journalists strived for the truth, an audience might twist the meaning of the written word or simply misinterpret an author's intended meaning.[130] Furthermore, Streit reminded the League that the press was not alone in distributing falsehoods. Prevarications could also travel by way of rumors, gossip, and even forms of willful state-sponsored espionage.[131]

Beyond all these complicating variables, Streit also objected to the way the Council had defined "false news" to begin with: "We are concerned with false news not because of the effect it may have, but because it is false." Streit asked the League to consider the ways in which they had been muddying the issue by reducing the dangers of falsehood to a question of its effects. After all, Streit reminded his audience that both truth and lies had the power to disrupt international peace: "In our experience nothing, indeed, is so disturbing or trouble-making as the truth."[132]

As far as Streit was concerned, the whole question of false news merely distracted from a deeper set of issues. One such issue included governmental bodies—including the League—that tried to hide the truth from the public. He argued: "Despite the discredit into which secret diplomacy had fallen in the holocaust into which it led a blindfolded world," all such bodies continued to hold far too many of its deliberations in private.[133] Streit even pointed out that the League had tried to limit the release of information about the Sino-Japanese conflict.[134] What is more, Streit went on to claim that most efforts to curtail "falsehood" quickly led to efforts to constrict or control the press. In that same frame, Streit was vehemently opposed the creation of this "court of honor for journalists," which he felt would amount to methods of control by fear and would only lead to the creation of scapegoats and witch hunts. As he stated: "We would not easily grant that fear serves truth more than falsity."[135]

Streit insisted that one way to ensure the printing of truth was further safeguarding the right of the press to print the truth. For many private and public actors wanted to control the press. Furthermore, he reminded the League that "few if any newspapers have ever been killed by the publication of [a] news item that was false, even if the fault was deliberate. Many have been ruined because they told the truth. It is a costly business to withstand all those who do not want the truth on certain things reported."[136] Streit also offered a solution to the problem of false news: "If we start with the principle that the thing to do is to have the Press in the hands of the journalists, we can immediately isolate the germ of the disease of false news."[137]

Streit ended by disavowing the attitude toward the press that the League had taken up in its query: "This attitude considers the Press not as a medium of information for everyone, but as a weapon, or at best, a sort of searchlight to turn on or off, and this way and that way, as suits policy." If this attitude prevailed, it was only a matter of time before claims of "falsity" could be used to discredit one's enemies—including journalists. Streit then restated the point he made in the beginning: "When Gutenberg began to print, he began by printing without adjective or adverb: *Fiat lux*. This Association stands to-day where the Press has ever stood, for everlasting daylight on everything and for everyone."[138]

Later, in a publication entitled *Union Now*, Streit had offered another articulation of his own philosophy of truth, "that Man's vast future lies in the democratic philosophy that would give every one an equal chance, an equal freedom to tell us all whatever truth he alone has seen or believes that he has seen, an equal obligation to express his truth with that clarity and simplicity that makes us all see it and thereby proves it true, and an equal right to refuse to accept whatever one alone still doubts is true, an equal veto against whatever one alone believes is false."[139] Rather than some facile relativism, Streit hoped to highlight the difference between peaceful conversations among opposing views and the climate wherein each party sought *to discredit the authenticity* of opposing views.

Beyond the difficulty of ascertaining the truth, a great deal of (violent) political acrimony was increasingly playing out in domains that were seemingly impervious to empirical evidence. In the 1920s and 1930s, there had been an increasing interest and absolute belief in the authenticity of the apocryphal *Protocols of the Elders of Zion*.[140] *Protocols*—which claimed to be a "leaked" document containing plans of a Jewish cabal aspiring to world domination—had been frequently circulated and reprinted in dozens of languages.[141] Each reprinting claimed that Jewish leaders would move first by seductions, offering the promises of liberalism, equality, and brotherhood. Then, through these false promises and illusionary diversions, *Christendom* would eventually fall.[142]

Scholars such as Benjamin W. Segel definitively proved that these documents were in fact forgeries, a cut-and-paste of other writing including "trashy" German novels, including those of the anti-Semitic Herman Goedsche, in particular, his chapter called "In the Jewish Cemetery of Prague."[143] Despite cooperative efforts of detective work and careful textual analysis, belief in the *Protocols* persisted, going through countless rounds of reprinting and translation into numerous languages.[144]

Shortly after addressing the "lying press" in *Mein Kampf*, Hitler addressed the question of *Protocols*' authenticity: "What many Jews unconsciously wish to do is here clearly set forth. . . . If the historical developments, which have taken place within the last few centuries be studied in the light of this book we will understand why the Jewish Press incessantly repudiates and denounces it. For the Jewish peril will be stamped out the moment the general public come into possession of that book and understand it."[145]

Hitler's rhetorical gymnastics, where efforts to disprove *Protocols* served as further confirmation of their "authenticity," call for a deeper deconstruction of the true/false binary. For one, at stake were the ways in which the whole conspiratorial power of anti-Semitism rested partly on the ways that information systems had confused the relationship between faith, facts, and the will to power. Where "truth" was muddy, disconcerting, and unpalatable, totalitarian forms of power offered comforting stereotypes, whipped up primordial prejudices, and offered *a total* unbroken, simple "world picture." No amount of fact-checking could alter that "soup" of preexisting fears and desires.

As Hannah Arendt stated: "No factual statement can really ever be beyond doubt. . . . Testimony is always suspect to an act of faith on the part of those who hear it."[146] Whereas lies can appeal to the "wishes" and "expectations," of the audience, in many cases, according to Arendt, "reality has the disconcerting habit of confronting us with the unexpected, for which we were not prepared."[147] In this way, efforts *to shed light* or to reveal *epic forms* of human truth must also compete with other circulating narratives, narratives less disruptive to preexisting faiths.

Using this frame, we might rethink the fact that it took so long for Lux's death to appear as a story and ask why in Lux's own moment the event passed so quickly from "mere information" into silence. When the Assembly discussed the reports on the inquiry into false news, most delegates seemed willing to entertain that the threat of the false required some form of *action*. There was, however, one voice in the Assembly that stood baldly against any control of the press: "To a Frenchman, the freedom of the Press was an inalienable democratic principle. They rejected the idea of censorship in any form. One of the great French polemical writers said, 'You cannot kill ideas with a gun.' The speaker than added: 'Neither can you eliminate them with a pair of scissors.'" He then turned to another question, namely that of silence and silencing: "There were, in truth, regular conspiracies of silence. Useful news was systematically eliminated. To know the truth and not to spread it was worse than to manufacture tendentious news or carelessly to spread abroad a piece of false information."[148] The voice was that of Francois De Tessan, member of the French Resistance, who died in the Buchenwald concentration camp during April 1944.[149]

Whither Lux?

Just a few months after Lux's burial, Anthony Eden spoke out in the Assembly on the importance of creating peace mentalities. On September 25, 1936, Eden stated: "Indeed, the seriousness of the times is such as to command frank speech, so that I shall not apologize to you for using less guarded language than is usual for our assembly." Eden continued by asking a question: "What pictures does the world present to us today, in September 1936?"[150] He then answered that the world was rife with nationalism, with antagonisms, and with renewed spending on armaments. Then he pleaded: "If disarmament is to be real, it must be not only military but mental, not only weapons but the war mentality must be laid aside." Of course, no mention of Lux appeared.

In 1980, Victor Lusinchi took the opportunity to report on an exhibition commemorating the birth of the League of Nations in a *New York Times* article: "Sixty years ago today, cheering crowds massed in the streets of Geneva as church bells tolled throughout the city to welcome world statesmen attending a ceremony to officially open the forum that would end all wars—The League of Nations."[151] Despite the panegyrics, Lusinchi also recounted the missteps, the appeasement of Nazism, and the failures to act at the Italian conquest of Ethiopia. He also spoke of other things the League had left out of its celebration; nowhere, for example, did the exhibit cast light on the treasons of Pierre Laval, who worked for the cause of fascism from within the League and collaborated with the Nazi regime in France.[152]

Lusinchi also noticed another conspicuously absent story line: "The exhibit does not chronicle the dramatic protest against the rising tide of Nazism and Fascism of an Austrian-born Jew, Stefan Lux, who committed suicide in a public gallery at the 1936 session. The crack of the pistol shot could be heard in the press workroom behind the press gallery."[153] Lusinchi then ended by recalling a quote he had overheard during the League years. When the League opened the doors to its newly designed building—the Palais des Nations in 1938—apparently "Vernon Bartlett, a British Journalist and one-time League functionary, was already wondering whether the big marble edifice was 'anything more than a magnificent tomb for a great idea.'"[154]

In fact, during World War II, the Palais stood nearly empty. The League's functions and functionaries dispersed to seek asylum in other countries, just like so many wartime émigrés.[155] That slow disassembly, the scattering of its parts and pieces across the world stage, had indeed been a swan song. The architects of the post–World War II world order decided not to resuscitate the League but rather to create an entirely new organization.[156] The organization born in the trenches passed away under a mushroom cloud.

6

The Word and the Sword Revisited

> The most radical and the only secure form of possession is destruction, for only what we have destroyed is safely and forever ours.
>
> HANNAH ARENDT, *The Origins of Totalitarianism*

The Return of the Sword

At the end of World War II, in the annals of the *Contemporary Jewish Record*, Alexandre Koyré wrote an essay, lined with disdain. He stated: "Never has there been so much lying as in our day. Never has lying been so shameless, so systematic, so unceasing."[1] However, he admitted that lying was as old as civilization itself. The earliest human histories contained stories of innumerable fabrications and betrayals, prevarications and willful untruths. And yet the contemporary and explicitly political lie, according to Koyré, had taken on new shapes and forms. It had twisted and contorted into novel monstrosities hitherto unseen. He stated: "The written and spoken word, the press, the radio, all technical progress is put to the service of the lie. Modern man—*genus totalitarian*—bathes in the lie, breathes the lie, is in thrall to the lie every moment of his existence."[2] The primary problem with this novel politics of lying, according to Koyré, was the following: "The official philosophies of the totalitarian regimes unanimously brand as nonsensical the idea that there exists a single objective truth valid for everybody."[3]

Of course, in one sense, he was right. Fascism—especially in its Nazi variant—had replaced science with pseudoscience, had spewed vitriolic untruths, and all in the name of disposing of millions of human lives, as if they were less than human. Years later, in her own work on the subject, Hannah Arendt provided a modification to Koyré's idea that somehow "lying" or "truth telling" was what distinguished bad regimes from the good. Arendt stated: "for opinion, and not truth, belongs among the indispensable prerequisites of all power. 'All governments rest on opinion,' James Madison said, [and] not even the most autocratic ruler or tyrant could ever rise to power, let alone keep it, without the support of those who are like-minded."[4] In other words in a world where opinion had become the lifeblood of political legitimacy, politics very rarely had use for the pure, unadorned "facts."[5]

We can read both Koyré and Arendt as part of a wider post–World War II conversation that grew from the desire to make sense of the nightmare of fascist violence and the mechanisms that had made it possible.[6] On the one hand, fascist regimes had used media to mobilize genocide. On the other hand, the tools of international discussion, arbitration, and publicity had not been able to prevent those horrors.[7] In these discussions the League also became a symbolic point of reference once again for the indicting the double failure of words—at once deceptive and dangerous and also effete and ineffectual.

These reverberations even found their way to the League's closing Assembly in 1946, where delegates gathered in the Palais des Nations to bequeath the global stage to the United Nations.[8] That final meeting became at once a memorial and a collective reckoning, with attempts to diagnose what had gone awry with the maiden experiment in global governance. In almost every case, the delegates also used their time at the microphone to admit that the organization had misplaced its faith in the peacekeeping power of words.

When the French delegate Joseph Paul-Boncour took the floor, he insisted that if the task of the final Assembly was to "bury the League," then the delegates should do so "in the purple shrouds reserved for the last sleep of dead gods."[9] In Paul-Boncour's speech, among the encomiums, the League acquired the honors of a passé iconography, that of gods and kings. And indeed, the League forged in the palatial dramaturgy of Versailles had faded into irrelevance in the more modern meeting halls of Dumbarton Oaks, San Francisco, and finally New York City. What is more, the overt religious symbolism of the Covenant had already given way to the corporate legality of the UN Charter.

Other discursive nuances had changed as well. Despite the fact that World War II had been even more destructive than the first, no one in 1946 spoke of war itself as an archaic and anticivilized force. Rather, the claim was that if the League was—like kingship itself—an anachronism, it was partly because it had failed to act. When Paul-Boncour listed the League's chief and fatal errors, the first and most egregious was the part the League had played in the appeasement of Germany.[10] He then went on to further decry how the League had also only ever "talked" in the case of Japan and Italy. There had been too many words in Geneva and never enough action. Finally, he ended by asserting "the reality, *the worldwide reality* [my emphasis] . . . was that war could be avoided only if all the pacific nations united to oppose their collective force to the force of the aggressor."[11]

Beyond Paul-Boncour, many delegates stood to affirm that the United Nations would be superior to the League in at least one way, namely, in that it made provisions for collective force.[12] As Turkish delegate Feridun Cemal Erkin stated, "there cannot exist a truly efficient international League without an armed force to support it."[13] Suddenly too, in outlining an early version of the doctrine of mutually assured destruction, the Cuban representative Guillermo de Blanck, pointed out how the discovery of nuclear power might make its own contribution to a more peaceful world: "To this I would add the conviction that the new force, both constructive and destructive, which has recently been discovered will contribute, in its destructive aspect, towards peace, as it would be absurd for certain peoples to decide to commit suicide in order to assassinate others." He then went on to speak of the other ways in which this new power might equalize the world: "In a few years thanks to atomic energy there will no longer be strong peoples and weak peoples. All will be strong; and that being so each will be able and will be bound to respect others and to make itself respected within the framework of the new universal organization. This was the aim of the League; the United Nations will now fulfill it."[14]

It was as if the delegates returned to records of 1920 and replaced every instance of the phrase "world public opinion," with that of "collective force." Of course, this emphasis on action did not signal the end of the importance of information. The United Nations created an Information Organization that mirrored the League's Information Section, but on a greater scale.[15] As Kenneth Cmiel has argued, even the idea that information should flow freely across borders (with provisions for protecting news correspondents) became an important dimension of the international human rights discourse.[16] Finally, the UN's own chronology emerged along with what scholars have identified as the birth of the information age proper.[17] And indeed, information networks (along with financial systems) were de facto more diffusive, more pervasive, and more immaterial in 1947 than they had been in 1919.

Despite the continued importance of immaterial information flows to the project of international governance, in recounting what went wrong again and again, delegates at the League's final Assembly (as well as at the San Francisco conference) blamed "words" and "talk" and "non-action" for the war. In fact, only one League delegate seemed to issue a warning about the potential disaster of a world held together with weapons of mass destruction. Costa du Rels of Bolivia issued a quiet warning: "How terrifying is the interdependence of nations now that they are confronted with the inescapable prospect of their own powers of destruction."[18] Beyond this cautionary statement, most delegates reaffirmed the positive power of "collective force."

Once again, the discussions about how to move the world forward after a violent global war, and what part international organizations might play in that world, took place through a reworking of the word/sword binary. We might conclude here, for the "world picture" over which the League had stood guard had, in a very real sense, ended. In the final Assembly of the League, Count Carton de Wiart of Belgium summarized the organization as a reflecting of its own moment. He stated: "The History of the League is the history of the twenty years between the two world wars. Between these two tragic periods it forms a sort of curve or trajectory of which the starting-point, peaks, hesitations and falls corresponded to the fervent desire for peace, constructive efforts, generous illusions, anxieties, disappointments and backslidings which the peoples and world opinion experienced between the two catastrophes."[19] And indeed, the League's history was revelatory of the extent to which the interwar crisis was born in part of the ways in which information networks linked up both quests for power and wealth as well as existential quests for certainty. In more discrete historical terms, the League's doctrines were less a ruse or set of illusions than a series of ordinary political intoxications in the long, information-driven twentieth century. They brewed alongside a host of archaic myths, each competing to bind both time and space with one single political "reality."[20]

And yet some questions linger. If the League's emphasis on the word was designed to produce symbolic capital for the revival of the "standards of civilization," the United Nations clearly had a different task. So what was that world over which the UN would stand guard? To answer that question, we might ponder what else was being discredited alongside the League's "failure to act." By discrediting the League's commitment to the "word," the architects of the UN also discredited a system that stated the outlawry of war among its chief ambitions. If we jump ahead, to the 1960s, when Hannah Arendt looked back at the world after 1945, she remarked on how the end of interwar totalitarian regimes had led to other violent legacies. In *On Violence*, Arendt stated: "The Second World War was not followed by peace but by a cold war and the establishment of the military-industrial complex." She spoke of the ways in which "war-making" had become the "principal structuring force in society," whereby all "economic systems, political philosophies, and corpora juris" had come to serve the war system.[21] The ideal of perpetual peace had transformed to a world of perpetual war, *always somewhere.*

Of course there were other differences at work. The United Nations admitted more members, sanctioned more official languages, and acknowledged a commitment to the eventual independence of what Vijay Prashad has called "the darker nations."[22] It was also technically much more "global" than the League had been.²³ What is more, we can find cases where—as with the League—the UN affected discrete positive change, or provided channels for marginalized voices to make themselves heard.²⁴ However, at its root, the UN still produced "reputation laundering" and forms of global symbolic capital for a world system where great powers observed and managed their hegemonic status and financial interests with perpetual military intervention.²⁵ What is more, this active and expansive global military presence did not put an end to ethnic cleansing, as a political strategy of so-called nation building.²⁶

The fate and structure of the United Nations, or even the postwar order, is not the primary subject here. The reason for bringing the seams of the transition between one world order and the next is simply to underline the extent to which the "production of truth," and of specific "world pictures," remained central to the workings of power on the world stage. Here then we might look more closely at how the League's final Assembly was already preparing for a change of script and scene.

If we return to the texts of the League's First Assembly, we read countless allusions to the horrors of the trenches, the agonies of barbed wire and twisted flesh, and the grief of mothers. In 1946, however, there was an eerie lack of attention to the even greater, almost unfathomable human loss and suffering of World War II. There were a few broad references here and there to the "horrors of war," but cleansed of the concrete and visceral references to the trenches so prevalent in 1920. In their place came allusions to the failures of nonaction and the unspecified universality of human rights.²⁷

This abstract language calls to mind Benjamin's claim that the violence of the modern world was possible in part because modernity had "removed the sight of dying." Suddenly, all the references to the actual course of human suffering disappeared from view. Elsewhere on the world stage, despite efforts of bearing witness, even the hellish details of the Holocaust often (not always) became reabsorbed into political agendas of all kinds.²⁸ By reducing the story lines of suffering to "political failures to act," the stories of World War II became mere "information," used to justify fresh battles. They also became ready advertisements for the "progress" of the world to come—the world of the International Monetary Fund and the World Bank, guarded and protected, by "peacekeeping" forces.²⁹

On Signals and Noise

When Koyré discussed how and why "lying" had become an acceptable political act under totalitarian regimes, he first listed all the "normal" circumstances wherein publics had slowly come to tolerate forms of prevarication.

He stated: "In business, the lie is more or less allowed. Here again custom imposes certain restrictions, tending to become ever narrower. Still, the strictest business usage does not blink at the patent falsifications of advertising."[30] In those cases, the lie remained tolerated but only under certain conditions. However, he continued, "the exception is war: then, and then only, the lie becomes a just instrument." Then, he posed a question: "But what if war, an abnormal, episodic, transient condition, should come to be permanent and taken for granted? The lie, once an emergency measure, now becomes the norm."[31] Koyré was interested specifically in how totalitarian regimes' commitment to perpetual violence had sanctioned their use of political lies. In one sense, it might be satisfying to assume the defeat of fascism in World War II marked the end of political prevarication and the return of the rule not only of justice and law, but also of truth. However, Koyré perhaps unwittingly described the fate of the truth in a world where politics itself had become a form of advertising. As such, lies fueled violence, and violence fueled acts of editing, eliding, and erasing any details that threatened to destabilize the world picture.

Again, Arendt provided some *illumination* on this point: "Even in Hitler's Germany and Stalin's Russia it was more dangerous to talk about concentration and extermination camps, whose existence was no secret, then to hold and to utter "heretical" views on anti-Semitism, racism and Communism."[32] For human truths—fragile human bodies, lives and limbs caught in barbed wire, stories without a political "point"—were threatening.[33] Ardent continued: "What seems even more disturbing is that to the extent to which unwelcome factual truths are tolerated in free countries they are often, consciously or unconsciously, transformed into opinions."[34] Ardent reminded us that even when the "facts" can be secured, it is rare that they linger without being mobilized to secure public opinion toward a specified end or form of action.

The League's own rich mixed history also frequently got reduced to its "failures to act" after 1945. Those failures—flat, unexamined, clichéd—provided a convenient narrative for the changing of the guard. The cash value of the League's "failures" also had a long political afterlife. Alexandru Grigorescu recently explored how after the terrorist attacks on September 11, 2001, George W. Bush summoned the legacy of the League of Nations at the General Assembly. In his effort to gain approval for the invasion of Iraq, Bush stated: "We created the United Nations Security Council, so that, unlike the League of Nations, our deliberations would be more than talk, our resolutions would be more than wishes. After generations of deceitful dictators and broken treaties and squandered lives, we dedicated ourselves to standards of human dignity shared by all, and to a system of security defended by all."[35]

According to Grigorescu, Bush used the League-as-talking-shop trope more than forty times over the following two months.[36]

When it came to the details, the Bush administration elided historical contexts, claiming that a failure to support the US invasion of Iraq would be as egregious as allowing Italy to invade Ethiopia in 1935.[37] All the precise variables separating those two very different cases disappeared beneath the assertion that "action" is a superior virtue to "talk." What is more, the American delegation to the UN offered only thin and highly spurious "evidence" of the existence of "weapons of mass destruction," in Iraq, which was supposed to justify the—highly unpopular—act of war. Finally, we were still left without a clear sense of why action was justified in some cases (Iraq) and not in others (Rwanda).

By tracing the League's reputational afterlife into the late twentieth century, we gain a sense of the extent to which politics continues either to create new or to revive old ghosts, in order to redefine who might be worthy of basic rights (within or across borders) and who should be stripped of them. It is in this way that we see not just the specters but the wide spectrum of fascisms, including how they cling barnacle-like to would-be democratic societies and institutions.

In his recent *On Tyranny*, Timothy Snyder responded to the post-2008 rise of "fake news," authoritarian leadership, and populist coalitions with historical lessons from World War II. In a statement that resembled Koyré's position in 1945, Snyder warned: "Fascists rejected reason in the name of will, denying objective truth in favor of a glorious myth articulated by leaders who claimed to give voice to the people."[38] While that summary casts light on how fascism took hold, it still discounts (as Arendt warned) that reason and truth can prove just as destructive as will and myth in the hands of certain "opinion makers."[39] It is also possible that fascist ideologies made a number of people feel like they "had a voice," and one that felt clear and singular amid a confusing and alienating soundscape of many competing voices.[40]

Tyranny never only presses down from above but also is something for which people reach out from below.[41] People submit not just out of fearful obedience, but also out of desires for order, power, vanity, meaning, certainty, or sheer belonging. As Paechter stated in *Nazi-Deutsch*: "In this evocative and magic language the ideal sentence is the slogan. When thousands in a Sportpalast meeting chant in unison, "Ein Reich, ein Volk, ein Fuhrer," they do not think of any verb or action. A ritual is performed; three nouns, suggesting an order of the world, evoke acceptance of the structure thus laid out. When the Italian Fascist choruses about the senseless "du-cedu-cedu-cedu," the people accept the validity of their status as followers."[42] Even if the crowds gathered on the premise of a lie, the collective utterance is of togetherness, as a partnership fashioned from the ribs of others.[43]

The transhistorical insight here is that both the emergence of and resistance to fascist urges have become inexorably entwined with how information systems have and continue to transform the nature and uses of "truth telling" and "storytelling."[44] As John R. Pierce has explained, after 1939, the use of radar became integral to coordinating, among other things, aerial battlefields. In order to discern the target, such as an enemy plane, using electronic instruments, it was necessary to reduce the "clutter" and "noise" of presumably irrelevant information—from static to interference. This was at first, according to Pierce, a question left to engineers to ponder and solve. After the war, however, information science and its companion field of communication theory continued to pursue the elimination of "noise"—the enemy of certainty—in other fields of knowledge. In that frame, those sciences came to code ambiguity as "entropy," in other words, as chaos and decay.[45] Any information that fell outside of the zero-one binary got discarded as irrelevant. The target in both technical and epistemological terms became identifying how to send, receive, and then act on clear messages: in other words, to provide unambiguous information for decision making.[46]

Without criticizing information science as such, we can see how the extension of its logic might serve totalitarian designs. There is still a wide field where we need forms of knowledge that cannot be easily distilled into campaign slogans or firing orders.[47] A story of the same enemy plane might include a mixed amalgamation of elements—the life of the pilot, the global commodity chains along which the equipment traveled, divided hearts, the cost of fuel, sordid backgrounds, secrets, and unrequited love.[48] These elements are, of course, superfluous to the immediate decision of firing a weapon. But precisely, they might make pulling the trigger more difficult. And too, the story lines that escape the prison house of binary code (signal/noise, true/false, local/global, us/them) are not only meaningless to the radar; they are also destabilizing for the despots, the censors, and the book burners.[49]

Acknowledgments

With my deep gratitude for those who offered extensive notes on this entire manuscript at various stages: Marc Flandreau, Michael Geyer, Monica Huerta, Martin Jay, Adam McKeown, Daniel Rodgers, and three generous anonymous reviewers. I also want to thank the following people for their comments on specific chapters or for helping me to solve certain intellectual or editorial puzzles: Elizabeth Ault, Leah Barnes, William Bullman, Elizabeth Carter, Frederick Dickinson, Stefan Eich, Jennifer Foray, Denis Gainty, Michael Gordin, Geoff Jones, Rupali Mishra, Priya Nelson, Michelle Niemann, Matthew Osborn, John Durham Peters, Anson Rabinbach, Amalia Ribi-Forclaz, Davide Rodogno, Aidan Russell, Eric Santner, Andrew Sartori, Sharon Shahaf, David Sylvan, Robert Tignor, Till Van Rhanden, and Frédéric Zumer. Without the quiet knowing and know-how of Jacques Obserson at the League of Nations archives, this book would never have been possible. For their research assistance, I thank my wonderful students Daniel Dossou-Nonvide, Judith Frei, and Marco Maringoni. A special thanks to my friend and department chair Mohammad-Mahmoud Ould Mohamedou for his support, both in terms of getting time away from teaching and in general. There were also three institutional hosts that offered a generous provisioning of space and time: the Max Planck Institute for the Study of Societies in Cologne, the University of Paris II, and the Lauder Institute at the University of Pennsylvania. Finally, I want to express my thanks to Philippe Burrin for his part in helping to ensure that I would be able to finish this manuscript from the productive serenity of Geneva. For those who affected this work in more personal ways, I would rather keep my sentiments toward you outside of the information system. I will find another occasion and another way to say them, I promise.

Notes

Preface

1. Biltoft, "Anatomy of Credulity and Incredulity."
2. Shapin, *Social History of Truth*.
3. For a beautiful exploration of both light and shadow in the "clouds," see Peters, *Marvelous Clouds*.
4. Geertz, "Distinguished Lecture."
5. Bloch, "Réflections d'un historien sur les fausses nouvelles de la guerre," 14.
6. Jay, "Positive and Negative Totalities."
7. Nietzsche, *Birth of Tragedy*, 80.
8. Let's go then, but only if it pleases you.

Chapter One

1. Jung, *Portable Jung*. See chapter 12, "The Spiritual Problem of the Modern Man."
2. Eksteins, *Rites of Spring*; Winter, *Sites of Memory, Sites of Mourning*. For a discussion of the "collective" dimensions of Freudian trauma theory, please see Caruth, *Unclaimed Experience*.
3. For an overview of the global reach of World War I, please see Strachan, *First World War*; F. Dickinson, "Toward a Global Perspective of the Great War."
4. Statistics cited in Goldstein, *First World War Peace Settlements*.
5. Jung, *Portable Jung*, 460.
6. See especially Lovejoy, *Great Chain of Being*.
7. For a look at other, more global models of feudalism, please see Blaut, *Colonizer's Model of the World*.
8. For the long historical emergence of "secular" modernity, please see C. Taylor, *Sources of the Self*.
9. Jung, *Portable Jung*, 460.
10. Jung, 460.
11. Jung, 473.
12. Jung, 471.
13. Jung, 66.

14. For a lyrical bird's-eye view of the interwar conjuncture as seen from Russia, please see Kotkin, "Modern Times."

15. Of course Jung was not the only one to see links in the ferment of new cultural forms and new political movements; see Gay, *Modernism*.

16. I have, however, been influenced by Brown, *Life against Death*, and too by Mazlish, *Psychoanalysis and History*.

17. For an excellent analysis of the role of media in linking social processes from place to place through time, please see Gitelman, *Always Already New*. As a conjectural aside, it is possible that Jung's very concept of the "collective unconscious" (the murky mirror image of Émile Durkheim's collective conscious) might have been shaped in part by the fact that Jung was practicing psychology at a moment in which minds, institutions, and markets were increasingly "synched" via sprawling networks of cables and wires. See Jung, *Portable Jung*, 460.

18. There are already ample studies of both the technical growth and the myriad consequences of global communications grids. For just a small sampling, see Müller, *Wiring the World*; Comor, *Global Political Economy of Communication*; Castells, *Information Age*; Headrick, *Invisible Weapon*; Kern, *Culture of Time and Space*.

19. For my previous work on the theory of the archives of international organizations, please see Biltoft, "Sundry Worlds within the World." For works on the nature of fascism and of mass media and mass society, please see the classics: P. Taylor and Harris, *Critical Theories of Mass Media*; Luckert and Bachrach, *State of Deception*; Horkheimer and Adorno, *Dialectic of Enlightenment*; Grazia, *Culture of Consent*; Grazia, "Mass Culture and Sovereignty"; Heller, *Iron Fists*; Swett, *Selling Modernity*; Welch, *Propaganda, Power and Persuasion*.

20. E. Rosenberg, *Transnational Currents*. For a deeper sense of the content of these exchanges as they crossed the Atlantic between the wars, see Rodgers, *Atlantic Crossings*.

21. Pemberton, "New Worlds for Old"; McCarthy, *British People and the League of Nations*; Pedersen, "Meaning of the Mandates System."

22. There is already a vast literature on this topic, including a book I consider among the best: Müller, *Wiring the World*.

23. For an articulation of a method that fuses the tools of world and institutional history, please see Biltoft, "Sundry Worlds within the World." For an overview of global intellectual history, please see Moyn and Sartori, *Global Intellectual History*. For what I consider to be the best representatives of the budding field of organizational anthropology, please see Shore, Wright, and Però, *Policy Worlds*; S. Wright, *Anthropology of Organizations*; Niezen and Sapignoli, *Palaces of Hope*. I also draw from the socio-anthropological concept of lifeworlds as they form in specific spaces. See in particular Seamon, *Life Takes Place*. See also Bachelard and Jolas, *Poetics of Space*; Platt, "Places of Experience and the Experiences of Place"; Horkheimer and Adorno, *Dialectic of Enlightenment*.

24. For a discussion of Walter Benjamin's essay "To the Planetarium," please see Wohlfarth, "Walter Benjamin and the Idea of a Technological Eros."

25. McLuhan, *Gutenberg Galaxy*.

26. Please see Case, *Age of Questions*. I see that text as an intriguing collation of how and why the age of questions folded into an age of "final solutions." For a variant of this theory of the "dark side of modernity," see Bauman, *Modernity and the Holocaust*; Moses, *Empire, Colony, Genocide*; Santner, *Royal Remains*; Lebovic, *Philosophy of Life and Death*.

27. Paxton, *Anatomy of Fascism*.

28. Eco, "Ur-fascism."

29. For a study of those impulses-turned-political-projects both left and right, please see Tismăneanu, *Devil in History*. For a similarly complex set of arguments that follows through with a discussion of contemporary forms of populism, please see Finchelstein, *From Fascism to Populism in History*. See also Buck-Morss, *Dreamworld and Catastrophe*.

30. Paxton, *Anatomy of Fascism*, 14–15.

31. For a rather clear-eyed if popular description of that process, please see Stanley, *How Fascism Works*.

32. For what I think is a compelling view of the nature of "reception" in these contexts, see Holub, *Crossing Borders*.

33. On this point, I want to thank Martin Jay for pointing to me to the extent to which political and juridical as opposed to journalistic or scientific "truths" are fundamentally different registers through which the "public sphere," is established or contested. In a sense, while they are symbiotic, they can never be fully reconciled; see Habermas, *Structural Transformation of the Public Sphere*; Jay, *Virtues of Mendacity*.

34. Kleinberg, "Just the Facts." See also Shapin, *Social History of Truth*; Cmiel and Peters, *Promiscuous Knowledge*.

35. Kern, *Culture of Time and Space*. See also Berman, *All That Is Solid Melts into Air*; Reich, Higgins, and Raphael, *Mass Psychology of Fascism*.

36. Foucault, *Order of Things*.

37. Pedersen, "Back to the League of Nations"; Mazower, *No Enchanted Palace*; Clavin, *Securing the World Economy*; Amrith and Sluga, "New Histories of the United Nations"; Jackson and O'Malley, *Institution of International Order*; Karl Nordenstreng and Seppa, "League of Nations and the Mass Media"; Tworek, "Peace through Truth?"

38. See, in particular, Pedersen, *Guardians*; Clavin, *Securing the World Economy*; Callahan, *Mandates and Empire*; Mazower, *No Enchanted Palace*; Decorzant, *La Société des Nations et la naissance*; Tournès, *Les États-Unis et la Société des Nations*; Burgess, *League of Nations and the Refugees from Nazi Germany*; Fink, "Defender of Minorities."

39. Schipper, Lagendijk, and Anastasiadou, "New Connections for an Old Continent."

40. Brendebach, Herzer, and Tworek, *International Organizations and the Media in the Nineteenth and Twentieth Centuries*; Pedersen, "Meaning of the Mandates System"; Pedersen, *Guardians*. For other excellent studies of the League as a center of international expertise, please see Jackson and O'Malley, *Institution of International*. In particular in that volume, see Sánchez Román, "From the Tigris to the Amazon." See also Clavin and Wessels, "Transnationalism and the League of Nations."

41. Brendebach, Herzer, and Tworek, *International Organizations and the Media in the Nineteenth and Twentieth Centuries*, especially intro and chapters 4, 5, and 6.

42. Of course by "words" and discussion, Wilson also meant the broader arcs of international liberalism, including the carrots of free trade and the sticks of economic sanctions. Wilson, *Politics of Woodrow Wilson*, 326.

43. See Northedge, *League of Nations*, 20–30; Knock, *To End All Wars*.

44. "Avalon Project," article 3.

45. See, again, the text of the Covenant, "Avalon Project."

46. League of Nations Archives (LNA), *Records of the First Assembly of the League of Nations*, 30.

47. Baker, *Woodrow Wilson and World Settlement*, 1:42.

48. Baker, 1:97–102.

49. LNA, *Records of the First Assembly of the League of Nations*, 87.

50. See the text of the Covenant, "Avalon Project," article 8.

51. League of Nations, *How to Make the League of Nations Known*, 64.

52. The literature on the "expertise" produced at the League is legion. For a collection of several good pieces on the subject, please see Jackson and O'Malley, *Institution of International Order*. There has been a particularly excellent series of studies on the League and economic expertise. For what I consider to be the best, please see Clavin, *Securing the World Economy*; Piétri, "L'œuvre d'un organisme technique de la Société des Nations"; Fior, *Institution Globale et Marchés Financiers*.

53. Long and Wilson, *Thinkers of the Twenty Years' Crisis*.

54. Carr, *Twenty Years' Crisis*.

55. Carr, 27.

56. Pedersen, "Back to the League of Nations."

57. For a discussion of print and the role of written alphabets, see McLuhan, *Gutenberg Galaxy*; Ong and Hartley, *Orality and Literacy*; and Innis, *Empire and Communications*. See also the introduction of Cmiel and Peters, *Promiscuous Knowledge*.

58. Appadurai, "Disjuncture and Difference in the Global Cultural Economy." But see especially Peters, *Speaking into the Air*.

59. For an exploration of the longer arc of nominalism and then its transformation alongside new technologies (here, photography), please see Jay, "Magical Nominalism"; Lee, *Questioning Nineteenth-Century Assumptions about Knowledge*; Mercer and O'Neill, *Early Modern Philosophy*.

60. Vesey, *Idealism, Past and Present*.

61. G. Steiner, *After Babel*.

62. Please see Aarsleff, *From Locke to Saussure*. See also Eschbach and Trabant, *History of Semiotics*.

63. Joseph, *Ferdinand de Saussure*. Marc Shell has also convincingly claimed that Saussure—who came from a Swiss banking family—was influenced by the fluctuating monetary systems from gold to fiat. I will take this point up again later on in the book. Shell, *Money, Language, and Thought*.

64. G. Steiner, *After Babel*.

65. For a discussion of print and the role of written alphabets, see McLuhan, *Gutenberg Galaxy*; Ong and Hartley, *Orality and Literacy*; and Innis, *Empire and Communications*.

66. G. Steiner, *After Babel*; Biltoft, "Pivotes Informacionales y Giros Linguisitos."

67. Joseph, Taylor, and Love, *Landmarks in Linguistic Thought II*.

68. Souza Filho, *Language and Action*.

69. Derrida, *Of Grammatology*; Innis and Watson, *Bias of Communication*; Ong and Hartley, *Orality and Literacy*.

70. Rancière, Melehy, and White, *Names of History*; Bourdieu and Thompson, *Language and Symbolic Power*. In the context of photography, please see Jay, "Magical Nominalism."

71. Austin, Urmson, and Sbisà, *How to Do Things with Words*.

72. LaCapra, *Writing History, Writing Trauma*; Caruth, *Unclaimed Experience*.

73. Rasula, *Destruction Was My Beatrice*.

74. Bernays and Miller, *Propaganda*, 52.

75. Winkler, *Nexus*; Mock, *Words That Won the War*.

76. Lippmann, *Public Opinion*, 18. Also see Creel, *How We Advertised America*; and Lasswell, *Propaganda Technique in the World War*.

77. Lasswell, *Propaganda Technique in the World War*; Winkler, *Nexus*.

78. Lippman, *Public Opinion*, 18.

79. Müller and Tworek, "Telegraph and the Bank."

80. Innis, *Empire and Communications*.

81. Headrick, *Invisible Weapon*.

82. See Tully, *Devil's Milk*; and Tully, "Victorian Ecological Disaster."

83. Michael Geyer and Bright, "Global Violence and Nationalizing Wars in Eurasia and America," 643.

84. See Weber, *Peasants into Frenchmen*; and B. Anderson, *Imagined Communities*; Madley, *American Genocide*; Coward, "Globalisation of Enclosure"; Turner, *Enclosures in Britain*; Klauser, *Surveillance and Space*.

85. For the case of the French press, see Bignon and Flandreau, "Economics of Badmouthing."

86. Herman and Chomsky, *Manufacturing Consent*.

87. For example, see Pedersen, *Guardians*; Mazower, *No Enchanted Palace*; Joyce, *Broken Star*; Biltoft, "Meek Shall Not Inherit the Earth"; Laqua, "Transnational Intellectual Cooperation."

88. Pedersen, "Meaning of the Mandates System"; Pedersen, *Guardians*.

89. Iriye, *Global Community*.

90. Dimier, "On Good Colonial Government"; Egerton, "Collective Security as Political Myth."

91. Pedersen, *Guardians*; Wheatley, "Mandatory Interpretation"; Callahan, *Mandates and Empire*. See also the entire special issue on the mandates in the *American Historical Review* 124, no. 5, but especially Lichtenstein and Myod, "One Hundred Years of Mandates."

92. For evidence from the League itself, see International Conference on Economic Statistics and League of Nations, *Proceedings of the International Conference Relating to Economic Statistics*.

93. Many states were left out, and the League's Secretariat was still mostly European. Dykmann, "How International Was the Secretariat of the League of Nations?"

94. Müller and Tworek, "Telegraph and the Bank."

95. For an overview, see Marvin, *When Old Technologies Were New*; and Standage, *Victorian Internet*. More importantly, for a deeper exploration of the newly fragile economics of truth, please see Flandreau, *Anthropologists in the Stock Exchange*.

96. Cmiel and Peters, *Promiscuous Knowledge*.

97. Kern, *Culture of Time and Space*.

98. Trivellato, *Familiarity of Strangers*.

99. There is also an older story here. See Darnton, *Poetry and the Police Communication Networks in Eighteenth-Century Paris*; and Headrick, *When Information Came of Age*.

100. McLuhan, *Understanding Media*, 7.

101. Wenzlhuemer, *Connecting the Nineteenth-Century World*.

102. For a non-Western perspective on this shift in global imagination, see F. Dickinson, "Toward a Global Perspective of the Great War."

103. "Robert Graves."

104. Geroulanos and Meyers, *Human Body in the Age of Catastrophe*.

105. Please see Manela, *Wilsonian Moment*. See also Gorman, *Emergence of International Society in the 1920s*.

106. Miller, *My Diary at the Conference of Paris*.

107. Henig, *League of Nations*.

108. Zimmern, *League of Nations and the Rule of Law*, 23.

109. Laqua, "Transnational Intellectual Cooperation."

110. Pemberton, *Global Metaphors*.

111. Case, *Age of Questions*.

112. D. Bell, *Reordering the World*; Powell, *Globalism*. For a precise contextual illumination of the way these binaries became mapped onto questions of the material and the immaterial, specifically through matrices of choice and primordial longing at the margins, see Bayart, *L'état en Afrique*; and Bayart, Warnier, et al., *Matière à politique*.

113. In contrast, resistance movements like the Boxer Rebellion in China or the Ghost Dance movement in the United States stood against the onslaught of Western (Christian) modernity with syncretic forms of spiritualism—claims of turning of bullets into water or calling on the dead. See Cohen, *History in Three Keys*; and R.-H. Anderson, *Lakota Ghost Dance of 1890*.

114. Seeing the League as *haunted* is different than declaring it tainted or collaborationist; here I have been influenced by Kleinberg, *Haunting History*.

115. Jay, "Positive and Negative Totalities." For an interwar exploration, see Sapir, *Totality*.

116. Spretnak, *Resurgence of the Real*.

117. Here I have been influenced by M. Mann, *Dark Side of Democracy*; Bauman, *Modernity and the Holocaust*.

118. For variants of twentieth-century utopianisms, please see Winter, *Dreams of Peace and Freedom*; Buck-Morss, *Dreamworld and Catastrophe*. This concept is defined as "a racially unified and hierarchically organized body in which the interests of individuals would be strictly subordinate to those of the nation, or Volk." Quoted in "Volksgemeinschaft."

119. Vismann, *Files*.

120. Vismann, 9.

121. Parikka, *What Is Media Archaeology?*

122. Cmiel and Peters, *Promiscuous Knowledge*.

123. Burgess, *League of Nations and the Refugees from Nazi Germany*.

124. Bauman, *Liquid Modernity*; Berman, *All That Is Solid Melts into Air*.

125. Quoted in the preface of Deleuze and Guattari, *Anti-Oedipus*, xiii.

Chapter Two

1. Price, *World Talks It Over*, ix.

2. For example, see Pedersen, *Guardians*; Mazower, *No Enchanted Palace*; Joyce, *Broken Star*; Biltoft, "Meek Shall Not Inherit the Earth"; Laqua, "Transnational Intellectual Cooperation."

3. For the workings of the Permanent Mandate Commission (PMC), please see Pedersen, *Guardians*; see also Wheatley, "Mandatory Interpretation"; Callahan, *Mandates and Empire*.

4. Dykmann, "How International Was the Secretariat of the League of Nations?

5. Please see a contemporary analysis of the League's support of the equality of states in Stallybrass, *Society of States*.

6. For "representations" of Ethiopia in the interwar moment, please see Ribi-Forclaz, *Humanitarian Imperialism*.

7. Coyajee, *India and the League of Nations*. Please see also Thakur, *Jan Smuts and the Indian Question*; Thakur, "Jan Smuts, Jawaharlal Nehru and the Legacies of Liberalism."

NOTES TO PAGES 18–22

8. Traz, *Spirit of Geneva*, xvii.
9. *League of Nations and the Press*, 7.
10. *League of Nations and the Press*, 17.
11. *League of Nations and the Press*, 19.
12. *League of Nations and the Press*, 33.
13. *League of Nations and the Press*, 29.
14. *League of Nations and the Press*, 29–30. See also League of Nations, *League of Nations Library*; League of Nations Library, *Ouvrages sur l'activité de la Société des Nations*.
15. *League of Nations and the Press*, 53. See also Aufricht, *Guide to League of Nations Publications*.
16. *League of Nations and the Press*, 60.
17. See the finding aids of the League of Nations archives, http://libraryresources.unog.ch/c.php?g=462663&p=3162919.
18. See correspondence between Sir Eric Drummond and Arthur Burrows, January 12, and January 20, 1921, LNA R 1365/10558/10558.
19. "Correspondence between the Secretariat of the League of Nations and the Remington Typewriter Company," December 1919, LNA box R 1534/2217/2217.
20. For a critical method of looking at an object from multiple perspectives, see Žižek, *Parallax View*.
21. J. Scott, *Seeing Like a State*; Boucock, *In the Grip of Freedom*; Page, *Political Authority and Bureaucratic Power*.
22. Pemberton, "New Worlds for Old."
23. Riles, "Infinity within the Brackets"; Wheatley, "Mandatory Interpretation"; Grazia and Paggi, "Story of an Ordinary Massacre"; Butler, *Psychic Life of Power*; Lefebvre, Wander, and Rabinovitch, *Everyday Life in the Modern World*; Stewart, *Ordinary Affects*.
24. Riles, "Infinity within the Brackets."
25. Pemberton, "New Worlds for Old"; E. Rosenberg, *Transnational Currents*.
26. Kittler, *Gramophone, Film, Typewriter*.
27. Marcot, *History of Remington Firearms*.
28. McCarthy, *British People and the League of Nations*, 17.
29. Otlet and Rayward, *International Organisation and Dissemination of Knowledge*.
30. A. Wright, *Cataloging the World*.
31. For the ways in which "public spheres" always serve specific interests despite claims of inclusivity and neutrality, please see Habermas, *Structural Transformation of the Public Sphere*.
32. Baker, *Woodrow Wilson and World Settlement*, 3:430.
33. Flandreau, *Anthropologists in the Stock Exchange*, especially chapter 1.
34. Derrida, *Of Grammatology*. In support of looking at League documents as "texts," please see Wheatley, "Mandatory Interpretation."
35. Hardt and Negri, "Biopolitical Production," 222.
36. Flandreau and Flores, "Bonds and Brands"; Poovey, *Genres of the Credit Economy*; Castaldo, *Trust in Market Relationships*; Lauer, *Creditworthy*.
37. Norris, *R. G. Dun and Co.*; Gaillard, *Century of Sovereign Ratings*; Flandreau and Flores, "Bonds and Brands"; Viktorin et al., *Nation Branding in Modern History*; Lauer, *Creditworthy*.
38. Pemberton, *Global Metaphors*; Dirlik, "Architectures of Global Modernity, Colonialism, and Places." See also Baudrillard, *Simulacra and Simulation*.
39. Quoted in Bernays and Miller, *Propaganda*, iv.

40. Greenblatt, *Marvelous Possessions*.

41. Heidegger, *Question concerning Technology, and Other Essays*, 128.

42. Heidegger, 132.

43. Heidegger, 134.

44. For a look at how such exhibitions reveal the changes in the values and mentalities of empire, please see Hale, *Races on Display*; Qureshi, *Peoples on Parade*.

45. For an excellent account of the League and world's fairs, see Allen, "Internationalist Exhibitionism."

46. Mitchell, *Colonising Egypt*, 6.

47. For discussions on the economics of truth, please see Flandreau, *Anthropologists in the Stock Exchange*. See also Calabrese and Sparks, *Toward a Political Economy of Culture*. I have made this claim also in Biltoft, "Sundry Worlds within the World."

48. Maier, *Recasting Bourgeois Europe*; Mallard, "Gift Revisited."

49. I also make this point in my forthcoming manuscript on the League of Nations. In thinking of the "world-making" function as one dimension of symbolic capital formation, I was influenced by D. Bell, *Reordering the World*; Mitchell, *Colonising Egypt*; Hoffenberg, *Empire on Display*.

50. Egerton, "Collective Security as Political Myth"; "League of Nations as an Instrument of Liberalism by Raymond B. Fosdick"; Ribi-Forclaz, *Humanitarian Imperialism*.

51. There is a link here to bodies of literature that see international organizations as producers of norms, knowledge, and forms of expertise. Decorzant, "La Société des Nations et l'apparition"; Barnett, *Rules for the World*; Shore, Wright, and Però, *Policy Worlds*.

52. Coase, *Firm, the Market, and the Law*; Williams, *Emergence of the Theory of the Firm*.

53. Barnett, *Rules for the World*.

54. Fridenson, "Les Organisations Un Nouvel Object."

55. For these crises both at the League and beyond, see Pedersen, *Guardians*; Ribi-Forclaz, *Humanitarian Imperialism*; Adas, *Machines as the Measure of Men*; Laqua, *Internationalism Reconfigured*.

56. Adas, *Machines as the Measure of Men*.

57. "On Transience" in Freud, Strachey, and Freud, *Standard Edition of the Complete Psychological Works of Sigmund Freud*, 8:305–7.

58. Gay, *Freud*.

59. Aydin, *Politics of Anti-Westernism in Asia*. See also Spengler and Atkinson, *Decline of the West*; Lazier, *God Interrupted*. The point about decline narratives is also made briefly in Pemberton, "New Worlds for Old," 312.

60. See "Lenin, VS." See also Charles Maier's description of the tension between the forces of revolution and those of conservation in Maier, *Recasting Bourgeois Europe*.

61. Hochschild, *King Leopold's Ghost*. Please see also Burbank and Cooper, *Empires in World History*; Streets-Salter and Getz, *Empires and Colonies in the Modern World*; Ballantyne and Burton, *Empires and the Reach of the Global*.

62. See Eksteins, *Rites of Spring*.

63. Linklater, "Standard of Civilisation."

64. Heidegger, *Question concerning Technology, and Other Essays*, 134.

65. Gorman, *Emergence of International Society in the 1920s*.

66. See "Lenin, VS." See also Maier, *Recasting Bourgeois Europe*.

67. Besant, *War Articles and Notes*, 135.

68. Mukerji, *Disillusioned India*, 222.
69. Ellis, *Origin, Structure and Working of the League of Nations*, 63.
70. Ellis, 33.
71. Ellis, 62.
72. Sartori, *Liberalism in Empire*; Mehta, *Liberalism and Empire*. See also Cohn, *Colonialism and Its Forms of Knowledge*.
73. See Cain, "Ellis, Charles Howard (Dick)."
74. Febvre and Burke, *New Kind of History*, 220.
75. Poovey, *Genres of the Credit Economy*; Müller and Tworek, "Telegraph and the Bank."
76. Freud, Strachey, and Freud, *Standard Edition of the Complete Psychological Works of Sigmund Freud*, 9:36.
77. International Conference on Economic Statistics and League of Nations, *Proceedings of the International Conference Relating to Economic Statistics*; League of Nations and Economic Intelligence Service, *Annuaire statistique de la Société des Nations*.
78. Smuts, *League of Nations*, 11. For an examination of Smuts's role in the concept of international organization, see Mazower, *No Enchanted Palace*.
79. Smuts, *League of Nations*, 27.
80. Maier, *Recasting Bourgeois Europe*.
81. For a longer term view of the role of reputation in that of state power, see Flandreau and Flores, "Bonds and Brands."
82. Z. Steiner, *Lights That Failed European International History*.
83. In a world of intangible assets, or, in Pierre Bourdieu's terms, an increasingly symbolic economy, "credit worthiness" and "credibility" were tightly linked. Bourdieu, "La production de la croyance."
84. Wilson's pronouncement for the right of peoples to self-determination sent numerous anticolonialist nationalists marching to Paris in 1919. Wilson never intended to liberate all colonies, but rather to avoid new direct annexations of the territories of the defeated powers. As for full national self-determination, that prize would go only to the European territories carved out from the old land empires in central and eastern Europe. See Manela, *Wilsonian Moment*. See also Pedersen, *Guardians*; Sharp, *Versailles Settlement*; and Prott, *Politics of Self-Determination*.
85. Pedersen, *Guardians*; Callahan, *Mandates and Empire*.
86. "Avalon Project."
87. Accominotti, Flandreau, Rezzik, and Zumer, "Black Man's Burden, White Man's Welfare."
88. Pedersen, "Meaning of the Mandates System."
89. Lowe, *Intimacies of Four Continents*.
90. Pedersen, *Guardians*.
91. Gaillard, *Century of Sovereign Ratings*.
92. Flores and Decorzant, "Going Multilateral?"; Decorzant, "La Société des Nations et l'apparition"; Clavin, *Securing the World Economy*.
93. Pauly, *League of Nations and the Foreshadowing of the International Monetary Fund*. See also Mazower, *No Enchanted Palace*.
94. Ellis, *Origin, Structure and Working of the League of Nations*, 63.
95. Pauly, *League of Nations and the Foreshadowing of the International Monetary Fund*.
96. My wonderful student Thomas Gidney is currently writing about this subject in "Anomaly among Anomalies."

97. Coyajee, *India and the League of Nations*. Please see also Thakur, *Jan Smuts and the Indian Question*; Thakur, "Jan Smuts, Jawaharlal Nehru and the Legacies of Liberalism"; Legg, "International Anomaly?"

98. Wagner, *Amritsar*, 2019.

99. The Indian delegation was typically composed of Englishmen from the India Office, representatives from the princely states, and then delegates chosen from among the Indian elite, especially those in posts in the British government.

100. For a discussion of the Indian delegation and practice of separating India and the dominions in League, see Coyajee, *India and the League of Nations*; Thakur, *Jan Smuts and the Indian Question*.

101. There is a vast literature on the progressive "failings" of the League of Nations. Please see Mazower, *No Enchanted Palace*; Prashad, *Darker Nations*; Callahan, *Mandates and Empire*.

102. League of Nations, *How to Make the League of Nations Known*.

103. On the nature of hegemony, see Gramsci, *Prison Notebooks*. See also Gran, *Beyond Eurocentrism*.

104. Amrith and Sluga, "New Histories of the United Nations"; Sluga and Clavin, *Internationalisms*.

105. Short, *Magic Lantern Empire*; Kalka, *Gaslight*; Stieglitz, *Lantern Slides*.

106. B. B. Dickinson, "Use of Lantern Slides in Teaching," 161.

107. LNA R 1340 22/34066/34066. The League made lantern slide presentations at various branches of the YMCA and League of Nations Unions. Dartmouth College also purchased a set.

108. For an exploration of how photography came to play a role in nineteenth-century legal conceptions of evidence and truth, see Huerta, "Evidence of Things Unseen." For other reflections on the role of photography in framing conceptions of reality, see Barthes, *Camera Lucida*; Sontag, *On Photography*. For a specific case study of the use of photography to frame international organizational moods and especially fund-raising agendas, see Rodogno, "Horrific Photo of a Drowned Syrian." See also Fehrenbach and Rodogno, *Humanitarian Photography*.

109. Sontag, *On Photography*, 3.

110. International Educational Cinematographic Institute and League of Nations, *Draft Protocol for Facilitating the International Circulation of Films of an Educational Character*; Druick, "International Educational Cinematographic Institute"; Higson and Maltby, *"Film Europe" and "Film America"*; Seabury, *Motion Picture Problems*.

111. Cmiel and Peters, *Promiscuous Knowledge*, chapter 4; Grazia, "Mass Culture and Sovereignty."

112. Barthes, *Camera Lucida*, 5.

113. Werner, "Archives of the Planet."

114. See "Albert-Kahn."

115. "Repetoires des photographes," May 1926, LNA R 1340 55079/34066.

116. Martin Lewis and Wigen, *Myth of Continents*.

117. "Repetoires des photographes," May 1926, LNA R 1340 55079/34066. For more on mapping and its claims to truth, see Black, *Visions of the World*; Rankin, *After the Map*; Norman and Thrower, *Maps and Civilization*; Harley, Laxton, and Andrews, *New Nature of Maps*.

118. Smuts, *League of Nations*, 34.

119. "Repetoires des photographes," May 1926, LNA R 1340 55079/34066.

120. "Repetoires des photographes," May 1926.

121. "Repetoires des photographes," May 1926.

NOTES TO PAGES 32–36

122. "Letter of Herbert Ames to Arthur Pelt," March 31, 1924, LNA R 1430 22/34066/34066.
123. "Memo," April 3, 1924, LNA R 1430 22/34066/34066.
124. "Letter of Arthur Pelt to Herbert Ames," May 29, 1924, LNA R 1340/22/34066/34066.
125. "Memo," March 31, 1924, LNA R 1430 22/34066/34066.
126. Quoted in Shields, "Greek-Turkish Population Exchange," 5.
127. "The Greek Refugee Loan," LNA R 1340 34066/34066.
128. "Greek Refugee Loan."
129. "Greek Refugee Loan."
130. "Greek Refugee Loan."
131. "Greek Refugee Loan."
132. Shields, "Greek-Turkish Population Exchange"; I siz, *Humanism in Ruins*; Clark, *Twice a Stranger*.
133. Here again I want to cite the importance to my thinking of Hardt and Negri, "Biopolitical Production," 222.
134. Bashford, "Population, Geopolitics, and International Organizations"; Bashford, "Nation, Empire, Globe"; Connelly, "Seeing beyond the State."
135. Correspondence between Herbert Ames and Director of Philip and Son, February 7, 1924, LNA R 1340 22/34066/34066.
136. Memos between Herbert Ames and Pablo de Azcárate May 16, 1924, LNA R 1340 22/34066/34066. See also Raymond Fosdick and Arthur Sweetzer, May 27, 1924, LNA R 1340 22/34066/34066.
137. The League held a conference for reducing tariffs for films with explicitly salutary educational content. At the same time, the League's Committee on International Intellectual Cooperation supported an inquiry to limit the circulation of "western films" into colonial territories. In short, they worried about the "psychological effect" that modern films might have on "backward populations." The file on the subject implied that seeing Western modes of life might inspire inappropriate desires, forms of restlessness, or unrest among colonial populations. International Educational Cinematographic Institute and League of Nations, *Draft Protocol for Facilitating the International Circulation of Films of an Educational Character*; Druick, "International Educational Cinematograph Institute." See also Higson and Maltby, *"Film Europe" and "Film America."* See also the contents of the file "The Effects of the Cinema on Backward Races," LNA R 2349 33439/32641.
138. See Akami, "Limits of Peace Propaganda." See also Asseraf, "Making Their Own Internationalism."
139. Barthes, *Camera Lucida*.
140. Hardt and Negri, "Biopolitical Production," 222.
141. "Marty Jay photographs deceive, but ... showing and telling, except for moments when the past—like the nature world itself—was reified and mobilized for the future." Walden, *Photography and Philosophy*, 16; Roberts, *Photography and Its Violations*.
142. Short, *Magic Lantern Empire*; Kalka, *Gaslight*. See also E. Ogden, *Credulity*.
143. Jay, "Magical Nominalism." See also Huerta, "Evidence of Things Unseen."
144. Valery, "Centenary of Photography," 194.
145. Valery, 193.
146. Jay, "Can Photographs Lie?," 18.
147. For how the debate over slavery in Ethiopia played out in this dispute, see Ribi-Forclaz, *Humanitarian Imperialism*.

148. Ethiopia and League of Nations, *Dispute between Ethiopia and Italy*; Italy and League of Nations, *Dispute between Ethiopia and Italy: Photographs*; Italy and League of Nations, *Dispute between Ethiopia and Italy: Communication*; Baer, *Test Case*. For a more general description of Italian colonial policy, see Larebo, *Building of an Empire*.

149. Ethiopia and League of Nations, *Dispute between Ethiopia and Italy*; Italy and League of Nations, *Dispute between Ethiopia and Italy: Photographs*; Italy and League of Nations, *Dispute between Ethiopia and Italy: Communication*; Baer, *Test Case: Italy, Ethiopia, and the League of Nations*; Larebo, *Building of an Empire*.

150. Traz, *Spirit of Geneva*, xv.

151. Traz, xvi.

152. Traz, xii.

153. Agamben, *Homo Sacer*, 23.

154. Boyer, *Spirit and System*.

155. See Jay, "Magical Nominalism." See also Sontag, *Regarding the Pain of Others*.

156. Committee on Intellectual Co-operation, *Modern Means of Spreading Information Utilised in the Cause of Peace*.

157. Inter-governmental Conference for the Conclusion of an International Convention concerning the Use of Broadcasting in the Cause of Peace and League of Nations, *International Convention*.

158. Opening Speech of M. Arnold Raestead, President of the Conference, September 16, 1936, LNA Conf.E.R.P./3.

159. Opening Speech of M. Arnold Raestead.

160. Opening Speech of M. Arnold Raestead.

161. Disarmament Information Committee, *Disarmament*; Conference for the Reduction and Limitation of Armaments and League of Nations, *Moral Disarmament*.

162. Horkheimer and Adorno, *Dialectic of Enlightenment*, 129.

163. Heidegger, *Parmenides*, 81.

164. G. Steiner, *Heidegger*; Badiou and Cassin, *Heidegger*.

165. Hitler, *My New Order*, 500.

166. On the competing universalisms contained within IOs, see Amrith and Sluga, "New Histories of the United Nations."

167. A. Rosenberg, *Myth of the Twentieth Century*, 1.

168. A. Rosenberg, i.

169. A. Rosenberg, x.

Chapter Three

1. "Tristan Tzara—Dada Manifesto (23rd March 1918)."

2. Rasula, *Destruction Was My Beatrice*.

3. Michael and Doerr, *Nazi-Deutsch*; Steinhoff, *George Orwell and the Origins of 1984*.

4. "Tristan Tzara—Dada Manifesto (23rd March 1918)."

5. Quoted in Grunberger, *12-Year Reich*, 47.

6. B. Anderson, *Imagined Communities*; J. Scott, *Seeing Like a State*; L. Bell and McLaughlin, "John E. Joseph."

7. Jameson, *Prison-House of Language*.

8. Manning, "Language and International Affairs," 296, my emphasis.

9. L. Bell and McLaughlin, "John E. Joseph"; Bourdieu and Thompson, *Language and Symbolic Power*; Foucault, *Archeology of Knowledge*.

10. Weber, *Peasants into Frenchmen*; B. Anderson, *Imagined Communities*; Smith, *Ethnic Origins of Nations*.

11. See the chapter on language in Cohn, *Colonialism and Its Forms of Knowledge*.

12. Dauzat, *Le français et l'anglais langues internationals*, 10.

13. For an elaboration of how the linguistic turn, turned on an informational pivot, please see Biltoft, "Pivotes Informacionales y Giros Linguisitos."

14. See MacMillan, *Paris 1919*; Miller, *My Diary at the Conference of Paris*.

15. Dauzat, *Le français et l'anglais langues internationals*, 10.

16. Dominion, *Frontiers of Language and Nationality in Europe*, 332.

17. Harold Nelson has argued that Wilson was optimistic not only that the victor powers could adjust the political frontiers in those regions to reflect the ethno-linguistic divisions, but that such an adjustment would provide the basis for a stable democratic order. Nelson, *Land and Power*, 61.

18. These included Czechoslovakia; Estonia; Albania; Latvia; Lithuania; Poland; the Kingdom of Serbs, Croats and Slovenes (Yugoslavia); Greece; Romania; Bulgaria; Hungary; Austria; Germany; and Turkey.

19. Robinson, *Were the Minorities Treaties a Failure?*, 43.

20. For a look at these maps, see Miller, *My Diary at the Conference of Paris*. See also Gullberg, *State, Territory, and Identity*; and Ádám, *Versailles System and Central Europe*.

21. For a clear explanation of this rationale for the Minority Treaties, see Fink, "Minority Rights as an International Question"; Macartney, *National States and National Minorities*.

22. League of Nations, *League of Nations and the Protection of Minorities*, 20.

23. Alderson, *Why the War Cannot Be Final*, n.p. Though published in 1915, this pamphlet came home from the Peace Conference in the personal belongings of Ray Stannard Baker. Document reference number WET 29.117.D, Seeley G. Mudd Manuscript Library, Princeton University.

24. For a description of the characters that came to the Peace Conference hoping to influence Wilson and other great power leaders, see MacMillan, *Paris 1919*.

25. For a description of the transatlantic development of city planning and scientific management, see Rodgers, *Atlantic Crossings*; Doray, *From Taylorism to Fordism*; J. Scott, *Seeing Like a State*.

26. With respect to language in science in general, rather than scientific management, see Gordin, *Scientific Babel*.

27. On the growth of cultural internationalism to 1918, see Iriye, *Cultural Internationalism and World Order*; and Kern, *Culture of Time and Space*.

28. Pollock, *Language of the Gods in the World of Men*; Eco, *Search for the Perfect Language*.

29. See Hobsbawm, *Nations and Nationalism since 1780*; relevant here, too, is Weber, *Peasants into Frenchmen*. For the use of language in state-building projects of the late nineteenth century, see J. Scott, *Seeing Like a State*. For language as part of imagined and invented traditions, see B. Anderson, *Imagined Communities*; Hobsbawm and Ranger, *Invention of Tradition*; Hobsbawm and Ranger, *Nationalism*; Smith, *Antiquity of Nations*.

30. For the growth of postwar linguistic determinism, see Mathiot, *Ethnolinguistics*.

31. To explore the ways in which these languages grew up with transnational efforts to scientific communities, see Gordin, *Scientific Babel*.

32. Montague C. Butler, "Which Shall It Be? The Problem of an International Language," pamphlet appended to a letter to the secretary-general from the British Esperanto Association, July 18, 1923, LNA R 1048/23516/28693.

33. LNA, *Records of the First Assembly of the League of Nations*, 180.

34. LNA, 178–80.

35. LNA, 219.

36. The other signatories included delegates from Romania, Belgium, Persia, Czechoslovakia, Colombia, China, Finland, Albania, Japan, Venezuela, Haiti, Poland, Italy, Chile, and India. LNA, 218–19. See also "Esperanto as an International Auxiliary Language," League of Nations Document, A.5.1922, 2.

37. For a complete biography of Zamenhof, see Forster, *Esperanto Movement*. For a beautiful biography of the Esperanto movement, see Schor, *Bridge of Words*.

38. See Janten, *Esperanto*.

39. Janten, *Esperanto*.

40. Shenton, *Cosmopolitan Conversation*, 469.

41. Guérard, *Short History of the International Language Movement*.

42. For a description of France's relation to the League of Nations in its first phase, see Mouton, *Le Société des Nations et les intérêts de la France*; Noble, *Policies and Opinions at Paris*; and Birebent, *Militants de la paix et de la SDN*.

43. LNA, *Records of the First Assembly of the League of Nations*, 413.

44. League of Nations, *Esperanto as an International Auxiliary Language*.

45. Nitobe, *Language Question and the League of Nations*, 6.

46. Nitobe, 11.

47. Nitobe, 13.

48. Nitobe, 14.

49. League of Nations, *Esperanto as an International Auxiliary Language*, 2. The League offered the use of its facilities for an International Conference on the Teaching of Esperanto in Schools in 1921, and League officials observed those proceedings.

50. "Questionnaire with Regard to the Teaching of Esperanto in Schools," LNA Document C.L. 5(a), 1922 XII.[A].

51. League of Nations, *Esperanto as an International Auxiliary Language*.

52. "Esperanto as an Auxiliary International Language, Report of the 5th Committee as Submitted to the Third Assembly," Records of the Third Assembly, Minutes of the Fifth Committee on Social and General Questions, Assembly document A.81, 1922 Xii.A.

53. M. de Rio Branco, "Contre l'octroi du patronage de la Société des Nations a l'Esperanto," pamphlet appended to letter from General Sebert to the secretary-general, January 14, 1922, LNA R 1048/23516/25988.

54. Gramsci, "Single Language and Esperanto."

55. Gramsci, 29.

56. "Pour la langue commercial auxiliaire universelle: Actes de la conférence internationale de chambres de commerce, foires d'échantillons, groupements economiques et offices du tourisme, réunie a venise du 2 au 4 Avril, 1923," Conference Proceedings, appendix to a letter from the president of the Italian Chamber of Commerce in Switzerland to the secretary-general, May 9, 1923, LNA R 1048/23516/25754.

57. Privat, *Esperanto in Fifty Lessons*; Privat, *Historio de la lingvo Esperanto*; Privat, *Life of Zamenhof*.

NOTES TO PAGES 47–52   137

58. Heath and Senn, "Edmond Privat and the Commission of the East in 1918"; Chaudhury, *Edmond Privat*; Privat, *Vie de Gandhi*; Privat, *Aux Indes avec Gandhi*.

59. Farrokh, *La pensée et l'action d'Edmond Privat*.

60. "Respecting the Representation of Members of the League of Nations at the Annual Assembly by Persons not their own Nationals," Cabinet Memo, April 10, 1923, CAB/24/159 (C.P. 191 23), British National Archives (TNA).

61. "Respecting the Representation of Members of the League of Nations."

62. "Respecting the Representation of Members of the League of Nations."

63. Minutes of the ICIC, June 6, 1923, LNA R 1048/23516/2906.

64. Minutes of the ICIC, August 1, 1923, LNA R 1048/23516/29913.

65. Minutes of the ICIC, August 1, 1923.

66. LNA, *Records of the Fifth Assembly*, 117.

67. Schor, *Bridge of Words*; Garvía, *Esperanto and Its Rivals*.

68. Vossler, *Spirit of Language in Civilization*, 162.

69. Wittgenstein and Anscombe, *Philosophical Investigations*, aphorism 11-20, 124.

70. Wittgenstein, Granger, and Russell, *Tractatus logico-philosophicus*

71. Fink, *Defending the Rights of Others*.

72. League of Nations, *Protection of Linguistic, Racial or Religious Minorities*, 13–17.

73. Cowan, "Who's Afraid of Violent Language?," 271; Biltoft, "Meek Shall Not Inherit the Earth."

74. Biltoft, "Meek Shall Not Inherit the Earth."

75. Colban to Dr. Van Hamel, January 29, 1925, LNA R 1698/42698/42698.

76. Dr. Van Hamel to Colban, January 29, 1925, LNA R 1698/42698/42698.

77. Cited in Stavans, *Resurrecting Hebrew*.

78. British Information Services, *Britain's Mandate for Palestine*; Gavish, *Survey of Palestine under the British Mandate*; Jones and Anglo-Palestinian Archives Committee, *Britain and Palestine*; United States and League of Nations, *Mandate for Palestine*; Leifer, *Balfour Declaration, the Palestine Mandate, and the United Nations Partition Resolution*; World Zionist Organization, *Establishment in Palestine of the Jewish National Home*; Great Britain and League of Nations, *Report by His Majesty's Government in the United Kingdom of Great Britain and Northern Ireland to the Council of the League of Nations*.

79. Letter HR to Eric Colban, January 26, 1925, LNA R 1698/42698/42698.

80. Eric Colban to Dr. Van Hamel, Minorities Section memo, July 4, 1925, LNA R 1698/42698/42698.

81. Azcárate, *League of Nations and National Minorities*, 4.

82. Azcárate, 49–51.

83. Antoine Meillet quoted in League of Nations Association of Jugoslavia, *Bulgars and Jugoslavs*, 9.

84. League of Nations, *League of Nations and the Protection of Minorities*.

85. Please see Dimier, "On Good Colonial Government"; Callahan, *Sacred Trust*; Upthegrove, *Empire by Mandate*); Callahan, *Mandates and Empire*; Margalith, *International Mandates*; Stoyanovsky, *Mandate for Palestine*; van Maanen-Helmer, *Mandates System in Relation to Africa and the Pacific Islands*; Fieldhouse, *Western Imperialism in the Middle East*.

86. Dimier, "On Good Colonial Government." See also Silverfarb, *Britain's Informal Empire in the Middle East*; "Entry of Iraq into the League of Nations," Secret Cabinet Memorandum Circulated by the Secretary of State for the Colonies, June 9, 1927, CAB/24/187, C.P. 178 (27), TNA.

87. See the *Official Journal of the League of Nations* 13 no. 7, 1347–49. For an account of the process, see Pedersen, "Getting Out of Iraq." See also Robinson, *Were the Minorities Treaties a Failure?*, 167. For a narrative of the process by which Iraq entered the League, see Q. Wright, *Mandates under the League of Nations*. See also Q. Wright, "Proposed Termination of the Iraq Mandate."

88. Chatterjee, *Nation and Its Fragments*.

89. Mukherjee, "Problem of Indian Minorities."

90. Macartney, *National States and National Minorities*, 440–41.

91. Azcárate, *League of Nations and National Minorities*, 97.

92. Azcárate, 17.

93. Decorzant, *La Société des Nations et la naissance*; Slobodian, *Globalists*; Biltoft, "Meek Shall Not Inherit the Earth"; Peterecz, "Picking the Right Man for the Job."

94. League of Nations, *Protection of Linguistic, Racial or Religious Minorities*, 42–45.

95. League of Nations, 42.

96. League of Nations, 45.

97. Wampole, *Rootedness*.

98. Azcárate, *League of Nations and National Minorities*, 120–22; Fink, "Defender of Minorities."

99. League of Nations Association of Jugoslavia, *Bulgars and Jugoslavs*, 19.

100. Standardization of Railway Nomenclature, box R 2568, LON; Standardization of Philosophical Terms, box R 1087, LON; Unification of Graphic Symbols, box R 2224, LON; Standardization of Scientific Terminology, box R 2190, 11839, folder 260, LON.

101. League of Nations Association of Jugoslavia, *Bulgars and Jugoslavs*, 19.

102. Nitobe, *Works of Inazo Nitobe*, 8:435.

103. "Circumstances of Introducing Roman Characters into Japanese Writing," pamphlet by A. Tanakadate, box R 2251, file 21496, folder 21496, LON. For a general discussion of the reform of Japanese writing, see Gottlieb, *Language and the Modern State*.

104. G. Lewis, *Turkish Language Reform*.

105. *International Communication*.

106. International Institute of Intellectual Co-operation and League of Nations, *L'adoption universelle des caractères latins*, n.p.

107. Otto Jespersen, *How to Teach a Foreign Language* (London: Allen and Unwin, 1928); Reynolds, "On Grammatical Trifles"; *Otto Jespersen: Facets of His Life and Work*.

108. International Institute of Intellectual Co-operation and League of Nations, *L'adoption universelle des caractères latins*, n.p.

109. Cited in International Institute of Intellectual Co-operation and League of Nations, n.p.

110. G. Lewis, *Turkish Language Reform*.

111. Aytürk, "Turkish Linguists against the West"; Poulton, *Top Hat, Grey Wolf, and Crescent*; Gökalp, *Turkish Nationalism and Western Civilization*; Heyd, *Language Reform in Modern Turkey*.

112. Sapir, *Language*, 125.

113. Firth, *Tongues of Men and Speech*, 89.

114. Firth, 95.

115. Pedersen, "Getting Out of Iraq"; Baram, "Case of Imported Identity"; Fink, "Minority Rights as an International Question."

116. Hutton, *Linguistics and the Third Reich*.

NOTES TO PAGES 57–61

117. Lins, *Dangerous Language*. See also Schor, *Bridge of Words*.
118. Hitler, *Mien Kampf*, 307.
119. Forster, *Esperanto Movement*.
120. W. J. Dodd, *National Socialism and German Discourse Unquiet Voices*, 105.
121. Paechter, *Nazi-Deutsch*, 5.
122. Paechter, 5.
123. Klemperer and Brady, *Language of the Third Reich*, 282–83. I found this same example was also noted in Press, "Language of Ideology."
124. Lebovic, *Philosophy of Life and Death*.
125. Mazower, *Hitler's Empire*.
126. Quoted in Garvía, *Esperanto and Its Rivals*, 151.
127. C. K. Ogden, *Debabelization*, 2.
128. Winston Churchill's speech at Harvard University on September 6, 1943, circulated to the members of the War Cabinet, September 20, 1943, CAB/66/40/48, Memorandum W.P. (43) 398, TNA.
129. Koeneke, *Empires of the Mind*.
130. Steinhoff, *George Orwell and the Origins of 1984*.
131. "Hugo Ball's Dada Manifesto, July 1916."
132. League of Nations, *Memorandum on Currency, 1913–1921*, 86.
133. International Conference for the Adoption of a Convention for the Suppression of Counterfeiting Currency et al., *Proceedings*, 98.

Chapter Four

1. Saussure, *Course in General Linguistics*, 119. On the influence of monetary thinking and policy on Saussure's view of language, see Shell, *Money, Language, and Thought*.
2. Again see Shell, *Money, Language, and Though*; Dyer, "Making Semiotic Sense of Money as a Medium of Exchange"; Gray, "Buying into Signs"; Wennerlind, "Money Talks."
3. For a discussion of the resonance between the processes underwriting both economic and linguistic phenomena, see Goux, *Symbolic Economies*.
4. Redish, "Anchors Aweigh."
5. Fisher, "Stabilizing the Dollar," 154.
6. Fisher, 156.
7. See especially Clavin, *Securing the World Economy*; Clavin and Wessels, "Transnationalism and the League of Nations"; Endres, *International Organizations and the Analysis of Economic Policy*; Decorzant, *La Société des Nations et la naissance*.
8. Clavin, *Securing the World Economy*. See also Clavin, "Money Talks."
9. Clavin, *Securing the World Economy*. See also Clavin and Wessels, "Another Golden Idol?"
10. On the "social" life of money, the most inspiring recent work in the macroeconomic history literature is Straumann, *Fixed Ideas of Money*. On the role of Sweden in pioneering alternative targets, see the classic contributions by Jonung, "Knut Wicksell's Norm of Price Stabilization"; and Jonung, "Cassel, Davidson and Heckscher on Swedish Monetary Policy." For other perspectives on France, please see Mouré, *Gold Standard Illusion*; in a more general context, see Flandreau, "Pillars of Globalization."
11. See "Correspondence with the International Federation of Eugenics Organizations,"

LNA R 5A/19309/19309." For Fischer's own work on Eugenics, see Fisher, *Impending Problems of Eugenics*. For looking transversally at the "social" meaning of money, see especially N. Dodd, *Sociology of Money*; and N. Dodd, *Concepts of Money*.

12. Arbuthnot, "This Generation Can Not Escape Paying the Cost of War," 417.

13. Arbuthnot, 417.

14. See, for example, Malcolm, *Scraps of Paper*.

15. Edsall, *Coming Scrap of Paper*, 22.

16. Edsall, 23.

17. The film is available online at https://www.youtube.com/watch?v=2kDvBJqHm_c. It was last consulted on January 23, 2017.

18. Desan, *Making Money*.

19. Fox and Ernst, *Money in the Western Legal Tradition*, 10.

20. Pocock, *Machiavellian Moment*; Desan, *Cultural History of Money in the Age of Enlightenment*.

21. White and Schuler, "Retrospectives."

22. Quoted in White and Schuler, "Retrospectives," 213.

23. In fact, he was very much still one in 1931, when he wrote *Treatise on Money*.

24. G. Mann, *In the Long Run We Are All Dead*; G. Mann, "Poverty in the Midst of Plenty."

25. Keynes, *Economic Consequences of the Peace*.

26. Cristiano, *Political and Economic Thought of the Young Keynes*.

27. Biltoft, "League of Nations and Alternative Economic Perspectives."

28. For an overview of Cassel's life and the main arc of his work, see Carlson, *State as a Monster*.

29. Cassel, *World's Monetary Problems*, 13.

30. Cassel, 28–29.

31. Cassel, 21.

32. For various views of this relationship, see Briggs and Burke, *Social History of the Media*; for a discussion of the relation between state building and "print capitalism," see B. Anderson, *Imagined Communities*. For an in-depth case study of the political economy of power struggles over the media in interwar France, see Bignon and Flandreau, "Price of Media Capture and the Debasement of the French Newspaper Industry."

33. Cassel, *World's Monetary Problems*, 23.

34. Cassel, 51.

35. Cassel, 13–14.

36. Cassel, 78.

37. See the brilliant book by Gorman, *Emergence of International Society in the 1920s*; see also Maier, *Recasting Bourgeois Europe*; Z. Steiner, *Lights That Failed European International History*.

38. Clavin, *Securing the World Economy*.

39. Other bodies propagated these visions as well, for example, Britain's famous Cunliffe Committee, on which the young Keynes served. See Cunliffe Committee and Macmillan Committee, *British Parliamentary Reports on International Finance*.

40. Bloomfield first referred to these "rules" of the game; see Bloomfield, *Monetary Policy under the International Gold Standard*.

41. Eichengreen and Flandreau, *Gold Standard in Theory and History*.

42. Bloomfield, *Monetary Policy under the International Gold Standard*.

43. Flandreau, "Central Bank Cooperation in Historical Perspective."

44. Hobsbawm and Ranger, *Invention of Tradition*.
45. Polanyi, *Great Transformation*.
46. Simmel, *Philosophy of Money*, 167.
47. See Kern, *Culture of Time and Space*.
48. Conant, "Development of Credit," 161.
49. Conant, 167–68.
50. Conant, 165.
51. Flandreau and Leeming, *Glitter of Gold*, 3.
52. Conant, "Development of Credit," 165.
53. For two excellent works on the subject of prejudice during the gold rush and its link to the "primitivism" of gold, see Hill, *Tarnished Gold*; Starr, Orsi, and California Historical Society, *Rooted in Barbarous Soil*.
54. Goux, *Symbolic Economies*.
55. Redish, "Anchors Aweigh."
56. Meder, "Giro Payments and the Beginnings of the Modern Cashless Payment System."
57. Flandreau, "Central Bank Cooperation in Historical Perspective."
58. Helleiner, *Making of National Money*, 3. It was only during the interwar period the most other independent states in Europe, Asia, and Latin America completed that process.
59. Helleiner, 3–4.
60. B. Anderson, *Imagined Communities*.
61. J. Scott, *Seeing Like a State*.
62. Mihm, *Nation of Counterfeiters*.
63. Smith, *Nationalism and Modernism*; B. Anderson, *Imagined Communities*.
64. Robertson, "Aesthetics of Authenticity." See also Poovey, *Genres of the Credit Economy*.
65. Mihm, *Nation of Counterfeiters*.
66. Spencer, *Man versus the State*, 14.
67. For Marx's discussion of money, see chapter 3 in Marx and Griffith, *Capital*.
68. See part 5 in Marx and Engels, *Capital*.
69. Simmel, *Philosophy of Money*, 169.
70. Macleod, *Theory of Credit*; Mitchell-Innes, "What Is Money."
71. Knapp, *State Theory of Money*, 2.
72. Note that proposals to have a price-index standard of value were already present in the bouillon debates of the early nineteenth century. On this point, see Flandreau and Centre for Economic Policy Research, *Pillars of Globalization*.
73. Bagehot, "New Standard of Value," 476–77.
74. Bagehot, 472.
75. For an innovative view of the seemingly paradoxical state-strengthening effects of fin de siècle global integration, see Flandreau, "Does Integration Globalize?" Also see Wallerstein, *Centrist Liberalism Triumphant*.
76. For a review of this debate in the context of Japan's adoption of the gold standard, see Schiltz, "Money on the Road to Empire."
77. For a summary of nineteenth century discussions, see Flandreau and Leeming, *Glitter of Gold* (especially the introduction, "King Bullion: The International Monetary Regime, 1848–73").
78. As a result, the debate continues among economic historians on whether the gold standard benefitted some and hazed others. For the view that gold adherence provided financial

benefits in the shape of lower borrowing costs, a classic contribution is Bordo and Rockoff, "Gold Standard as a 'Good Housekeeping Seal of Approval.'" For the contrarian view that investors saw beyond the veil of gold, and did not "reward" states on a gold standard with better terms, see Flandreau and Zumer, *Making of Global Finance 1880–1913*.

79. Flandreau, "Crises and Punishment."
80. Arrighi, *Long Twentieth Century*.
81. Lenin, *Imperialism*.
82. See Bryan, *Gold Standard at the Turn of the Twentieth Century*. For the international contradictions of liberalism, see Manent, *Intellectual History of Liberalism*; Mehta, *Liberalism and Empire*; and especially Sartori, *Liberalism in Empire*.
83. Michael Geyer and Bright, "Global Violence and Nationalizing Wars in Eurasia and America."
84. Fisher, "Stabilizing the Dollar," 157.
85. According to Cassel, "it is often believed that the recovery of trade which is now so urgently needed could best be furthered by the establishment of an international standard of money." See Cassel, *World's Monetary Problems*, 75–76.
86. Request of René de Saussure to the secretary-general of the League of Nations, to consider "La Monnaie Fictive Internationale," October 12, 1920, LON box R 1479, document 7469, dossier 7469; Saussure, *La structure logique*.
87. "Supervisory Commission: Currency in Which Contributions Are Paid: Note by the Secretary General," June 12, 1934, LNA 5310/9866/9866.
88. Willis, *History of the Latin Monetary Union*. For a discussion of how the gold standard won out over the international currency schemes of the nineteenth century, see M. H. Geyer and Paulmann, *Mechanics of Internationalism*.
89. Cassel, *World's Monetary Problems*, 77.
90. The classic work is League of Nations, Financial Economic and Transit Department, and Nurkse, *International Currency Experience*, esp. 27. For a textbook narrative, see Endres and Fleming, *International Organizations and the Analysis of Economic Policy*, 58–60. For a study shedding new light on the actual composition of central bank reserves under the gold exchange standard and focusing on competition among key currencies (sterling v. the dollar), see Eichengreen and Flandreau, "Rise and Fall of the Dollar."
91. League of Nations, Financial Economic and Transit Department, and Nurkse, *Course and Control of Inflation*, 4.
92. Cassel, *World's Monetary Problems*, 86–87.
93. Cassel, 325.
94. Fergusson, *When Money Dies*.
95. Clavin, "Money Talks." More specifically, see Clavin, *Securing the World Economy*; and Clavin, "Austrian Hunger Crisis."
96. On this topic, see Y. Decorzant and J. Flores, "Public Borrowing in Harsh Times: The League of Nations Loans Revisited," Working Paper 12091, University of Geneva, 2012. See also Biltoft, "Meek Shall Not Inherit the Earth."
97. League of Nations, Financial Economic and Transit Department, and Nurkse, *Course and Control of Inflation*, 18.
98. Biltoft, "Meek Shall Not Inherit the Earth."
99. Balderston, *World Economy and National Economies in the Interwar Slump*.
100. Letter from M. Brian to the secretary-general of the League of Nations, June 5, 1926,

reproduced in International Conference for the Adoption of a Convention for the Suppression of Counterfeiting Currency et al., *Proceedings*, 219.

101. See Banque Nationale de Belgique, *Bulletin hebdomadaire d'information et de documentation*. Also see Klay, "Hungarian Counterfeit Francs"; "Great Forgery Plot in Hungarian Capital."

102. "Uncovering the Hungarian Bank-Note Scandal."

103. On the episode and its international repercussions, see Banque Nationale de Belgique, *Bulletin hebdomadaire d'information et de documentation*, no. 19, October 21, 1926.

104. This act of nationalism had an earlier resonance, as Hungary dumped currency in order to secure its own monetary sovereignty in the 1860s. See *Emperor of Austria versus Louis Kossuth*.

105. League of Nations, Financial Economic and Transit Department, and Nurkse, *Course and Control of Inflation*.

106. Peterecz, *Jeremiah Smith*; Boross, *Inflation and Industry in Hungary*; League of Nations, *Financial Reconstruction of Hungary*.

107. Peterecz, "Picking the Right Man for the Job."

108. Hagen, "Before the 'Final Solution.'"

109. Petruccelli, "Banknotes from the Underground." Incidentally, 1926 was also the year that the first run of the Hungarian *Pengo* went into print. Ironically, it was also so easy to counterfeit that it had to launch another run by 1927.

110. In this strain, request the unpublished working paper by Nicolas Delalande, "Protecting State Credit: Speculation, Trust and Sovereignty in 1920s France," Conference Proceedings Government Debt Crises: Politics, Economics, and History, Geneva Switzerland, IHEID, 2012.

111. Irwin and National Bureau of Economic Research, *Did France Cause the Great Depression?*; Eichengreen, *Golden Fetters*.

112. Delalande, "Protecting State Credit."

113. International Conference for the Adoption of a Convention for the Suppression of Counterfeiting Currency et al., *Proceedings*, 221–22.

114. International Conference for the Adoption of a Convention for the Suppression of Counterfeiting Currency et al., 223.

115. *Counterfeiting Currency*.

116. Petruccelli, "Banknotes from the Underground."

117. International Conference for the Adoption of a Convention for the Suppression of Counterfeiting Currency et al., *Proceedings*, 223–24.

118. Eichengreen, *Golden Fetters*.

119. International Conference for the Adoption of a Convention for the Suppression of Counterfeiting Currency et al., *Proceedings*, 50–51.

120. League of Nations, *Mixed Committee for the Suppression of Counterfeiting Currency*, 6.

121. Robertson, "Aesthetics of Authenticity."

122. League of Nations, *Mixed Committee for the Suppression of Counterfeiting Currency*, 6.

123. League of Nations, 18.

124. Benjamin, *Work of Art in the Age of Mechanical Reproduction*. Benjamin offered some insights relevant for understanding the social and political significance of counterfeit in the age of mass reproduction. In that text he described how the "authenticity" of the object became a matter of its relation to its historical roots, its time and place tradition.

125. "Uncovering the Hungarian Bank-Note Scandal."

126. Fisher, *Money Illusion*, 135. For Fisher's earlier musings on the real and the nominal, see *Purchasing Power of Money*.

127. Freud, *Future of an Illusion*, 39.

128. International Conference for the Adoption of a Convention for the Suppression of Counterfeiting Currency et al., *Proceedings*, 48.

129. International Conference for the Adoption of a Convention for the Suppression of Counterfeiting Currency et al., 77.

130. International Conference for the Adoption of a Convention for the Suppression of Counterfeiting Currency et al., 47–48.

131. League of Nations, *Mixed Committee for the Suppression of Counterfeiting Currency*, 7.

132. International Conference for the Adoption of a Convention for the Suppression of Counterfeiting Currency et al., *Proceedings*, 52.

133. International Conference for the Adoption of a Convention for the Suppression of Counterfeiting Currency et al., 71.

134. Biblioklept, "'Counterfeit Money'—Charles Baudelaire."

135. International Conference for the Adoption of a Convention for the Suppression of Counterfeiting Currency et al., *Proceedings*, 250.

136. See "Ratification of the Convention for the Suppression of Counterfeiting Currency," LNA box 4585, file 10399.

137. Clavin, *Failure of Economic*.

138. League of Nations, Financial Economic and Transit Department, and Nurkse, *International Currency Experience*, 105–6.

139. Eichengreen, *Golden Fetters*; Clavin and Wessels, "Another Golden Idol?"

140. League of Nations et al., *Interim Report of the Gold Delegation*.

141. League of Nations, Financial Economic and Transit Department, and Nurkse, *International Currency Experience*, 39–40.

142. League of Nations et al., *Interim Report of the Gold Delegation*, 20.

143. Clavin and Wessels, "Another Golden Idol?"; Clavin, *Securing the World Economy*.

144. Cassel, *Downfall of the Gold Standard*, 1.

145. Cassel, 2.

146. Cassel, 2.

147. Cassel, 5.

148. Cassel, 13.

149. Cassel, 14.

150. Cassel, 213.

151. Cassel, 212.

152. Cassel, 214.

153. Adam and Mazal Holocaust Collection, *Art of the Third Reich*; Barron et al., "Degenerate Art."

154. Fergusson, *When Money Dies*; James, *Reichsbank and Public Finance in Germany*; Stolper, *German Economy*.

155. Possony, *Die Wehrwirtschaft des totalen Krieges*; Carroll, "Design for Total War"; Wolfe, "Development of Nazi Monetary Policy." See too the wonderful Tooze, *Wages of Destruction*.

156. Robert, *Hitler's Counterfeit Reich*; Malkin, *Krueger's Men*.

157. Wolfe, "Development of Nazi Monetary Policy."

158. P. Morrison, *Poetics of Fascism*.

159. Douglas, *Premises of Social Credit*.
160. Pound, *Guide to Kulchur*, 298. Thanks to David Sylvan for this reference.
161. Pound, *What Is Money For*.
162. Pound, *What Is Money For*.
163. "Three Coins from Freud | HMS," https://hms.harvard.edu/news/harvard-medicine/harvard-medicine/handed-down/three-coins-freud, accessed January 6, 2016.
164. League of Nations, *League Hands Over*.

Chapter Five

1. Speaking of the poetic and the coincidental, there were several other historical figures with the surname Lux who made or attempted to make "radical" contributions in their moment. The German Adam Lux (about whom Stefan Zweig wrote a play in 1928) participated in the French Revolution and died by guillotine. Joseph August Lux was a twentieth-century Austrian author, playwright, and photographer. The Nazis arrested J. A. Lux and sent him to Dachau, after which they also ordered the burning of his published works. Please see Zweig and Tremousa, *Adam Lux*; Gooch, "Germany and the French Revolution"; Jarzombek, "Joseph August Lux."
2. Carter and Muir, *Printing and the Mind of Man*.
3. Wainewright, *Reporting on Hitler*.
4. Durkheim and Neuburger, *Le suicide*.
5. See LNA box R 5230/15/24650/17433; and also Sargent, "Desperate Mission of Stefan Lux." This story is also cited in Reinharz and Shavit, *Road to September 1939*. Mention of Lux also appears in Lester, *Suicide and the Holocaust*.
6. "Suicide Shot Rings at League Session."
7. Sargent, "Desperate Mission of Stefan Lux."
8. All that remains are a few sparse documents, Lux's letter to Joseph Avenol (in German) and a few press clippings covering the event. See LNA box R 5230/15/24650/17433.
9. For a narrative of the question of false news and its meanings for international journalism, please see Tworek, "Peace through Truth?"
10. Mazower, *Dark Continent*.
11. Caspar, *Gegen die Lügenpresse*; Schellenberg, "Lügenpresse?"; Luckert and Bachrach, *State of Deception*; Lilienthal and Neverla, *Lügenpresse Anatomie eines politischen Kampfbegriffs*.
12. Of relevance to my understanding here is Jay, *Virtues of Mendacity*. See also Arendt's essay "Lying in Politics," in Arendt, *Crisis of the Republic*.
13. Here I take inspiration from dimensions of the concept of "social editing" in Flandreau, *Anthropologists in the Stock Exchange*; in conversation with T. Morrison and Coates, *Origin of Others*; and Horkheimer and Adorno, *Dialectic of Enlightenment*.
14. For a description of the intellectual climate and fate of intellectuals under German-occupied France, please see Burrin, *Living with Defeat*.
15. For the details of Benjamin's death, please see Eiland and Jennings, *Walter Benjamin*. See also Hannah Arendt's introduction in Benjamin, *Illuminations*.
16. For questions of writing traumatic events, see LaCapra, *Writing History, Writing Trauma*.
17. Benjamin, *Illuminations*. I mention this because Hannah Arendt's thoughts on truth and lying in politics will be important for this chapter. However, the translation of Benjamin's essay in that volume has several problems. Thus I will be using Benjamin, *Walter Benjamin: Selected Writings*, vol. 3.

18. Benjamin, *Walter Benjamin*, 3:143.

19. Benjamin, 3:144.

20. Benjamin, 3:147.

21. Benjamin, 3:147.

22. Benjamin, 3:147–48.

23. Jay, "'Aesthetic Ideology' as Ideology." In conversation with literature on "the attention economy," see, for one, Marazzi, Hardt, and Conti, *Capital and Language*.

24. Benjamin's perspective on information anticipated and influenced that of Max Horkheimer and Theodor W. Adorno. In their treatise on the culture industry, they also argued that details from media technologies rarely disrupted or dislodged the "whole." Horkheimer and Adorno, *Dialectic of Enlightenment*.

25. Jay, "'Aesthetic Ideology' as Ideology."

26. Benjamin, *Walter Benjamin*, 3:149.

27. Benjamin, 3:149.

28. Benjamin, 3:146.

29. Please see Stewart, *Ordinary Affects*; Lefebvre, Wander, and Rabinovitch, *Everyday Life in the Modern World*. See also Biltoft, "Sundry Worlds within the World."

30. Benjamin, *Walter Benjamin*, 3:149.

31. Benjamin, 3:151.

32. Arendt, *Between Past and Future*, 262–63.

33. Benjamin, *Walter Benjamin*, 3:149.

34. For that history, please see Beavan, *Fingerprints*.

35. Benjamin, *Walter Benjamin*, 3:151.

36. Benjamin, 3:144.

37. Benjamin, 3:143–44.

38. Benjamin, 3:152.

39. Benjamin, 3:152.

40. While this is not the claim she makes, there are some historical dimensions to the rise of obituaries in the lovely book by Johnson entitled *Dead Beat*. See also Fowler, *Obituary as Collective Memory*.

41. Horkheimer and Adorno, *Dialectic of Enlightenment*, 136.

42. Benjamin, *Walter Benjamin*, 3:151.

43. Benjamin, 3:151.

44. Two books written shortly after the event were Hahn, *Vor Den Augen Der Welt!*; and *Porqué se mató el periodista Stéfan Lux*.

45. Sargent, "Desperate Mission of Stefan Lux," 188.

46. For a story of the role of the *Manchester Guardian* in the interwar moment in Britain, please see Cockett, *Twilight of Truth*. See also Wainewright, *Reporting on Hitler*.

47. Sargent, "Desperate Mission of Stefan Lux," 193.

48. Sargent, 190.

49. Sargent, 196–97.

50. Sargent, 190.

51. "Suicide Shot Rings at League Session." Also quoted in Sargent, "Desperate Mission of Stefan Lux," 190.

52. For a various accounts, see "Revolver Shot in Geneva Assembly Hall"; "League Assembly 'Closes' Abyssinian Issue"; "Epidemics Claim 213 in Chungking in June."

NOTES TO PAGES 96–100

53. "Suicide Shot Rings at League Session."
54. "League in Panic as Jew Shoots Self in Gallery"; "Foreign Lands"; "Jewish Writer Dies in Protest against Nazis."
55. See press clipping in LNA R 5230/15/24650/17433.
56. Press clipping in LNA R 5230/15/24650/17433.
57. "League in Turmoil as Czech Ends Life: Shoots Self to Protest Nazi Anti-Semitism; Reform Discussed," *Philadelphia Inquirer.*
58. "Revolver Shot in Geneva Assembly Hall."
59. "Epidemics Claim 213 in Chungking in June"; "Revolver Shot in Geneva Assembly Hall."
60. "League Hall Sees Suicide."
61. "League Hall Sees Suicide."
62. "League in Panic as Jew Shoots Self in Gallery."
63. Text transcribed from film. For a review of the film, please see A. O. Scott, "Film Review."
64. For views of the links between the League of Nations and the "Jewish question," please see Fink, *Defending the Rights of Others*; Burgess, *League of Nations and the Refugees from Nazi Germany*; Feinberg, *Jewish League of Nations Societies*; League of Nations Union, *Jewish Problem.*
65. Sargent, "Desperate Mission of Stefan Lux."
66. Sargent.
67. Sargent, 197.
68. Birchard and Thomas, *Cecil B. DeMille's Hollywood*; Ringgold and Bodeen, *Films of Cecil B. DeMille*; *King of Kings.*
69. Schildkraut and Lania, *My Father and I.*
70. Sargent, "Desperate Mission of Stefan Lux," 199.
71. Deák, *Weimar Germany's Left-Wing Intellectuals.*
72. They did so, however, under the new title *Die neue Weltbühne*; please see Armer, *Die Wiener Weltbühne.*
73. Sargent, "Desperate Mission of Stefan Lux," 197.
74. See telegraph from Dr. Arthur Heller, July 6, 1936, in LNA R 5230/15/24650/17433, "Efin Lux Pas Mort Pour Juif Mai pour l'idee Humanitare et LAST NOT LEAST POUR SOCIET DE NATIONS STOP J Espere Que Cette Action Heroique Ne Restera Sans Effet=Dr Arthur Heller."
75. My translation, letter from Stefan Lux to Joseph Avenol, July 2, 1936, in LNA R 5230/15/24650/17433.
76. See correspondence between Secretariat et Le Department Politique Fédéral des affaires étrangères, July 14, 1936, LNA R 5230/15/24650/17433.
77. Sargent also states that she sent a copy of that letter to the then-archivist in Geneva. However, that letter still does not appear in the file folder. As such, for the sake of simplicity, and in homage to the work she did, I draw here on her transcription. For the full translation, see Sargent, "Desperate Mission of Stefan Lux," 193.
78. Sargent, 193–94.
79. Sargent, 193–94.
80. Sargent, 193–94. See also Rancière, Melehy, and White, *Names of History.*
81. Sargent, "Desperate Mission of Stefan Lux," 194.
82. McDonough, *Hitler, Chamberlain and Appeasement*; Mommsen and Kettenacker, *Fascist Challenge and the Policy of Appeasement.*
83. Sargent, "Desperate Mission of Stefan Lux," 195.
84. Sargent, 195.

85. Sargent, 196.

86. See Correspondence between the League and the *Israelitisches Wochenblatt*, July 9 and 10, LNA R 5230/15/24650/17433.

87. See letter concerning the credentials on Stefan Lux, July 4, 1936, received at the League July 9, 1936, LNA R 5230/15/24650/17433.

88. See a memo on security questions pertaining to the Lux incident, July 7, 1936, LNA R 5230/15/24650/17433.

89. For a detail account of this story line and how Avenol transformed his beliefs into practice while at the League, please see Barros, *Betrayal from Within*.

90. Sargent, "Desperate Mission of Stefan Lux," 191.

91. Goeschel, *Suicide in Nazi Germany*, 98.

92. Goeschel, 98.

93. Horkheimer and Adorno, *Dialectic of Enlightenment*, 153.

94. "Suicide Shot Rings at League Session."

95. *Der Opfertod von Genf: Die Tat des Stephan Lux vor der Völkerbundsversammlung*, in the *Israelitisches Wochenblatt für die Schweiz*, July 10, 1936. See press clipping in LNA R 5230/15/24650/17433.

96. "League in Panic as Jew Shoots Self in Gallery."

97. Brustein, *Roots of Hate*; Burrin and Lloyd, *Nazi Anti-Semitism*; Hagen, "Before the 'Final Solution.'"

98. Segel and Levy, *Lie and a Libel*.

99. *Der Opfertod von Genf*.

100. Frend, *Martyrdom and Persecution in the Early Church*; Metzger and Murphy, *Apocryphal/Deuterocanonical Books of the Old Testament*.

101. Doran, "Revolt of the Maccabees"; Himmelfarb, "Judaism and Hellenism in 2 Maccabees."

102. Himmelfarb, "Judaism and Hellenism in 2 Maccabees"; Momigliano, "Second Book of Maccabees."

103. Luckhurst and McDonagh, *Transactions and Encounters*.

104. Ariès, *Hour of Our Death*, 116.

105. Ariès, 116.

106. My translation from the German (in consultation of Judith Frei), *Der Opfertod von Genf*.

107. My translation from the German (in consultation with Judith Frei), *Der Opfertod von Genf*.

108. Tartakoff, "Synagogues, Cemeteries, and Frontiers."

109. Tartakoff.

110. My translation from the French, *Der Opfertod von Genf*.

111. The journalist had even delayed his travel plans from Geneva to London in order to await his copy of Lux's letter, only to discover that the League sent it on to England via the post. See inquiry letter to M. Stencek concerning Mr. Dell, July 4, 1936, LNA R 5230/15/24650/17433.

112. *Der Opfertod von Genf*.

113. My translation of Dell's speech from the French; see LNA R 5230/15/24650/17433.

114. LNA R 5230/15/24650/17433, 78. For the journey of Bell's disillusionment, please see Renshaw, "Disillusionment of Robert Dell."

NOTES TO PAGES 105–112

115. I use the edition of *Mein Kampf* available at http://www.greatwar.nl/books/meinkampf/meinkampf.pdf, 204.

116. Conference for the Reduction and Limitation of Armaments and League of Nations, *Moral Disarmament.*

117. "Report of the Third Committee," in LNA R 3310/39043/31113.

118. LNA R 3310 13/39043/31113.

119. LNA R 3310/13/39034/31113.

120. LNA R 3310/13/39034/31113.

121. LNA R 3310 13/31668/31113.

122. LNA R 3310 13/31668/31113.

123. LNA R 3310/13/39034/31113. For context of the state of journalism in Valot's France during those years, please see Bignon and Flandreau, *Price of Media Capture and the Looting of Newspapers in Interwar France.*

124. LNA R 3310/13/39034/31113.

125. Bloch, *Strange Defeat*; Nord, *France 1940.*

126. Bloch, "Réflections d'un historien sur les fausses nouvelles de la guerre," 17.

127. LNA R 3310/13/39034/31113.

128. See "Cooperation of the Press in the Organization of Peace," 1, LNA R 3310/13/39034/31113.

129. "Cooperation of the Press in the Organization of Peace," 1.

130. "Cooperation of the Press in the Organization of Peace," 2.

131. "Cooperation of the Press in the Organization of Peace," 1.

132. "Cooperation of the Press in the Organization of Peace," 2.

133. "Cooperation of the Press in the Organization of Peace," 10.

134. "Cooperation of the Press in the Organization of Peace," 2.

135. "Cooperation of the Press in the Organization of Peace," 12.

136. "Cooperation of the Press in the Organization of Peace," 12.

137. "Cooperation of the Press in the Organization of Peace," 12.

138. "Cooperation of the Press in the Organization of Peace," 12.

139. Streit, *Union Now*, 137.

140. Streit, 137.

141. Streit, 137.

142. Streit, 5.

143. Streit, 5.

144. Streit, 5.

145. *Mein Kampf*, http://www.greatwar.nl/books/meinkampf/meinkampf.pdf, 255.

146. Arendt, *Crisis of the Republic*, 6.

147. Arendt, 6–7.

148. "Cooperation of the Press in the Organization of Peace," 12.

149. For an account of memories of the Holocaust in France, please see Kritzman and Mazal Holocaust Collection, *Auschwitz and After.*

150. LNA Records of the Assembly, 1936, 47.

151. Lusinchi, "Exhibit in Geneva."

152. Lusinchi.

153. Lusinchi.

154. Lusinchi.

155. The ILO went to Montreal; the Economic and Financial Section moved to Princeton, NJ; the Health and Opium sections went to Washington, DC; and finally, the Treasury moved to London League of Nations. League of Nations, *League Hands Over*, 8–11.

156. Hilderbrand, *Dumbarton Oaks*.

Chapter Six

1. Quoted in Koyré, "Political Function of the Modern Lie," 143.
2. Koyré, 143.
3. Koyré, 143.
4. Arendt, *Between Past and Future*, 233.
5. See again the distinction between political and other forms of truth in Jay, *Virtues of Mendacity*.
6. Horkheimer and Adorno, *Dialectic of Enlightenment*.
7. Potter, "League Publicity"; see also a discussion of the issue in McCarthy, *British People and the League of Nations*.
8. League of Nations, *Board of Liquidation*. See also Biltoft "Intangible Values."
9. League of Nations and Assembly, *Records of the Twentieth (Conclusion) and Twenty-First Ordinary Sessions of the Assembly*, 35.
10. LNA, Records of the Final Assembly, 35–36.
11. LNA, 35.
12. LNA, 36.
13. LNA, 45.
14. LNA, 50.
15. United Nations and Inter-organization Board for Information Systems, *Directory of United Nations Information Systems*.
16. Cmiel, "Human Rights, Freedom of Information, and the Origins of Third-World Solidarity."
17. Lilley and Trice, *History of Information Science*; Castells, *Rise of the Network Society*.
18. League of Nations and Assembly, *Records of the Twentieth (Conclusion) and Twenty-First Ordinary Sessions of the Assembly*, 28.
19. League of Nations, *League Hands Over*, 43.
20. Versluis, *New Inquisitions*.
21. Arendt, *On Violence*, 9–11.
22. Prashad, *Darker Nations*.
23. Kennedy, *Parliament of Man*; Lazier, "Earthrise."
24. Though again, this was with mixed results. C. Anderson, *Eyes off the Prize*.
25. See Hardt and Negri, *Empire*; Hardt and Negri, "Biopolitical Production."
26. Levene, "Why Is the Twentieth Century the Century of Genocide?"
27. For the ambiguities of human rights discourse, please see again Levene.
28. Please see the brilliant Dean, *Moral Witness*. See also her earlier Dean, *Aversion and Erasure*.
29. Wasson and Grieveson, *Cinema's Military Industrial Complex*; Baran and Sweezy, *Monopoly Capital*; Slobodian, *Globalists*.
30. Koyré, "Political Function of the Modern Lie," 145.
31. Koyré, 145.

32. Arendt, *Between Past and Future*, 236.
33. Netz, *Barbed Wire*.
34. Arendt, *Between Past and Future*, 236.
35. Quoted in Grigorescu, "Mapping the UN–League of Nations Analogy," 34.
36. Grigorescu.
37. Grigorescu.
38. Snyder, *On Tyranny*, 11.
39. On this, see Kleinberg, "Just the Facts."
40. Peters, *Speaking into the Air*.
41. Butler, *Psychic Life of Power*; please see also Havel, *Living in Truth*. And thanks to John Peters for encouraging me to read it.
42. Paechter, *Nazi-Deutsch*, 6.
43. Again for the ways in which information systems transformed forms of and longing for intimacy, please see Peters, *Speaking into the Air*.
44. For a brilliant case study of how information has interacted with authoritarian governance and resistance to it in Syria, please see Wedeen, *Ambiguities of Domination Politics*.
45. Lilley and Trice, *History of Information Science*.
46. See Pierce, *Introduction to Information Theory*, chapter 2. For an another excellent overview, see Lilley and Trice, *History of Information Science*.
47. Jay, *Virtues of Mendacity*.
48. Particularly influential as a model of this sort of history is Chakrabarty, *Provincializing Europe*; also see Eley, *Crooked Line from Cultural History to the History of Society*.
49. Van Rahden, *Demokratie*.

Bibliography

Aarsleff, Hans. *From Locke to Saussure: Essays on the Study of Language and Intellectual History.* Minneapolis: University of Minnesota Press, 1985.
Accominotti, Olivier, Marc Flandreau, Riad Rezzik, and Frederic Zumer. "Black Man's Burden, White Man's Welfare: Control, Devolution and Development in the British Empire, 1880–1914." *European Review of Economic History* 14, no. 1 (2010): 47–70.
Ádám, Magda. *The Versailles System and Central Europe.* Burlington, VT: Ashgate, 2004.
Adam, Peter, and Mazal Holocaust Collection. *Art of the Third Reich.* New York: H. N. Abrams, 1992.
Adas, Michael. *Machines as the Measure of Men: Science, Technology, and Ideologies of Western Dominance.* Ithaca, NY: Cornell University Press, 1990.
Agamben, Giorgio. *Homo Sacer: Sovereign Power and Bare Life.* Stanford, CA: Stanford University Press, 2016.
Akami, T. "The Limits of Peace Propaganda: The Information Section of the League of Nations and Its Tokyo Office." In *Exorbitant Expectations: International Organizations and the Media in the Nineteenth and Twentieth Centuries,* ed. Jonas Brendebach, Martin Herzer, and Heidi Tworek, 70–90. New York: Routledge, 2019.
"Albert-Kahn: Les Collections." Le musée départemental Albert-Kahn. http://collections.albert-kahn.hauts-de-seine.fr/, accessed March 27, 2020.
Alderson, Albert William. *Why the War Cannot Be Final: Its True and Only Cause; The Only Way to Obtain Finality in Armaments and War; The Deciding Factor for Peace or War; The Eternal Enemy; Empires and Expansion, Etc.* London: P. S. King and Son, 1915.
Allen, David. "Internationalist Exhibitionism: The League of Nations at the New York World's Fair, 1939–1940." In *Exorbitant Expectations: International Organizations and the Media in the Nineteenth and Twentieth Centuries,* ed. Jonas Brendebach, Martin Herzer, and Heidi Tworek, 91–117. New York: Routledge, 2019.
Amrith, Sunil, and Glenda Sluga. "New Histories of the United Nations." *Journal of World History* 19, no. 3 (October 29, 2008): 251–74.
Anderson, Benedict R. O'G. *Imagined Communities: Reflections on the Origin and Spread of Nationalism.* New York: Verso, 1991.

Anderson, Carol. *Eyes off the Prize: The United Nations and the African American Struggle for Human Rights, 1944–1955*. Cambridge: Cambridge University Press, 2009.

Anderson, Rani-Henrik. *The Lakota Ghost Dance of 1890*. Lincoln: University of Nebraska Press, 2008.

Appadurai, Arjun. "Disjuncture and Difference in the Global Cultural Economy." *Theory, Culture and Society* 7, nos. 2–3 (June 1, 1990): 295–310.

Arbuthnot, C. C. "This Generation Can Not Escape Paying the Cost of War." *Scientific Monthly* 7, no. 5 (1918): 413–34.

Arendt, Hannah. *Between Past and Future: Eight Exercises in Political Thought*. New York: Penguin Books, 1968.

———. *Crisis of the Republic*. New York: Harcourt, Brace, 1973.

———. *On Violence*. New York: Harcourt, Brace, and World, 1974.

Ariès, Philippe. *The Hour of Our Death: The Classic History of Western Attitudes toward Death over the Last One Thousand Years*. New York: Vintage Books, 2008.

Armer, Jörg. *Die Wiener Weltbühne: Wien, 1932–1933 / Die neue Weltbühne: Prag/Paris, 1933–1939; Bibliographie einer Zeitschrift*. München: K. G. Saur, 1992.

Arrighi, Giovanni. *The Long Twentieth Century: Money, Power, and the Origins of Our Times*. London: Verso, 2010.

Asseraf, Arthur. "Making Their Own Internationalism: Algerian Media and a Few Others the League of Nations Ignored, 1919–1943." In *Exorbitant Expectations: International Organizations and the Media in the Nineteenth and Twentieth Centuries*, ed. Jonas Brendebach, Martin Herzer, and Heidi Tworek, 177–93. New York: Routledge, 2019.

Aufricht, Hans. *Guide to League of Nations Publications: A Bibliographical Survey of the Work of the League, 1920–1947*. New York: AMS, 1966.

Austin, J. L., J. O. Urmson, and Marina Sbisà. *How to Do Things with Words: The William James Lectures Delivered at Harvard University in 1955*. Oxford: Clarendon, 2011.

"Avalon Project—the Covenant of the League of Nations." Yale University, Avalon Project, Documents in Law, History and Diplomacy. http://avalon.law.yale.edu/20th_century/leagcov.asp, accessed March 31, 2017.

Aydin, Cemil. *The Politics of Anti-Westernism in Asia: Visions of World Order in Pan-Islamic and Pan-Asian Thought*. New York: Columbia University Press, 2007.

Aytürk, İlker. "Turkish Linguists against the West: The Origins of Linguistic Nationalism in Atatürk's Turkey." *Middle Eastern Studies* 40, no. 6 (2010): 1–25.

Azcárate, Pablo de. *League of Nations and National Minorities, an Experiment*. Washington, DC: Carnegie Endowment for International Peace, 1945.

Bachelard, Gaston, and M. Jolas. *The Poetics of Space*. Boston: Beacon, 1994.

Badiou, Alain, and Barbara Cassin. *Heidegger: His Life and His Philosophy*. New York: Columbia University Press, 2016.

Baer, George W. *Test Case: Italy, Ethiopia, and the League of Nations*. Hoover Institution Publication 159. Stanford, CA: Hoover Institution Press, 1976.

Bagehot, Walter. "A New Standard of Value." *Economic Journal* 2, no. 7 (1892): 472–77.

Baker, Ray Stannard. *Woodrow Wilson and World Settlement*. 3 vols. Garden City, NY: Doubleday, Page, 1922.

Balderston, Theo. *The World Economy and National Economies in the Interwar Slump*. Houndmills, Basingstoke, Hampshire: Palgrave Macmillan, 2003.

Ballantyne, Tony, and Antoinette M. Burton. *Empires and the Reach of the Global, 1870–1945.* Cambridge, MA: Harvard University Press, 2014.

Banque Nationale de Belgique. *Bulletin hebdomadaire d'information et de documentation,* no. 19 (October 21, 1926).

Baram, Amatzia. "A Case of Imported Identity: The Modernizing Secular Ruling Elites of Iraq and the Concept of Mesopotamian-Inspired Territorial Nationalism, 1922–1992." *Poetics Today* 15, no. 2 (Summer 1994): 279–319.

Baran, Paul A., and Paul M. Sweezy. *Monopoly Capital: An Essay on the American Economic and Social Order.* New York: Monthly Review Press, 1966.

Barnett, Michael N. *Rules for the World: International Organizations in Global Politics.* Ithaca, NY: Cornell University Press, 2004.

Barron, Stephanie, et al. *"Degenerate Art": The Fate of the Avant-Garde in Nazi Germany.* Los Angeles: Los Angeles County Museum of Art / H. N. Abrams, 1991.

Barros, James. *Betrayal from Within: Joseph Avenol, Secretary-General of the League of Nations, 1933–1940.* New Haven, CT: Yale University Press, 1969.

Barthes, Roland. *Camera Lucida: Reflections on Photography.* New York: Hill and Wang, 2010.

Bashford, Alison. "Nation, Empire, Globe: The Spaces of Population Debate in the Interwar Years." *Comparative Studies in Society and History* 49 (2007): 170–201.

———. "Population, Geopolitics, and International Organizations in the Mid Twentieth Century." *Journal of World History* 19, no. 3 (2008): 327–47.

Baudrillard, Jean. *Simulacra and Simulation.* Ann Arbor: University of Michigan Press, 2018.

Bauman, Zygmunt. *Liquid Modernity.* Cambridge, UK: Polity, 2000.

———. *Modernity and the Holocaust.* Cambridge, UK: Polity, 2013.

Bayart, Jean-François. *L'état en Afrique: La politique du ventre.* Paris: Fayard, 2013.

Bayart, Jean-François, Jean-Pierre Warnier, Nicolas Argenti, Fondation nationale des sciences politiques, and Centre d'études et de recherches internationales. *Matière à politique: Le pouvoir, les corps, les choses.* Paris: Karthala, 2004.

Beavan, Colin. *Fingerprints: The Origins of Crime Detection and the Murder Case That Launched Forensic Science.* New York: Hyperion, 2001.

Bell, Duncan. *Reordering the World: Essays on Liberalism and Empire.* Princeton, NJ: Princeton University Press, 2016.

Bell, Lindsay, and Mireille McLaughlin. "John E. Joseph: Language and Politics." *Language Policy* 7, no. 4 (2008): 393–95.

Benjamin, Walter. *Illuminations: Essays and Reflections.* Edited by Hannah Arendt, translated by Harry Zohn. New York: Schocken Books, 1969.

———. *Walter Benjamin: Selected Writings.* Cambridge, MA: Belknap Press of Harvard University Press, 2006.

———. Benjamin, Walter. *The Work of Art in the Age of Mechanical Reproduction.* London: Penguin, 2008.

Berman, Marshall. *All That Is Solid Melts into Air: The Experience of Modernity.* New York: Simon and Schuster, 1982.

Bernays, Edward L., and Mark Crispin Miller. *Propaganda.* New York: Ig, 2005.

Besant, Annie. *War Articles and Notes.* London: Theosophical Publishing Society, 1915.

Biblioklept. "'Counterfeit Money'—Charles Baudelaire." *Biblioklept* (blog), September 17, 2014. https://biblioklept.org/2014/09/16/counterfeit-money-charles-baudelaire/.

Bignon, Vincent, and Marc Flandreau. "The Economics of Badmouthing: Libel Law and the Underworld of the Financial Press in France before World War I." *Journal of Economic History* 71, no. 3 (2011): 616–53.

———. "The Price of Media Capture and the Debasement of the French Newspaper Industry during the Interwar." *Journal of Economic History* 74 (2014): 799–830.

———. *The Price of Media Capture and the Looting of Newspapers in Interwar France.* London: Centre for Economic Policy Research, 2012.

Biltoft, Carolyn N. "The Anatomy of Credulity and Incredulity; or, A Hermeneutics of Misinformation." *Harvard Kennedy School Misinformation Review*, no. 2 (April 30, 2020): 1–11. https://doi.org/10.37016/mr-2020-016.

———. "Decoding the Balance Sheet: Gifts, Goodwill and the Liquidation of the League of Nations." *Capitalism* 1, no. 2 (forthcoming).

———. "The League of Nations and Alternative Economic Perspectives." In *Handbook of Alternative Theories of Economic Development*, ed. Erik S. Reinert, Jayati Ghosh, and Rainer Kattel, 270–95. Cheltenham, UK: Edward Elgar, 2016.

———. "The Meek Shall Not Inherit the Earth: Nationalist Economies, Ethnic Minorities at the League of Nations." In *National Economies: Volks-Wirtschaft, Racism and Economy in Europe between the Wars (1918–1939/45)*, ed. Christoph Kreutzmüller, Michael Wildt, and Moshe Zimmermann, 138–54. Newcastle upon Tyne: Cambridge Scholars, 2015.

———. "Pivotes informacionales y giros linguisitos: Filosofías geopolíticas del lenguaje en la Liga de las Naciones." *Ayer*, forthcoming.

———. "Sundry Worlds within the World: De-centered Histories and Institutional Archives." *Journal of World History* 31, no. 4 (forthcoming).

Birchard, Robert S., and Kevin Thomas. *Cecil B. DeMille's Hollywood.* Lexington: University Press of Kentucky, 2004.

Birebent, Christian. *Militants de la paix et de la SDN: Les mouvements de soutien à la Société des Nations en France et au Royaume-Uni, 1918–1925.* Paris: Harmatta, 2007.

Black, Jeremy. *Visions of the World: A History of Maps.* London: Mitchell Beazley, 2005.

Blaut, James Morris. *The Colonizer's Model of the World: Geographical Diffusionism and Eurocentric History.* New York: Guilford, 1993.

Bloch, Marc. "Réflections d'un historien sur les fausses nouvelles de la guerre." *Revue de synthèse historique* 7 (1921): 13–35.

———. *Strange Defeat: A Statement of Evidence Written in 1940.* New York: Norton, 1999.

Bloomfield, Arthur I. *Monetary Policy under the International Gold Standard, 1880–1914.* New York, 1959.

Bordo, Michael D., and Hugh Rockoff. "The Gold Standard as a 'Good Housekeeping Seal of Approval.'" *Journal of Economic History* 56, no. 2 (June 1996): 389–428.

Boross, Elizabeth A. *Inflation and Industry in Hungary: 1918–1929.* Berlin: Haude und Spener, 1994.

Boucock, Cary. *In the Grip of Freedom: Law and Modernity in Max Weber.* Toronto: University of Toronto Press, 2008.

Bourdieu, Pierre. "La production de la croyance [contribution à une économie des biens symboliques]." *Actes de la recherche en sciences sociales* 13, no. 1 (1977): 3–43.

Bourdieu, Pierre, and John B. Thompson. *Language and Symbolic Power.* Cambridge, MA: Harvard University Press, 1991.

Boyer, Dominic. *Spirit and System: Media, Intellectuals, and the Dialectic in Modern German Culture.* Chicago: University of Chicago Press, 2005.

Brendebach, Jonas, Martin Herzer, and Heidi Tworek, eds. *Exorbitant Expectations: International Organizations and the Media in the Nineteenth and Twentieth Centuries.* New York: Routledge, 2019.

Briggs, Asa, and Peter Burke. *A Social History of the Media: From Gutenberg to the Internet.* Cambridge, UK: Polity, 2002.

British Information Services. *Britain's Mandate for Palestine.* New York: British Information Services, 1944.

Brown, Norman O. *Life against Death: The Psychoanalytical Meaning of History.* Middletown, CT: Wesleyan University Press, 1988.

Brustein, William. *Roots of Hate: Anti-Semitism in Europe before the Holocaust.* Cambridge: Cambridge University Press, 2003.

Bryan, Steven. *The Gold Standard at the Turn of the Twentieth Century: Rising Powers, Global Money, and the Age of Empire.* New York: Columbia University Press, 2010.

Buck-Morss, Susan. *Dreamworld and Catastrophe: The Passing of Mass Utopia in East and West.* Cambridge: MIT Press, 2002.

Burbank, Jane, and Frederick Cooper. *Empires in World History: Power and the Politics of Difference.* Princeton, NJ: Princeton University Press, 2010.

Burgess, Greg. *League of Nations and the Refugees from Nazi Germany: James G. McDonald and Hitler's Victims.* London: Bloomsbury, 2016.

Burrin, Philippe. *Living with Defeat: France under the German Occupation, 1940–1944.* London: Arnold, 1996.

Burrin, Philippe, and Janet Lloyd. *Nazi Anti-Semitism: From Prejudice to the Holocaust.* New York: New Press, 2005.

Butler, Judith. *The Psychic Life of Power: Theories in Subjection.* Stanford, CA: Stanford University Press, 1997.

Cain, Frank. "Ellis, Charles Howard (Dick) (1895–1975)." In *Australian Dictionary of Biography.* Canberra: National Centre of Biography, Australian National University. http://adb.anu.edu.au/biography/ellis-charles-howard-dick-10113/text17703, accessed May 5, 2017.

Calabrese, Andrew, and Colin Sparks. *Toward a Political Economy of Culture: Capitalism and Communication in the Twenty-First Century.* Lanham, MD: Rowman and Littlefield, 2004.

Callahan, Michael D. *Mandates and Empire: The League of Nations and Africa, 1914–1931.* Brighton: Sussex Academic, 2008.

———. *A Sacred Trust: The League of Nations and Africa, 1929–1946.* Brighton: Sussex Academic, 2004.

Carlson, Benny. *The State as a Monster: Gustav Cassel and Eli Heckscher on the Role and Growth of the State.* Lanham, MD: University Press of America, 1994.

Carr, Edward Hallett. *The Twenty Years' Crisis, 1919–1939: An Introduction to the Study of International Relations.* 1939. London: Macmillan, 1946.

Carroll, Berenice A. "Design for Total War: The Contest for 'Wehrwirtschaft' under the Third Reich." The Hague: Mouton, 1968.

Carter, John, and Percy H. Muir, eds. *Printing and the Mind of Man: A Descriptive Catalogue Illustrating the Impact of Print on the Evolution of Western Civilization during Five Centuries.* London: Cassell, 1967.

Caruth, Cathy. *Unclaimed Experience: Trauma, Narrative, and History.* Baltimore: Johns Hopkins University Press, 2016.

Case, Holly. *The Age of Questions, or, A First Attempt at an Aggregate History of the Eastern, Social, Woman, American, Jewish, Polish, Bullion, Tuberculosis, and Many Other Questions over the Nineteenth Century, and Beyond.* Princeton, NJ: Princeton University Press, 2018.

Caspar, Wilhelm. *Gegen die Lügenpresse.* N.p.: n.p., 1914.

Cassel, Gustav. *The Downfall of the Gold Standard.* Oxford: Clarendon, 1936.

———. *The World's Monetary Problems: Two Memoranda.* New York: E. P. Dutton, 1921.

Castaldo, Sandro. *Trust in Market Relationships.* London: Edward Elgar, 2008.

Castells, Manuel. *The Information Age: Economy, Society, and Culture.* Vol. 1. Chichester, West Sussex: Wiley-Blackwell, 2010.

———. *The Rise of the Network Society.* Malden, MA: Blackwell, 1996.

Chakrabarty, Dipesh. *Provincializing Europe: Postcolonial Thought and Historical Difference.* Princeton, NJ: Princeton University Press, 2000.

Chatterjee, Partha. *The Nation and Its Fragments: Colonial and Postcolonial Histories.* Princeton, NJ: Princeton University Press, 1993.

Chaudhury, Pranab Chandra Roy. *Edmond Privat, a Forgotten Friend of India.* Ahmedabad: Navajivan, 1976.

Clark, Bruce. *Twice a Stranger: The Mass Expulsions That Forged Modern Greece and Turkey.* Cambridge, MA: Harvard University Press, 2009.

Clavin, Patricia. "The Austrian Hunger Crisis and the Genesis of International Organization after the First World War." *International Affairs* 90, no. 2 (2014): 265–78.

———. *The Failure of Economic Diplomacy: Britain, Germany, France and the United States, 1931–36.* Houndmills, Basingstoke, Hampshire: Macmillan; New York: St. Martin's, 1996.

———. "'Money Talks': Competition and Cooperation with the League of Nations, 1929–40." In *Money Doctors: The Experience of International Financial Advising 1850–2000*, ed. Marc Flandreau, 219–48. London: Routledge, 2003.

———. *Securing the World Economy: The Reinvention of the League of Nations, 1920–1946.* Oxford: Oxford University Press, 2013.

Clavin, Patricia, and Jens-Wilhelm Wessels. "Another Golden Idol? The League of Nations' Gold Delegation and the Great Depression, 1929–1932." *International History Review* 26, no. 4 (2004): 765–95.

———. "Transnationalism and the League of Nations: Understanding the Work of Its Economic and Financial Organisation." *Contemporary European History* 14, no. 4 (2005): 465–92.

Cmiel, Kenneth. "Human Rights, Freedom of Information, and the Origins of Third-World Solidarity." In *Truth Claims: Representation and Human Rights*, ed. Mark Bradley and Patrice Petro, 106–30. New Brunswick, NJ: Rutgers University Press, 2002.

Cmiel, Kenneth, and John Durham Peters. *Promiscuous Knowledge: Information, Image, and Other Truth Games in History.* Chicago: University of Chicago Press, 2020.

Coase, R. H. *The Firm, the Market, and the Law.* Chicago: University of Chicago Press, 1990.

Cockett, Richard. *Twilight of Truth: Chamberlain, Appeasement and the Manipulation of the Press.* London: Weidenfeld and Nicolson, 1989.

Cohen, Paul A. *History in Three Keys: The Boxers as Event, Experience, and Myth.* New York: Columbia University Press, 1997.

Cohn, Bernard S. *Colonialism and Its Forms of Knowledge: The British in India.* Princeton, NJ: Princeton University Press, 1996.

Committee on Intellectual Co-operation. *Modern Means of Spreading Information Utilised in the Cause of Peace: Report, Etc.* Geneva: League of Nations, 1938.

Comor, Edward A. *The Global Political Economy of Communication: Hegemony, Telecommunication, and the Information Economy.* New York: St. Martin's, 1994.

Conant, Charles A. "The Development of Credit." *Journal of Political Economy* 7, no. 2 (1899): 161–81.

Conference for the Reduction and Limitation of Armaments, and League of Nations. *Moral Disarmament.* Series of League of Nations Publications, 1932.IX.52. Geneva: League of Nations, 1932.

Connelly, Matthew. "Seeing beyond the State: The Population Control Movement and the Problem of Sovereignty." *Past and Present* 193, no. 1 (November 2006): 197–233.

Counterfeiting Currency. Geneva: League of Nations Imp. d'Ambilly, 1926.

Cowan, Jane K. "Who's Afraid of Violent Language? Honour, Sovereignty and Claims-Making in the League of Nations." *Anthropological Theory* 3, no. 3 (2003), 271–91.

Coward, Martin. "The Globalisation of Enclosure: Interrogating the Geopolitics of Empire." *Third World Quarterly* 26, no. 6 (2005): 855–71.

Coyajee, J. C. *India and the League of Nations.* Madras: Thompson, 1932.

Creel, George. *How We Advertised America: The First Telling of the Amazing Story of the Committee on Public Information That Carried the Gospel of Americanism to Every Corner of the Globe.* New York: Harper and Brothers, 1920.

Cristiano, Carlo. *The Political and Economic Thought of the Young Keynes: Liberalism, Markets and Empire.* New York: Routledge, 2014.

Cunliffe Committee and Macmillan Committee. *British Parliamentary Reports on International Finance: The Cunliffe Committee and the Macmillan Committee Reports; Repr. of the Ed. London 1918, 1931.* New York: Arno, 1978.

Darnton, Robert. *Poetry and the Police Communication Networks in Eighteenth-Century Paris.* Cambridge, MA: Belknap Press of Harvard University Press, 2010.

Dauzat, Albert. *Le français et l'anglais langues internationals.* Paris: Larousse, 1915.

Deák, István. *Weimar Germany's Left-Wing Intellectuals: A Political History of the Weltbühne and Its Circle.* Berkeley: University of California Press, 1968.

Dean, Carolyn J. *Aversion and Erasure.* Ithaca, NY: Cornell University Press, 2017.

———. *The Moral Witness: Trials and Testimony after Genocide.* Ithaca, NY: Cornell University Press, 2019.

Decorzant, Yann. *La Société des Nations et la naissance d'une conception de la régulation économique internationale.* Brussels: Peter Lang, 2011.

———. "La Société des Nations et l'apparition d'un nouveau réseau d'expertise économique et financière (1914–1923)." *Critique internationale*, no. 52 (2011): 35–50.

Deleuze, Gilles, and Felix Guattari. *Anti-Oedipus: Capitalism and Schizophrenia.* Minneapolis: University of Minnesota Press, 1983.

Dell, Robert. *Germany Unmasked.* London: Hopkinson, 1934.

Derrida, Jacques. *Of Grammatology.* Baltimore: Johns Hopkins University Press, 2016.

Desan, Christine. *A Cultural History of Money in the Age of Enlightenment.* London: Bloomsbury Academic, 2019.

———. *Making Money: Coin, Currency, and the Coming of Capitalism.* Oxford: Oxford University Press, 2014.

Dickinson, B. B. "The Use of Lantern Slides in Teaching." *Geographical Teacher* 4, no. 4 (1908): 161–63.

Dickinson, Frederick R. "Toward a Global Perspective of the Great War: Japan and the Foundations of a Twentieth-Century World." *American Historical Review* 119, no. 4 (October 1, 2014): 1154–83.

Dimier, Veronique. "On Good Colonial Government: Lessons from the League of Nations." *Global Society: Journal of Interdisciplinary International Relations* 18, no. 3 (July 2004): 279–99.

Dirlik, Arif. "Architectures of Global Modernity, Colonialism, and Places." *Modern Chinese Literature and Culture* 17, no. 1 (2005): 33–61.

Disarmament Information Committee. *Disarmament.* Geneva: League of Nations, 1936.

Dodd, Nigel. *Concepts of Money: Interdisciplinary Perspectives from Economics, Sociology and Political Science.* Critical Studies in Economic Institutions 8. Cheltenham, UK: Edward Elgar, 2005.

———. *The Sociology of Money: Economics, Reason and Contemporary Society.* New York: Continuum, 1994.

Dodd, W. J. *National Socialism and German Discourse: Unquiet Voices.* Cham: Palgrave Macmillan, 2018.

Dominion, Leon. *The Frontiers of Language and Nationality in Europe.* New York: American Geographical Society of New York / H. Holt, 1917.

Doran, Robert. "The Revolt of the Maccabees." *National Interest*, no. 85 (2006): 99–103.

Doray, Bernard. *From Taylorism to Fordism: A Rational Madness.* London: Free Association, 1988.

Douglas, C. H. *The Premises of Social Credit.* New York: Economic Forum, 1933.

Druick, Zoe. "The International Educational Cinematographic Institute, Reactionary Modernism, and the Formation of Film Studies." *Revue Canadienne d'études cinématographiques / Canadian Journal of Film Studies* 16, no. 1 (2007): 80–97.

Durkheim, Émile, and Robert Neuburger. *Le suicide: Étude de sociologie.* Paris: Editions Payot et Rivages, 2009.

Dyer, Alan W. "Making Semiotic Sense of Money as a Medium of Exchange." *Journal of Economic Issues* 23, no. 2 (1989): 503–10.

Dykmann, Klauss. "How International Was the Secretariat of the League of Nations?" *International History Review* 37, no. 4 (August 8, 2015): 721–44.

Eco, Umberto. *The Search for the Perfect Language.* London: Fontana, 1997.

———. "Ur-fascism." *New York Review of Books*, June 22, 1995. https://www.nybooks.com/articles/1995/06/22/ur-fascism/.

Edsall, Edward W. *The Coming Scrap of Paper.* London: G. Allen and Unwin, 1915.

Egerton, George W. "Collective Security as Political Myth: Liberal Internationalism and the League of Nations in Politics and History." *International History Review* 5, no. 4 (1983): 496–524.

Eichengreen, Barry J. *Golden Fetters: The Gold Standard and the Great Depression, 1919–1939.* New York: Oxford University Press, 1992.

Eichengreen, Barry J., and Marc Flandreau. *The Gold Standard in Theory and History.* London: Routledge, 1997.

———. "The Rise and Fall of the Dollar (or When Did the Dollar Replace Sterling as the Leading Reserve Currency?)." *European Review of Economic History* 13 (2009): 377–411.

Eiland, Howard, and Michael W. Jennings. *Walter Benjamin: A Critical Life.* Cambridge, MA: Belknap Press of Harvard University Press, 2016.

Eksteins, Modris. *Rites of Spring: The Great War and the Birth of the Modern Age.* Toronto: Vintage Canada, 2012.

Eley, Geoff. *A Crooked Line from Cultural History to the History of Society.* Ann Arbor: University of Michigan Press, 2005.

Ellis, Charles Howard. *The Origin, Structure and Working of the League of Nations.* Boston: Houghton Mifflin, 1928.

Endres, A. M. *International Organizations and the Analysis of Economic Policy, 1919–1950.* Cambridge: Cambridge University Press, 2002.

Endres, Anthony M., and Grant A. Fleming. *International Organizations and the Analysis of Economic Policy, 1919–1950.* Cambridge: Cambridge University Press, 2002.

The Emperor of Austria versus Louis Kossuth: A Few Words of Common Sense Based on Documentary Evidence and Historical Facts. London: Trübner, 1861.

"Epidemics Claim 213 in Chungking in June." *China Press* (Shanghai), July 4, 1936.

Eschbach, Achim, and Jürgen Trabant. *History of Semiotics.* Philadelphia: J. Benjamins, 1983.

Ethiopia and League of Nations. *Dispute between Ethiopia and Italy: Request by the Ethiopian Government.* Geneva: League of Nations, 1935.

Farrokh, Mohammad. *La pensée et l'action d'Edmond Privat, 1889–1962: Contribution a l'histoire des ideés politiques en Suisee.* Berne: Peter Lang, 1991.

Febvre, Lucien, and Peter Burke. *A New Kind of History: From the Writings of Febvre.* London: Routledge, 1973.

Fehrenbach, Heide, and Davide Rodogno. *Humanitarian Photography: A History.* Cambridge: Cambridge University Press, 2016.

Feinberg, Nathan. *The Jewish League of Nations Societies: A Chapter in the History of the Struggle of the Jews for Their Rights.* Jerusalem: Magness, 1967.

Fergusson, Adam. *When Money Dies: The Nightmare of the Weimar Collapse.* London: Kimber, 1975.

Fieldhouse, D. K. *Western Imperialism in the Middle East 1914–1958.* Oxford: Oxford University Press, 2006.

Finchelstein, Federico. *From Fascism to Populism in History.* Berkeley: University of California Press, 2017.

Fink, Carole. "Defender of Minorities: Germany in the League of Nations, 1926–1933." *Central European History* 5, no. 4 (December 1972): 330–57.

———. *Defending the Rights of Others: The Great Powers, the Jews, and International Minority Protection, 1878–1938.* Cambridge: Cambridge University Press, 2004.

———. "Minority Rights as an International Question." *Contemporary European History* 9, no. 3 (November 2000): 385–400.

Fior, Michel. *Institution globale et marchés financiers: La Société des Nations face à la reconstruction de l'Europe, 1918–1931.* Brussels: Peter Lang, 2008.

Firth, J. R. *The Tongues of Men and Speech.* Westport, CT: Greenwood, 1986.

Fisher, Irving. *Impending Problems of Eugenics.* New York: Science Press, 1921.

———. *The Money Illusion.* New York: Adelphi, 1928.

———. *The Purchasing Power of Money: Its Determination and Relation to Credit Interest and Crises.* New York: Macmillan, 1911.

———. "Stabilizing the Dollar." *American Economic Review* 9, no. 1 (1919): 154–60.

Flandreau, Marc. *Anthropologists in the Stock Exchange: A Financial History of Victorian Science.* Chicago: University of Chicago Press, 2016.

———. "Central Bank Cooperation in Historical Perspective: A Skeptical View." *Economic History Review*, no. 4 (1997): 735–63.

———. "Crises and Punishment." In *Money Doctors: The Experience of International Financial Advising 1850–2000*, ed. Flandreau, 13–48. London: Routledge, 2005.

———. "Does Integration Globalize? Financial Crises and Financial Geography 1831–1914." In *Economic Globalization, International Organizations and Crisis Management*, ed. Richard Tilly and Paul J. J. Welfens, 107–26. Berlin: Springer, 2000.

———. "Pillars of Globalization: A History of Monetary Policy Targets 1797–1997." In *The Role of Money: Money and Monetary Policy in the 21st Century*, ed. A. Beyer and L. Reichlin, 208–43. Frankfurt: ECB, 2008.

Flandreau, Marc, and Centre for Economic Policy Research (Great Britain). *Pillars of Globalization: A History of Monetary Policy Targets, 1797–1997*. London: Centre for Economic Policy Research, 2007.

Flandreau, Marc, and Juan H. Flores. "Bonds and Brands: Foundations of Sovereign Debt Markets, 1820–1830." *Journal of Economic History* 69, no. 3 (September 2009): 646–84.

Flandreau, Marc, and Owen Leeming. *The Glitter of Gold: France, Bimetallism, and the Emergence of the International Gold Standard, 1848–1873*. Oxford: Oxford University Press, 2004.

Flandreau, Marc, and Frédéric Zumer. *The Making of Global Finance 1880–1913*. Paris: OECD, 2004.

Flores, Juan H., and Yann Decorzant. "Going Multilateral? Financial Markets' Access and the League of Nations Loans, 1923–8." *Economic History Review* 69, no. 2 (2015): 653–78.

"Foreign Lands." *Jewish Exponent* (Philadelphia), July 10, 1936. https://www.jewishexponent.com/.

Forster, Peter G. *The Esperanto Movement*. The Hague: Mouton, 1982.

Foucault, Michel. *The Archeology of Knowledge*. London: Routledge, 1989.

———. *The Order of Things: An Archaeology of the Human Sciences*. London: Routledge, 2010.

Fowler, Bridget. *The Obituary as Collective Memory*. New York: Routledge, 2009.

Fox, David, and Wolfgang Ernst. *Money in the Western Legal Tradition: Middle Ages to Bretton Woods*. Oxford: Oxford University Press, 2016.

Freidman, Walter A. *The Tactics of Traveling Salesmen: Using Geniality to Master the Marketplace*. Boston: Harvard Business School Press, 1998.

Frend, William H. C. *Martyrdom and Persecution in the Early Church: A Study of a Conflict from the Maccabees to Donatus*. Oxford: Blackwell, 1965.

Freud, Sigmund. *The Future of an Illusion*. London: Hogarth, 1928.

Freud, Sigmund, James Strachey, and Anna Freud. *The Standard Edition of the Complete Psychological Works of Sigmund Freud*. Vol. 8. *1905*. London: Vintage/Hogarth, 2001.

———. *The Standard Edition of the Complete Psychological Works of Sigmund Freud*. Vol. 9. London: Vintage, 2001.

Fridenson, Patrick. "Les Organisations Un Nouvel Object." *Annales ESC*, December 1989, 146–77.

Gaillard, Norbert. *Century of Sovereign Ratings*. New York: Springer, 2014.

Garvía, Roberto. *Esperanto and Its Rivals: The Struggle for an International Language*. Philadelphia: University of Pennsylvania Press, 2015.

Gavish, Dov. *A Survey of Palestine under the British Mandate, 1920–1948*. London: Routledge-Curzon, 2005.

Gay, Peter. *Freud: A Life for Our Time*. London: MAX, 2006.

———. *Modernism*. London: William Heinemann, 2007.
Geertz, Clifford. "Distinguished Lecture: Anti Anti-relativism." *American Anthropologist* 86, no. 2 (1984): 263–78.
Geroulanos, Stefanos, and Todd Meyers. *The Human Body in the Age of Catastrophe: Brittleness, Integration, Science, and the Great War*. Chicago: University of Chicago Press, 2018.
Geyer, Martin H., and Johannes Paulmann. *The Mechanics of Internationalism: Culture, Society, and Politics from the 1840s to the First World War*. London: German Historical Institute and Oxford University Press, 2001.
Geyer, Michael, and Charles Bright. "Global Violence and Nationalizing Wars in Eurasia and America: The Geopolitics of War in the Mid-Nineteenth Century." *Comparative Studies in Society and History: An International Quarterly* 38 (1996): 619–57.
Gidney, Thomas. "'An Anomaly among Anomalies': Colonial Membership of the League of Nations." PhD diss., Graduate Institute of International and Development Studies, Geneva, in progress.
Gitelman, Lisa. *Always Already New: Media, History, and the Data of Culture*. Cambridge, MA: MIT Press, 2008.
Goeschel, Christian. *Suicide in Nazi Germany*. Oxford: Oxford University Press, 2015.
Gökalp, Ziya. *Turkish Nationalism and Western Civilization: Selected Essays*. London: Allen and Unwin, 1959.
Goldstein, Erik. *The First World War Peace Settlements, 1919–1925*. London: Routledge, 2013.
Gooch, G. P. "Germany and the French Revolution." *Transactions of the Royal Historical Society* 10 (1916): 51–76.
Gordin, Michael D. *Scientific Babel: How Science Was Done before and after Global English*. Chicago: University of Chicago Press, 2015.
Gorman, Daniel. *The Emergence of International Society in the 1920s*. Cambridge: Cambridge University Press, 2012.
Gottlieb, Nanette. *Language and the Modern State: The Reform of Written Japanese*. Nissan Institute / Routledge Japanese Studies Series. London: Routledge, 1991.
Goux, Jean-Joseph. *Symbolic Economies: After Marx and Freud*. Ithaca, NY: Cornell University Press, 1990.
Gramsci, Antonio. *Prison Notebooks*. Edited and translated by Joseph A. Buttigieg and Antonio Callari. New York: Columbia University Press, 1992.
———. "A Single Language and Esperanto." In *Selections from the Cultural Writings*, 26–31. Cambridge, MA: Harvard University Press, 1985.
Gran, Peter. *Beyond Eurocentrism: A New View of Modern World History*. Syracuse, NY: Syracuse University Press, 1996.
Gray, Richard T. "Buying into Signs: Money and Semiosis in Eighteenth-Century German Language Theory." *German Quarterly* 69 (1996): 1–14.
Grazia, Victoria F. de. *The Culture of Consent*. Cambridge: Cambridge University Press, 2002.
———. "Mass Culture and Sovereignty: The American Challenge to European Cinemas, 1920–1960." *Journal of Modern History* 61, no. 1 (March 1989): 53–87.
Grazia, Victoria de, and Leonardo Paggi. "Story of an Ordinary Massacre: Civitella Della Chiana, 29 June, 1944." *Cardozo Studies in Law and Literature* 3, no. 2 (Autumn 1991): 153–69.
Great Britain and League of Nations. *Report by His Majesty's Government in the United Kingdom of Great Britain and Northern Ireland to the Council of the League of Nations on the*

Administration of Palestine and Trans-Jordan Reformatted from the Original and Including Government of Palestine Report: Report on Palestine Administration. London: HMSO, 1922.

"Great Forgery Plot in Hungarian Capital: Forgers Counterfeit Italian Currency (Reuter's Message), London, January 11," *Barrier Miner*, January 13, 1926.

Greenblatt, Stephen. *Marvelous Possessions: The Wonder of the New World, with a New Preface.* Chicago: University of Chicago Press, 2017.

Grigorescu, Alexandru. "Mapping the UN–League of Nations Analogy: Are There Still Lessons to Be Learned from the League?" *Global Governance* 11, no. 1 (January 1, 2005): 25–42.

Grunberger, Richard. *The 12-Year Reich: A Social History of Nazi Germany, 1933–1945.* New York: Da Capo, 1995.

Guérard, Albert Léon. *A Short History of the International Language Movement.* London: T. F. Unwin, 1922.

Gullberg, Tom. *State, Territory, and Identity: The Principle of National Self-Determination, the Question of Territorial Sovereignty in Carinthia and Other Post-Habsburg Territories after the First World War.* Turku, Finland: Åbo Akademi University Press, 2000.

Habermas, Jürgen. *The Structural Transformation of the Public Sphere: An Inquiry into a Category of Bourgeois Society.* Cambridge, UK: Polity, 2014.

Hagen, William W. "Before the 'Final Solution': Toward a Comparative Analysis of Political Anti-Semitism in Interwar Germany and Poland." *Journal of Modern History* 68, no. 2 (1996): 351–81.

Hahn, Arnold. *Vor Den Augen Der Welt! Warum Starb Stefan Lux? Sein Leben, Seine Tat, Seine Briefe.* Prague: Liga gegen d. Antisemitismus, 1936.

Hale, Dana S. *Races on Display: French Representations of Colonized Peoples, 1886–1940.* Bloomington: Indiana University Press, 2008.

Hardt, Michael, and Antonio Negri. "Biopolitical Production." In *Biopolitics: A Reader*, ed. Timothy Campbell and Adam Sitze, 215–36. Durham, NC: Duke University Press, 2013.

———. *Empire.* Cambridge, MA: Harvard University Press, 2000.

Harley, John Brian, Paul Laxton, and J. H. Andrews. *The New Nature of Maps: Essays in the History of Cartography.* Baltimore: Johns Hopkins University Press, 2002.

Havel, Václav. *Living in Truth: 22 Essays Published on the Occasion of the Award of the Erasmus Prize to Vaclav Havel.* London: Faber and Faber, 1990.

Headrick, Daniel R. *The Invisible Weapon: Telecommunications and International Politics, 1851–1945.* New York: Oxford University Press, 1991.

———. *When Information Came of Age: Technologies of Knowledge in the Age of Reason and Revolution, 1700–1850.* Oxford: Oxford University Press, 2000.

Heath, Roy E., and Alfred Erich Senn. "Edmond Privat and the Commission of the East in 1918." *Journal of Baltic Studies* 6, no. 1 (1975): 9–16.

Hecht, Susanna B. *The Scramble for the Amazon and the "Lost Paradise" of Euclides Da Cunha.* Chicago: University of Chicago Press, 2013.

Heidegger, Martin. *Parmenides.* Bloomington: Indiana University Press, 1998.

———. *The Question concerning Technology, and Other Essays.* New York: Harper Perennial, 2013.

Helleiner, Eric. *The Making of National Money: Territorial Currencies in Historical Perspective.* Ithaca, NY: Cornell University Press, 2003.

Heller, Steven. *Iron Fists: Branding the 20th Century Totalitarian State.* London: Phaidon, 2011.

Henig, Ruth B. *The League of Nations.* New York: Barnes and Noble, 1973.

Herman, Edward S., and Noam Chomsky. *Manufacturing Consent: The Political Economy of the Mass Media*. London: Bodley Head, 2008.

Heyd, Uriel. *Language Reform in Modern Turkey*. Oriental Notes and Studies 5. Jerusalem: Israel Oriental Society, 1954.

Higson, Andrew, and Richard Maltby. *"Film Europe" and "Film America": Cinema, Commerce and Cultural Exchange, 1920–1939*. Exeter: University of Exeter Press, 1999.

Hilderbrand, Robert C. *Dumbarton Oaks: The Origins of the United Nations and the Search for Postwar Security*. Chapel Hill: University of North Carolina Press, 2001.

Hill, Winifred Storrs. *Tarnished Gold: Prejudice during the California Gold Rush*. San Francisco: International Scholars, 1996.

Himmelfarb, Martha. "Judaism and Hellenism in 2 Maccabees." *Poetics Today* 19, no. 1 (1998): 19–40.

Hitler, Adolf. *Mein Kampf*. Translated by R. Manheim. Cambridge, MA: Riverside, 1943.

———. *My New Order*. New York: Reynal and Hitchcock, 1941.

Hobsbawm, E. J. *Nations and Nationalism since 1780: Program, Myth, Reality*. Cambridge: Cambridge University Press, 1992.

Hobsbawm, E. J., and T. O. Ranger. *The Invention of Tradition*. Cambridge: Cambridge University Press, 1983.

———. *Nationalism*. Oxford Readers. Oxford: Oxford University Press, 1994.

Hochschild, Adam. *King Leopold's Ghost: A Story of Greed, Terror and Heroism in Colonial Africa*. London: Picador, 2019.

Hoffenberg, Peter H. *An Empire on Display: English, Indian, and Australian Exhibitions from the Crystal Palace to the Great War*. Berkeley: University of California Press, 2001.

Holub, Robert C. *Crossing Borders: Reception Theory, Poststructuralism, Deconstruction*. Madison: University of Wisconsin Press, 1992.

Horkheimer, Max, and Theodor W. Adorno. *Dialectic of Enlightenment: Philosophical Fragments*. Edited by Gunzelin Schmid Noerr. Translated by Edmund Jephcott. Stanford, CA: Stanford University Press, 2007.

Huerta, Monica. "'The Evidence of Things Unseen': Law, Photography, and Expression." PhD diss., University of California, Berkeley, 2014.

"Hugo Ball's Dada Manifesto, July 1916." *Wired*. https://www.wired.com/beyond-the-beyond/2016/07/hugo-balls-dada-manifesto-july-2016/, accessed March 30, 2020.

Hutton, Christopher. *Linguistics and the Third Reich: Mother-Tongue Fascism, Race and the Science of Language*. London: Routledge, 2014.

I sız, Aslı. *Humanism in Ruins: Entangled Legacies of the Greek-Turkish Population Exchange*. Stanford, CA: Stanford University Press, 2018.

Innis, Harold Adams. *Empire and Communications*. London: Rowman and Littlefield, 2007.

Innis, Harold Adams, and Alexander John Watson. *The Bias of Communication*. Toronto: University of Toronto Press, 2012.

Inter-governmental Conference for the Conclusion of an International Convention concerning the Use of Broadcasting in the Cause of Peace and League of Nations. *International Convention concerning the Use of Broadcasting in the Cause of Peace, Geneva, September 23rd, 1936*. Valletta: Dept. of Information, 1967.

International Communication: A Symposium on the Language Problem. London: K. Paul, Trench, Trubner, 1931.

International Conference for the Adoption of a Convention for the Suppression of Counterfeiting

Currency et al., eds. *Proceedings of the International Conference for the Adoption of a Convention for the Suppression of Counterfeiting Currency, Geneva, April 9th to 20th, 1929*. Geneva, 1930.

International Conference on Economic Statistics and League of Nations. *Proceedings of the International Conference Relating to Economic Statistics, Geneva, November 26th to December 14th, 1928*. Geneva: League of Nations, 1929.

International Educational Cinematographic Institute and League of Nations. *Draft Protocol for Facilitating the International Circulation of Films of an Educational Character*. Geneva: League of Nations, 1932.

International Institute of Intellectual Co-operation and League of Nations. *L'adoption universelle des caractères latins*. Paris: Société des nations, Institut international de coopération intellectuelle, 1934.

Iriye, Akira. *Cultural Internationalism and World Order*. Baltimore: Johns Hopkins University Press, 1997.

———. *Global Community: The Role of International Organizations in the Making of the Contemporary World*. Berkeley: University of California Press, 2002.

Irwin, Douglas A., and National Bureau of Economic Research. *Did France Cause the Great Depression?* Cambridge, MA: National Bureau of Economic Research, 2010. http://papers.nber.org/papers/w16350, accessed January 4, 2016.

Italy and League of Nations. *Dispute between Ethiopia and Italy: Communication from the Italian Government*. Geneva: League of Nations, 1936.

———. *Dispute between Ethiopia and Italy: Photographs (Annex to Vol. II—Documents)*. Geneva: League of Nations, 1935.

Jackson, Simon, and Alanna O'Malley. *The Institution of International Order: From the League of Nations to the United Nations*. New York: Routledge, 2018.

James, Harold. *The Reichsbank and Public Finance in Germany, 1924–1933: A Study of the Politics of Economics during the Great Depression*. Frankfurt am Main: F. Knapp, 1985.

Jameson, Fredric. *The Prison-House of Language: A Critical Account of Structuralism and Russian Formalism*. Princeton, NJ: Princeton University Press, 2015.

Janten, Pierre. *Esperanto: Language, Literature, and Community*. Edited by Humphrey Tonkin. Translated by Humphrey Tonkin, Jane Edwards, and Karen Weiner-Johnson. Albany: State University of New York Press, 1973.

Jarzombek, Mark. "Joseph August Lux: Werkbund Promoter, Historian of a Lost Modernity." *Journal of the Society of Architectural Historians* 63, no. 2 (2004): 202–19.

Jay, Martin. "'The Aesthetic Ideology' as Ideology; or, What Does It Mean to Aestheticize Politics?" *Cultural Critique*, no. 21 (1992): 41–61.

———. "Can Photographs Lie? Reflections on a Perennial Anxiety." *Critical Studies* 2 (July 2016): 6–19.

———. "Magical Nominalism: Photography and the Re enchantment of the World." *Culture, Theory and Critique* 50, nos. 2–3 (July 1, 2009): 165–83.

———. "Positive and Negative Totalities: Implicit Tensions in Critical Theory's Vision of Interdisciplinary Research." *Thesis Eleven* 3, no. 1 (May 1, 1981): 72–87.

———. *The Virtues of Mendacity: On Lying in Politics*. Charlottesville: University of Virginia Press, 2012.

Jespersen, Otto. *How to Teach a Foreign Language*. London: Allen and Unwin, 1928.

"Jewish Writer Dies in Protest against Nazis: Reporter Suicide in League Assembly; War Danger Scored by Woman; Jewish Writer a Suicide." *Washington Post*, July 4, 1936.

Johnson, Marilyn. *The Dead Beat: Lost Souls, Lucky Stiffs, and the Perverse Pleasures of Obituaries.* New York: HarperCollins, 2007.
Jones, A. Philip, and Anglo-Palestinian Archives Committee. *Britain and Palestine, 1914–1948: Archival Sources for the History of the British Mandate.* Oxford: Oxford University Press for the British Academy, 1979.
Jonung, Lars. "Cassel, Davidson and Heckscher on Swedish Monetary Policy: A Confidential Report to the Riksbank in 1931." *Economy and History* 22, no. 2 (July 1, 1979): 85–101.
———. "Knut Wicksell's Norm of Price Stabilization and Swedish Monetary Policy in the 1930s." *Journal of Monetary Economics* 5, no. 4 (1979): 459–96.
Joseph, John Earl. *Ferdinand de Saussure: Critical Assessments of Leading Linguists.* Critical Assessments of Leading Linguists. London: Routledge, 2013.
———. *Saussure.* Oxford: Oxford University Press, 2012.
Joseph, John Earl, Talbot J. Taylor, and Nigel Love. *Landmarks in Linguistic Thought II: The Western Tradition in the Twentieth Century.* London: Routledge, 2001.
Joyce, James Avery. *Broken Star: The Story of the League of Nations (1919–1939).* Swansea: C. Davies, 1978.
Jung, Carl Gustav. *The Portable Jung.* New York: Penguin Books, 1986.
Kalka, Joachim. *Gaslight: An Album of the Nineteenth Century.* London: Penguin Books, 2017.
Kennedy, Paul M. *The Parliament of Man: The Past, Present, and Future of the United Nations.* Toronto: Harper Perennial, 2007.
Kern, Stephen. *The Culture of Time and Space, 1880–1918.* Cambridge, MA: Harvard University Press, 2003.
Keynes, John Maynard. *The Economic Consequences of the Peace: Premium Edition.* Hamburg, Germany: Management Laboratory Press, 2009.
The King of Kings. Modern Sound Pictures, Voyager Company, 1927. Copyright Collection (Library of Congress), and LC Purchase Collection (Library of Congress).
Kittler, Friedrich A. *Gramophone, Film, Typewriter.* Stanford, CA: Stanford University Press, 2006.
Klauser, Francisco Reto. *Surveillance and Space.* Newcastle: Sage, 2017.
Klay, Andor. "Hungarian Counterfeit Francs: A Case of Post–World War I Political Sabotage." *Slavic Review* 33, no. 1 (1974): 107–13.
Kleinberg, Ethan. *Haunting History: For a Deconstructive Approach to the Past.* Stanford, CA: Stanford University Press, 2017.
———. "Just the Facts: The Fantasy of a Historical Science." *History of the Present* 6, no. 1 (2016): 87–103.
Klemperer, Victor, and Martin Brady. *Language of the Third Reich: LTI ; Lingua Tertii Imperii.* New York: Bloomsbury Academic, 2013.
Knapp, Georg Friedrich. *State Theory of Money.* London: Macmillan, 1924.
Knock, Thomas J. *To End All Wars: Woodrow Wilson and the Quest for a New World Order.* New York: Oxford University Press, 1992.
Koeneke, Rodney. *Empires of the Mind: I. A. Richards and Basic English in China, 1929–1979.* Stanford, CA: Stanford University Press, 2004.
Kotkin, Stephen. "Modern Times: The Soviet Union and the Interwar Conjuncture." *Kritika: Explorations in Russian and Eurasian History* 2, no. 1 (Winter 2001): 111–64.
Koyré, Alexandre. "The Political Function of the Modern Lie." *October* 160 (June 1, 2017): 143–51.

Kritzman, Lawrence D., and Mazal Holocaust Collection. *Auschwitz and After: Race, Culture, and "the Jewish Question" in France.* New York: Routledge, 1995.

LaCapra, Dominick. *Writing History, Writing Trauma.* Baltimore: Johns Hopkins University Press, 2001.

Laqua, Daniel. *Internationalism Reconfigured: Transnational Ideas and Movements between the World Wars.* London: I. B. Tauris, 2011.

———. "Transnational Intellectual Cooperation, the League of Nations, and the Problem of Order." *Journal of Global History* 6, no. 2 (July 2011): 223–47.

Larebo, Haile. *The Building of an Empire: Italian Land Policy and Practice in Ethiopia, 1935–1941.* Oxford: Clarendon, 1999.

Lasswell, Harold D. *Propaganda Technique in the World War.* Mansfield Centre, CT: Martino, 2013.

Lauer, Josh. *Creditworthy: A History of Consumer Surveillance and Financial Identity in America.* New York: Columbia University Press, 2017.

Levene, Mark. "Why Is the Twentieth Century the Century of Genocide?" *Journal of World History* 11, no. 2 (2000): 305–36.

Lazier, Benjamin. "Earthrise; or, The Globalization of the World Picture." *American Historical Review* 116, no. 3 (2011): 602–30.

———. *God Interrupted: Heresy and the European Imagination between the World Wars.* Princeton, NJ: Princeton University Press, 2012.

"League Assembly 'Closes' Abyssinian Issue." *China Weekly Review* (Shanghai), July 11, 1936.

"League Hall Sees Suicide: Geneva Act Laid to Protest; Czechoslovakian Jew Fires Shot as World Delegates Push Peace Aims." *Los Angeles Times,* July 4, 1936, 5.

"League in Panic as Jew Shoots Self in Gallery: Czech Writer Fires Bullet into His Chest." *Chicago Daily Tribune,* July 4, 1936, 5.

League of Nations. *Board of Liquidation: Final Report Presented to States Members of the League of Nations in Accordance with the Requirement of the Final Article of the Resolution for the Dissolution of the League of Nations Adopted by the Assembly on April 18th, 1946, at Its Twenty-First Ordinary Session.* Geneva, 1947.

———. *Esperanto as an International Auxiliary Language: Report of the General Secretariat to the Third Assembly, League of Nations Publication.* Paris: Presses Universitaires de France, 1922.

———. *The Financial Reconstruction of Hungary: General Survey and Principal Documents.* 1926.

———. *How to Make the League of Nations Known and to Develop the Spirit of International Co-operation: Recommendations by the Sub-committee of Experts, International Committee on Intellectual Co-operation, League of Nations.* Geneva: Kundig, 1927.

———. *International Educational Cinematographic Institute: Draft Protocol for Facilitating the International Circulation of Films of an Educational Character.* Geneva: League of Nations, 1932.

———. *The League Hands Over.* Geneva: League Secretariat, 1946.

———. *The League of Nations and the Protection of Minorities of Race, Language and Religion.* Geneva: Information Section, League of Nations Secretariat, 1928.

———. *The League of Nations Library.* Geneva: League of Nations, 1939.

———. *Memorandum on Currency, 1913–1921.* Geneva: A. Kundig, 1922.

———. *Mixed Committee for the Suppression of Counterfeiting Currency: Report and Draft Convention.* Geneva: League of Nations, 1927.

———. *Protection of Linguistic, Racial or Religious Minorities by the League of Nations: Resolutions and Extracts from the Minutes of the Council, Resolutions and Reports Adopted by the Assembly, Relating to the Procedure to Be Followed in Questions concerning the Protection of Minorities*. Geneva, 1929.

———. *Records of the Twentieth (Conclusion) and Twenty-First Ordinary Sessions of the Assembly: Text of the Debates at the Plenary Meetings and Minutes of the First and Second Committees*. Geneva: League of Nations, 1946.

League of Nations and Assembly. *Records of the Twentieth (Conclusion) and Twenty-First Ordinary Sessions of the Assembly: Text of the Debates at the Plenary Meetings and Minutes of the First and Second Committees*. Geneva: League of Nations, 1946.

League of Nations and Economic Intelligence Service. *Annuaire statistique de la Société des Nations / Statistical Year-Book of the League of Nations*. Geneva: League of Nations, 1936.

League of Nations, et al. *Interim Report of the Gold Delegation and Report of the Gold Delegation, League of Nations*. New York: Arno, 1979.

The League of Nations and the Press: International Press Exhibition, Cologne, May to October 1928. Geneva: Information Section / League of Nations, 1928.

"The League of Nations as an Instrument of Liberalism by Raymond B. Fosdick." *Atlantic*, October 1920. http://www.theatlantic.com/past/docs/issues/20oct/fosdick.htm, accessed December 6, 2016.

League of Nations Association of Jugoslavia. *Bulgars and Jugoslavs*. Belgrade: Librairie Slave, 1928.

League of Nations, Financial Economic and Transit Department, and Ragnar Nurkse. *The Course and Control of Inflation: A Review of Monetary Experience in Europe after World War I*. Geneva: League of Nations, 1946.

———. *International Currency Experience: Lessons of the Interwar Period*. Geneva: League of Nations, 1944.

League of Nations Library. *Ouvrages sur l'activité de la Société des Nations catalogués à la Bibliothèque du Secrétariat*. Geneva: League of Nations, 1928.

League of Nations Union. *The Jewish Problem: A Report by the Executive Committee of the League of Nations Together with an Appendix Containing Suggestions concerning Refugees Generally*. London: League of Nations Union, 1943.

Lebovic, Nitzan. *The Philosophy of Life and Death: Ludwig Klages and the Rise of a Nazi Biopolitics*. New York: Palgrave, 2013.

Lee, Richard E. *Questioning Nineteenth-Century Assumptions about Knowledge, III: Dualism*. Boulder: Paradigm, 2010.

Lefebvre, Henri, Philip Wander, and S. Rabinovitch. *Everyday Life in the Modern World*. New York: Harper, 1971.

Legg, Stephen. "An International Anomaly? Sovereignty, the League of Nations and India's Princely Geographies." *Journal of Historical Geography* 43 (January 2014): 96–110.

Leifer, Elihu I. *The Balfour Declaration, the Palestine Mandate, and the United Nations Partition Resolution (1917–1947): A Factual Monograph*. Rev. ed. N.p.: Elihu I. Leifer, 2007.

Lenin, Vladimir Il'ich. *Imperialism, the Highest Stage of Capitalism: A Popular Outline*. New York: International, 1939.

"Lenin, VI: 1915; The Principles of Socialism and the War of 1914–1915." https://www.marxists.org/archive/lenin/works/1915/s-w/ch01.htm, accessed March 31, 2017.

Lester, David. *Suicide and the Holocaust*. New York: Nova Science, 2005.
Lewis, Geoffrey. *The Turkish Language Reform: A Catastrophic Success*. Oxford: Oxford University Press, 1999.
Lewis, Mark. *The Birth of the New Justice: The Internationalization of Crime and Punishment, 1919–1950*. Oxford: Oxford University Press, 2014.
Lewis, Martin W., and Kären E. Wigen. *The Myth of Continents: A Critique of Metageography*. Berkeley: University of California Press, 2003.
Lichtenstein, Alex, and Michael Myod. "One Hundred Years of Mandates." *American Historical Review* 124, no. 5 (December 2019): 1673–75.
Lilienthal, Volker, and Irene Neverla. *Lügenpresse: Anatomie eines politischen Kampfbegriffs*. Cologne: Kiepenheuer und Witsch, 2017.
Lilley, Dorothy B., and Ronald W. Trice. *A History of Information Science, 1945–1985*. San Diego: Academic, 1989.
Linklater, Andrew. "The 'Standard of Civilisation' in World Politics." *Human Figurations* 5, no. 2 (July 2016). http://hdl.handle.net/2027/spo.11217607.0005.205.
Lins, Ulrich. *Dangerous Language—Esperanto under Hitler and Stalin*. London: Palgrave Macmillan, 2016.
Lippmann, Walter. *Public Opinion*. New York: Harcourt, Brace, 1922.
Long, David, and Peter Wilson. *Thinkers of the Twenty Years' Crisis: Inter-war Idealism Reassessed*. Oxford: Clarendon / Oxford University Press, 1995.
Lovejoy, Arthur Oncken. *The Great Chain of Being: A Study of the History of an Idea*. Cambridge, MA: Harvard University Press, 1964.
Lowe, Lisa. *The Intimacies of Four Continents*. Durham, NC: Duke University Press, 2015.
Luckert, Steven, and Susan Bachrach. *State of Deception: The Power of Nazi Propaganda*. Washington, DC: Holocaust Publications, 2009.
Luckhurst, Roger, and Josephine McDonagh. *Transactions and Encounters: Science and Culture in the Nineteenth Century*. Manchester: Manchester University Press, 2002.
Lusinchi, Victor. "Exhibit in Geneva Recalling Era of the League of Nations: Recording Part of Exhibit A Collapsing House of Cards." *New York Times*, November 16, 1980. https://www.nytimes.com/1980/11/16/archives/exhibit-in-geneva-recalling-era-of-the-league-of-nations-recording.html.
Macartney, C. A. *National States and National Minorities*. New York: Russell and Russell, 1968.
Macleod, Henry Dunning. *The Theory of Credit, Vol. 1 of 2*. New York: Forgotten Books, 2012.
MacMillan, Margaret. *Paris 1919: Six Months That Changed the World*. New York: Random House, 2002.
Madley, Benjamin. *An American Genocide: The United States and the California Indian Catastrophe, 1846–1873*. New Haven, CT: Yale University Press, 2017.
Maier, Charles S. *Recasting Bourgeois Europe: Stabilization in France, Germany, and Italy in the Decade after World War I*. Princeton, NJ: Princeton University Press, 1975.
Malcolm, Ian. *Scraps of Paper: German Proclamations in Belgium and France*. London: Hodder and Stoughton, 1916.
Malkin, Lawrence. *Krueger's Men: The Secret Nazi Counterfeit Plot and the Prisoners of Block 19*. New York: Little, Brown, 2006.
Mallard, Grégoire. "The Gift Revisited: Marcel Mauss on War, Debt, and the Politics of Reparations." *Sociological Theory* 29, no. 4 (December 1, 2011): 225–47.

Manela, Erez. *The Wilsonian Moment: Self-Determination and the International Origins of Anticolonial Nationalism*. Oxford: Oxford University Press, 2007.
Manent, Pierre. *An Intellectual History of Liberalism*. Princeton, NJ: Princeton University Press, 1994.
Mann, Geoff. *In the Long Run We Are All Dead: Keynesianism, Political Economy, and Revolution*. London: Verso, 2017.
———. "Poverty in the Midst of Plenty: Unemployment, Liquidity, and Keynes' Scarcity Theory of Capital." *Critical Historical Studies* 2, no. 1 (March 1, 2015): 45–83.
Mann, Michael. *The Dark Side of Democracy: Explaining Ethnic Cleansing*. Cambridge: Cambridge University Press, 2009.
Manning, Clarence Augustus. "Language and International Affairs." *Sewanee Review* 32, no. 3 (1924): 295–311.
Marazzi, Christian, Michael Hardt, and Gregory Conti. *Capital and Language: From the New Economy to the War Economy*. Los Angeles: Semiotext(e), 2008.
Marcot, Roy M. *The History of Remington Firearms*. New York: Chartwell Books, 2011.
Margalith, Aaron M. *The International Mandates*. Baltimore: Johns Hopkins Press, 1930.
Marx, Karl, and Friedrich Engels. *Capital*. Vol. 3, *The Process of Capitalist Production as a Whole*. Cutchogue, NY: Buccaneer Books, 1988.
Marx, Karl, and Tom Griffith. *Capital*. Vol. 1. Warwick: Wordsworth, 2013.
Marvin, Carolyn. *When Old Technologies Were New*. Oxford: Oxford University Press, 1990.
Mathiot, Madeleine. *Ethnolinguistics: Boas, Sapir and Whorf Revisited*. The Hague: Mouton, 1979.
Mazlish, Bruce. *Psychoanalysis and History*. Englewood Cliffs, NJ: Prentice-Hall, 1963.
Mazower, Mark. *Dark Continent: Europe's Twentieth Century*. New York: A. A. Knopf / Distributed by Random House, 1999.
———. *Hitler's Empire: How the Nazis Ruled Europe*. New York: Penguin, 2009.
———. *No Enchanted Palace: The End of Empire and the Ideological Origins of the United Nations*. Princeton, NJ: Princeton University Press, 2009.
McCarthy, Helen. *The British People and the League of Nations: Democracy, Citizenship and Internationalism c. 1918–45*. Manchester: Manchester University Press, 2016.
McDonough, Frank. *Hitler, Chamberlain and Appeasement*. Cambridge: Cambridge University Press, 2011.
McLuhan, Marshall. *The Gutenberg Galaxy*. Toronto: University of Toronto Press, 2011.
———. *Understanding Media: The Extensions of Man*. New York: New American Library, 1966.
Meder, Stephan. "Giro Payments and the Beginnings of the Modern Cashless Payment System." In *Money in the Western Legal Tradition: Middle Ages to Bretton Woods*, ed. David Fox and Wolfgang Ernst, 441–87. Oxford: Oxford University Press, 2016.
Mehta, Uday Singh. *Liberalism and Empire: A Study in Nineteenth-Century British Liberal Thought*. Chicago: University of Chicago Press, 1999.
Mercer, Christina, and Eileen O'Neill. *Early Modern Philosophy: Mind, Matter, and Metaphysics*. Oxford: Oxford University Press, 2005.
Metzger, Bruce Manning, and Roland E. Murphy. *The Apocryphal/Deuterocanonical Books of the Old Testament*. New York: Oxford University Press, 1991.
Michael, Robert, and Karin Doerr. *Nazi-Deutsch / Nazi German: An English Lexicon of the Language of the Third Reich*. Westport, CT: Greenwood, 2002.

Mignolo, Walter. *The Darker Side of Western Modernity: Global Futures, Decolonial Options.* Durham, NC: Duke University Press, 2011.
Mihm, Stephen. *A Nation of Counterfeiters: Capitalists, Con Men, and the Making of the United States.* Cambridge, MA: Harvard University Press, 2007.
Miller, David Hunter. *My Diary at the Conference of Paris, with Documents.* New York: Appeal, 1924.
Mitchell, Timothy. *Colonising Egypt.* Cambridge: Cambridge University Press, 2007.
Mitchell-Innes, Harold. "What Is Money." *Banking Law Journal,* 1913, 377–408.
Mock, James R. *Words That Won the War: The Story of the Committee on Public Information, 1917–1919.* New York: Russell and Russell, 1968.
Momigliano, Arnaldo. "The Second Book of Maccabees." *Classical Philology* 70, no. 2 (1975): 81–88.
Mommsen, Wolfgang J., and Lothar Kettenacker. *The Fascist Challenge and the Policy of Appeasement.* London: G. Allen and Unwin, 1983.
Morrison, Paul. *The Poetics of Fascism: Ezra Pound, T. S. Eliot, Paul de Man.* New York: Oxford University Press, 1996.
Morrison, Toni, and Ta-Nehisi Coates. *The Origin of Others.* Cambridge, MA: Harvard University Press, 2017.
Moses, A. Dirk. *Empire, Colony, Genocide.* New York: Berghahn Books, 2008.
Mouré, Kenneth. *The Gold Standard Illusion: France, the Bank of France, and the International Gold Standard, 1914–1939.* Oxford: Oxford University Press, 2002.
Mouton, Marie-Renée. *Le Société des Nations et les intérêts de la France: 1920–1924.* Bern: P. Lang, 1995.
Moyn, Samuel. *The Last Utopia: Human Rights in History.* Cambridge, MA: Belknap Press of Harvard University Press, 2012.
Moyn, Samuel, and Andrew Sartori. *Global Intellectual History.* New York: Columbia University Press, 2013.
Muir, Ramsay. *The Interdependent World and Its Problems.* London: Constable, 1932.
Mukerji, Dhan Gopal. *Disillusioned India.* New York: E. P. Dutton, 1930.
Mukherjee, R. K. "The Problem of Indian Minorities." *Indian Review* 31, no. 4 (1930): 231–35.
Müller, Simone M. *Wiring the World: The Social and Cultural Creation of Global Telegraph Networks.* New York: Columbia University Press, 2016.
Müller, Simone, and Heidi Tworek. "The Telegraph and the Bank: On the Interdependence of Global Communications and Capitalism, 1866–1914." *Journal of Global History* 10, no. 2 (2015): 259–83.
Nelson, Harold I. *Land and Power: British and Allied Policy on Germany's Frontiers, 1916–19.* London: Routledge, 1963.
Netz, Reviel. *Barbed Wire: An Ecology of Modernity.* Middletown, CT: Wesleyan University Press, 2009.
Nietzsche, Friedrich. *The Birth of Tragedy Out of the Spirit of Music.* New York: Penguin, 1993.
Niezen, Ronald, and Maria Sapignoli. *Palaces of Hope: The Anthropology of Global Organizations.* Cambridge: Cambridge University Press, 2017.
Nitobe, Inazō. *The Language Question and the League of Nations.* Geneva: H. Vollet, 1921.
———. *The Works of Inazo Nitobe.* Tokyo: University of Tokyo Press, 1978.
Noble, George Bernard. *Policies and Opinions at Paris, 1919: Wilsonian Diplomacy, the Versailles Peace, and French Public Opinion.* New York: H. Fertig, 1968.

Nord, Philip G. *France 1940: Defending the Republic.* New Haven, CT: Yale University Press, 2015.
Nordenstreng, Karl, and Tara Seppa. "The League of Nations and the Mass Media: The Rediscovery of a Forgotten Story." New Delhi: International Association for Mass Communication Research, August 1986. https://sites.tuni.fi/uploads/2019/12/f0b91383-the_league_of_nations_and_the_mass_media.pdf, accessed July 26, 2020.
Norman, Joseph, and William Thrower. *Maps and Civilization: Cartography in Culture and Society.* Chicago: University of Chicago Press, 2007.
Norris, James D. *R. G. Dun and Co. 1841–1900: The Development of Credit-Reporting in the Nineteenth Century.* Westport, CT: Greenwood, 1978.
Northedge, F. S. *The League of Nations: Its Life and Times, 1920–1946.* New York: Holmes and Meier, 1986.
Ogden, C. K. *Debabelization, with a Survey of Contemporary Opinion on the Problem of a Universal Language.* London: K. Paul, Trench, Trubner, 1931.
Ogden, Emily. *Credulity: A Cultural History of US Mesmerism.* Chicago: University of Chicago Press, 2018.
Ong, Walter J., and John Hartley. *Orality and Literacy: The Technologizing of the Word.* London: Methuen, 1982.
Otlet, Paul, and W. Boyd Rayward. *International Organisation and Dissemination of Knowledge: Selected Essays of Paul Otlet.* Amsterdam: Elsevier, 1990.
Otto Jespersen: Facets of His Life and Work. Amsterdam Studies in the Theory and History of Linguistic Science 52. Amsterdam: J. Benjamins, 1989.
Paechter, Heinz. *Nazi-Deutsch: A Glossary of Contemporary German Usage, with Appendices on Government, Military and Economic Institutions.* New York: Ungar, 1944.
Page, Edward. *Political Authority and Bureaucratic Power: A Comparative Analysis.* Knoxville: University of Tennessee Press, 1985.
Parikka, Jussi. *What Is Media Archaeology?* Cambridge, UK: Polity, 2012.
Pauly, Louis W. *The League of Nations and the Foreshadowing of the International Monetary Fund.* Princeton, NJ: International Finance Section, Department of Economics, Princeton University, 1996.
Paxton, Robert Owen. *The Anatomy of Fascism.* New York: Vintage Books, 2005.
Pedersen, Susan. "Back to the League of Nations." *American Historical Review* 112, no. 4 (2007): 1091–117.
———. "Getting Out of Iraq—in 1932: The League of Nations and the Road to Normative Statehood." *American Historical Review* 115, no. 4 (2010): 975–1000.
———. *The Guardians: The League of Nations and the Crisis of Empire.* Oxford: Oxford University Press, 2015.
———. "The Meaning of the Mandates System: An Argument." *Geschichte und Gesellschaft* 32, no. 4 (2006): 560–82.
Pemberton, Jo-Anne. *Global Metaphors: Modernity and the Quest for One World.* London: Pluto, 2001.
———. "New Worlds for Old: The League of Nations in the Age of Electricity." *Review of International Studies* 28, no. 2 (2002): 311–36.
Peterecz, Zoltán. *Jeremiah Smith, Jr. and Hungary, 1924–1926: The United States, the League of Nations, and the Financial Reconstruction of Hungary.* Poznan: Wydawnictwo Albatros, 2013.
———. "Picking the Right Man for the Job: Jeremiah Smith, Jr. and American Private Influence

in the Financial Reconstruction of Hungary." *Hungarian Journal of English and American Studies* 15, no. 2 (2009): 285–305.

Peters, John Durham. *The Marvelous Clouds: Toward a Philosophy of Elemental Media*. Chicago: University of Chicago Press, 2016.

———. *Speaking into the Air: A History of the Idea of Communication*. Chicago: University of Chicago Press, 1999.

Petruccelli, D. "Banknotes from the Underground: Counterfeiting and the International Order in Interwar Europe." *Journal of Contemporary History* 51, no. 3 (July 2016): 507–30.

Pierce, John R. *An Introduction to Information Theory: Symbols, Signals and Noise*. New York: Dover, 1997.

Piétri, Nicole. "L'œuvre d'un organisme technique de La Société des Nations: Le Comité Financier et la reconstruction de l'Autriche (1921–1926)." In *The League of Nations in Retrospect / La Societe des Nations retrospective: Proceedings of the Symposium Organized by the United Nations Library and Geneva*, 319–42. New York: Walter de Gruyter, 1983.

Platt, Katherine. "Places of Experience and the Experiences of Place." In *The Longing for Home*, ed. Leroy S. Rouner, 112–27. Notre Dame, IN: University of Notre Dame Press, 1996.

Pocock, J. G. A. *The Machiavellian Moment: Florentine Political Thought and the Atlantic Republican Tradition*. Princeton, NJ: Princeton University Press, 1975.

Polanyi, Karl. *The Great Transformation: The Political and Economic Origins of Our Time*. Boston: Beacon, 2001.

Pollock, Sheldon. *The Language of the Gods in the World of Men: Sanskrit, Culture, and Power in Premodern India*. Berkeley: University of California Press, 2009.

Poovey, Mary. *Genres of the Credit Economy: Mediating Value in Eighteenth- and Nineteenth-Century Britain*. Chicago: University of Chicago Press, 2008.

Porqué se mató el periodista Stéfan Lux: Apuntes para la historia de un mártir del siglo XX. Buenos Aires: Columna, 1937.

Possony, Stefan Thomas. *Die Wehrwirtschaft des totalen Krieges*. Vienna: Gerold, 1938.

Potter, Pitman B. "League Publicity: Cause or Effect of League Failure?" *Public Opinion Quarterly* 2, no. 3 (July 1938): 399–412.

Pound, Ezra. *Guide to Kulchur*. New York: New Directions, 1952.

———. *What Is Money For?* London: Greater Britain Publications, 1939.

Powell, Jason L. *Globalism*. New Brunswick, NJ: Transaction, 2011.

Prashad, Vijay. *The Darker Nations: A People's History of the Third World*. New York: New Press / Distributed by W. W. Norton, 2007.

Press, Steven Michael. "The Language of Ideology: Lingual Manipulation of Readers in German Literature of the Third Reich." *Vanderbilt Undergraduate Research Journal* 1 (May 10, 2005). https://ejournals.library.vanderbilt.edu/index.php/vurj/index.

Price, Burr. *The World Talks It Over*. New York: R. D. Henkle, 1927.

Privat, Edmond. *Aux Indes avec Gandhi*. Paris: Éditions Denoël, 1960.

———. *Esperanto in Fifty Lessons*. New York: Fleming H. Revell, 1908.

———. *Historio de la lingvo Esperanto*. Leipzig: F. Hirt and Sohn, 1923.

———. *The Life of Zamenhof*. London: G. Allen and Unwin, 1931.

———. *Vie De Gandhi*. Genève: Labor et fides, 1949.

Prott, Volker. *The Politics of Self-Determination: Remaking Territories and National Identities in Europe, 1917–1923*. Oxford: Oxford University Press, 2016.

Poulton, Hugh. *Top Hat, Grey Wolf, and Crescent: Turkish Nationalism and the Turkish Republic.* New York: New York University Press, 1997.
Qureshi, Sadiah. *Peoples on Parade: Exhibitions, Empire, and Anthropology in Nineteenth-Century Britain.* Chicago: University of Chicago Press, 2011.
Rancière, Jacques, Hassan Melehy, and Hayden White. *The Names of History: On the Poetics of Knowledge.* Minneapolis: University of Minnesota Press, 1994.
Rankin, William. *After the Map: Cartography, Navigation, and the Transformation of Territory in the Twentieth Century.* Chicago: University of Chicago Press, 2018.
Rasula, Jed. *Destruction Was My Beatrice: Dada and the Unmaking of the Twentieth Century.* New York: Basic Books, 2015.
Redish, Angela. "Anchors Aweigh: The Transition from Commodity Money to Fiat Money in Western Economies." *Canadian Journal of Economics / Revue Canadienne d'Economique* 26, no. 4 (1993): 777–95.
Reich, Wilhelm, Mary Higgins, and Chester M. Raphael. *The Mass Psychology of Fascism.* London: Souvenir, 2018.
Reinalda, Bob, Jutta Joachim, and Bertjan Verbeek. *International Organizations and Implementation: Enforcers, Managers, Authorities?* London: Routledge, 2010.
Reinharz, Jehuda, and Yaacov Shavit. *The Road to September 1939: Polish Jews, Zionists, and the Yishuv on the Eve of World War II.* Waltham, MA: Brandeis University Press, 2018.
Renshaw, Daniel. "The Disillusionment of Robert Dell: The Intellectual Journey of a Catholic Socialist." *Intellectual History Review*, no. 278 (2017): 1–22.
"Revolver Shot in Geneva Assembly Hall: Suicide Attempt; A Photographer's Outburst; French Attitude to the League." *Times of India* (Mumbai), July 4, 1936.
Reynolds, Audrey Lois. On Grammatical Trifles: Otto Jespersen and His Linguistic Milieu. Evanston, IL: Northwestern University Press, 1969.
Ribi-Forclaz, Amalia. *Humanitarian Imperialism: The Politics of Anti-slavery Activism, 1880–1940.* Oxford: Oxford University Press, 2015.
Riles, Annelise. "Infinity within the Brackets." *American Ethnologist* 25, no. 3 (August 1, 1998): 378–98.
Ringgold, Gene, and DeWitt Bodeen. *The Films of Cecil B. DeMille.* Secaucus, NJ: Citadel, 1974.
Robert, Karl. *Hitler's Counterfeit Reich: Behind the Scenes of Nazi Economy.* New York: Alliance Book, 1941.
"Robert Graves: Recalling the Last War, Preparing for the Next." *Antiwar Literary and Philosophical Selections* (blog), June 29, 2011. https://rickrozoff.wordpress.com/2011/06/29/robert-graves-recalling-war/.
Roberts, John. *Photography and Its Violations.* New York: Columbia University Press, 2014.
Robertson, Frances. "The Aesthetics of Authenticity: Printed Banknotes as Industrial Currency." *Technology and Culture* 46, no. 1 (2005): 31–50.
Robinson, Jacob. *Were the Minorities Treaties a Failure?* New York: Institute of Jewish Affairs of the American Jewish Congress and the World Jewish Congress, 1943.
Rodgers, Daniel T. *Atlantic Crossings: Social Politics in a Progressive Age.* Cambridge, MA: Belknap Press of Harvard University Press, 2001.
Rodogno, Davide. "'A Horrific Photo of a Drowned Syrian Child': Humanitarian Photography and NGO Media Strategies in Historical Perspective." *International Review of the Red Cross* 97, no. 900, "The Evolution of Warfare" (November 2015): 1121–55.

Rosenberg, Alfred. *The Myth of the Twentieth Century: An Evaluation of the Spiritual-Intellectual Confrontations of Our Age.* Ostra Vetere, Italy: Ostara, 2017.

Rosenberg, Emily S. *Transnational Currents in a Shrinking World, 1870–1945.* Cambridge, MA: Belknap Press of Harvard University Press, 2012.

Sampson, Henry. *A History of Advertising from the Earliest Times.* Bristol: Thoemmes, 2002.

Sánchez Román, José Antonio. "From the Tigris to the Amazon: Peripheral Expertise, Impossible Cooperation and Economic Multilateralism at the League of Nations, 1920–1946." In *The Institution of International Order: From the League of Nations to the United Nations,* ed. Simon Jackson and Alanna O'Malley, 43–64. New York: Routledge, 2018.

Santner, Eric L. *The Royal Remains: The People's Two Bodies and the Endgames of Sovereignty.* Chicago: University of Chicago Press, 2011.

Sapir, Edward. *Language: An Introduction to the Study of Speech.* Teddington, UK: Echo Library, 2006.

———. *Totality.* Baltimore: Waverly, 1930.

Sargent, Betty. "The Desperate Mission of Stefan Lux." *Georgia Review* 55/56 (2001): 187–201.

Sartori, Andrew. *Liberalism in Empire: An Alternative History.* Berkeley: University of California Press, 2014.

Saussure, Ferdinand de. *Course in General Linguistics.* Rpt. ed. LaSalle, IL: Open Court, 1998.

———. *La structure logique des mots dans les langues naturelles considérée au point de vue de son application aux langues artificielles.* Bern: Büchler, 1919.

Schellenberg, Britta. "Lügenpresse?" In *Rechtsextremismus und "Nationalsozialistischer Untergrund,"* 309–39. Edition Rechtsextremismus. Wiesbaden: Springer, 2016.

Schildkraut, Joseph, and Leo Lania. *My Father and I [by] Joseph Schildkraut, as Told to Leo Lania.* New York: Viking, 1959.

Schipper, Frank, Vincent Lagendijk, and Irene Anastasiadou. "New Connections for an Old Continent: Rail, Road and Electricity in the League of Nations Organization for Communication and Transit." In *Materializing Europe: Transnational Infrastructures and the Project of Europe,* edited by A. Badenoch and A. Fickers, 133–43. London: Palgrave, 2010.

Schiltz, Michael. "Money on the Road to Empire: Japan's Adoption of Gold Monometallism, 1873–97." *Economic History Review* 65, no. 3 (2012): 1147–68.

Schor, Esther H. *Bridge of Words: Esperanto and the Dream of a Universal Language.* New York: Metropolitan Books, 2016.

Scott, A. O. "Film Review: An Inventor Trapped in Nazi Evil." *New York Times,* January 24, 2003, sec. Movies. https://www.nytimes.com/2003/01/24/movies/film-review-an-inventor-trapped-in-nazi-evil.html.

Scott, James C. *Seeing Like a State: How Certain Schemes to Improve the Human Condition Have Failed.* New Haven, CT: Yale University Press, 1998.

Seabury, William Marston. *Motion Picture Problems: The Cinema and the League of Nations.* New York: Avondale, 1929.

Seamon, David. *Life Takes Place: Phenomenology, Lifeworlds, and Place Making.* New York: Routledge, 2018.

Segel, B. W., and Richard S. Levy. *Lie and a Libel: The History of the Protocols of the Elders of Zion.* Lincoln: University of Nebraska Press, 1995.

Shapin, Steven. *A Social History of Truth: Civility and Science in Seventeenth-Century England.* Chicago: University of Chicago Press, 1994.

Sharp, Alan. *The Versailles Settlement: Peacemaking in Paris, 1919.* Houndmills: Palgrave, 2001.
Shell, Marc. *Money, Language, and Thought: Literary and Philosophical Economies from the Medieval to the Modern Era.* Berkeley: University of California Press, 1982.
Shenton, Herbert Newhard. *Cosmopolitan Conversation: The Language Problems of International Conferences.* New York: Columbia University Press, 1933.
Shields, Sarah. "The Greek-Turkish Population Exchange: Internationally Administered Ethnic Cleansing." *Middle East Report*, no. 267 (2013): 2–6.
Shore, Cris, Susan Wright, and Davide Però. *Policy Worlds: Anthropology and the Analysis of Contemporary Power.* New York: Berghahn Books, 2011.
Short, John Phillip. *Magic Lantern Empire: Colonialism and Society in Germany.* Ithaca, NY: Cornell University Press, 2012.
Silverfarb, Daniel. *Britain's Informal Empire in the Middle East: A Case Study of Iraq, 1929–1941.* New York: Oxford University Press, 1986.
Simmel, Georg. *The Philosophy of Money.* New York: Taylor and Francis, 2011.
Slobodian, Quinn. *Globalists: The End of Empire and the Birth of Neoliberalism.* Cambridge, MA: Harvard University Press, 2018.
Sluga, Glenda, and Patricia Clavin. *Internationalisms: A Twentieth-Century History.* Cambridge: Cambridge University Press, 2016.
Smith, Anthony D. *The Antiquity of Nations.* Cambridge, UK: Polity, 2004.
———. *The Ethnic Origins of Nations.* Oxford, UK: B. Blackwell, 1987.
———. *Nationalism and Modernism: A Critical Survey of Recent Theories of Nations and Nationalism.* London: Routledge, 1998.
Smuts, Jan Christiaan. *League of Nations: A Practical Suggestion.* Charleston, SC: Nabu, 2010.
Snyder, Timothy. *On Tyranny: Twenty Lessons from the Twentieth Century.* New York: Duggan Books, 2017.
Sontag, Susan. *On Photography.* New York: Picador, 2010.
———. *Regarding the Pain of Others.* New York: Picador, 2017.
Souza Filho, Danilo Marcondes de. *Language and Action.* Amsterdam: J. Benjamins, 1984.
Spencer, Herbert. *The Man versus the State.* Caldwell, ID: Caxton, 1940.
Spengler, Oswald, and Charles Francis Atkinson. *The Decline of the West.* Vol. 2. New York: A. Knopf, 1996.
Spretnak, Charlene. *Resurgence of the Real—Body, Nature and Place in a Hypermodern World.* London: Routledge, 1999.
Stallybrass, W. T. S. *A Society of States: Sovereignty, Independence and Equality in a League of Nations.* New York: E. P. Dutton, 1919.
Standage, Tom. *The Victorian Internet: The Remarkable Story of the Telegraph and the Nineteenth Century's On-line Pioneers.* London: Bloomsbury, 1998.
Stanley, Jason. *How Fascism Works: The Politics of Us and Them.* New York: Random House, 2018.
Starr, Kevin, Richard J. Orsi, and California Historical Society. *Rooted in Barbarous Soil: People, Culture, and Community in Gold Rush California.* Berkeley: University of California Press, 2000.
Stavans, Ilan. *Resurrecting Hebrew.* New York: Nextbook, 2008.
Steiner, George. *After Babel: Aspects of Language and Translation.* Oxford: Oxford University Press, 2006.

———. *Heidegger*. London: Fontana, 1987.
Steiner, Zara S. *The Lights That Failed European International History, 1919–1933*. Oxford: Oxford University Press, 2005.
Steinhoff, William. *George Orwell and the Origins of 1984*. Ann Arbor: University of Michigan Press, 1976.
Stewart, Kathleen. *Ordinary Affects*. Durham, NC: Duke University Press, 2007.
Stieglitz, Alfred. *Lantern Slides*. New York: n.p., 1896.
Stolper, Gustav. *German Economy, 1870–1940: Issues and Trends*. London: Routledge, 2018.
Stoyanovsky, J. *The Mandate for Palestine: A Contribution to the Theory and Practice of International Mandates*. London: Longmans, Green, 1976.
Strachan, Hew. *The First World War*. Oxford: Oxford University Press, 2001.
Straumann, Tobias. *Fixed Ideas of Money: Small States and Exchange Rate Regimes in Twentieth-Century Europe*. Cambridge UK: Cambridge University Press, 2010.
Streets-Salter, Heather, and Trevor R. Getz. *Empires and Colonies in the Modern World: A Global Perspective*. Oxford: Oxford University Press, 2016.
Streit, Clarence K. *Union Now: A Proposal for a Federal Union of the Democracies of the North Atlantic*. Hannover: HZ, 2006.
"Suicide Shot Rings at League Session: Czech Journalist Startles the Delegates by Firing Bullet into Chest on Floor; Protests for Reich Jews Planned Act to Call Attention to Their Plight, Says Letter Found in His Briefcase." *New York Times*, July 4, 1936.
Swett, Pamela E. *Selling Modernity: Advertising in Twentieth-Century Germany*. Durham, NC: Duke University Press, 2007.
Tartakoff, Laura Ymayo. "Synagogues, Cemeteries, and Frontiers: Anti-Semitism in Switzerland." *Society* 54, no. 1 (2017): 56–63.
Taylor, Charles. *Sources of the Self: The Making of the Modern Identity*. Cambridge: Cambridge University Press, 2012.
Taylor, Paul A., and Jan L. Harris. *Critical Theories of Mass Media: Then and Now*. Maidenhead: Open University Press, 2008.
Thakur, Vineet. *Jan Smuts and the Indian Question*. Pietermaritzburg: University of KwaZulu-Natal Press, 2018.
———. "Jan Smuts, Jawaharlal Nehru and the Legacies of Liberalism." *E-International Relations* (blog), May 18, 2018. https://www.e-ir.info/2018/05/18/jan-smuts-jawaharlal-nehru-and-the-legacies-of-liberalism/.
Tismăneanu, Vladimir. *The Devil in History: Communism, Fascism, and Some Lessons of the Twentieth Century*. Berkeley: University of California Press, 2014.
Tooze, Adam. *The Wages of Destruction: The Making and Breaking of the Nazi Economy*. New York: Penguin Books, 2008.
Tournès, Ludovic. *Les États-Unis et la Société des Nations (1914–1946): Le système face à l'émergence d'une superpuissance*. Bern: Peter Lang, 2016.
Traz, Robert de. *The Spirit of Geneva*. Oxford: Oxford University Press, 1935.
"Tristan Tzara—Dada Manifesto (23rd March 1918)." UbuWeb Papers. http://www.ubu.com/papers/tzara_dada-manifesto.html, accessed March 30, 2020.
Trivellato, Francesca. *The Familiarity of Strangers: The Sephardic Diaspora, Livorno, and Cross-Cultural Trade in the Early Modern Period*. New Haven, CT: Yale University Press, 2009.
Tully, John A. *The Devil's Milk: A Social History of Rubber*. New York: Monthly Review Press, 2011.

———. "A Victorian Ecological Disaster: Imperialism, the Telegraph, and Gutta-Percha." *Journal of World History* 20 (2009): 559–79.
Turner, Michael Edward. *Enclosures in Britain: 1750–1830*. Basingstoke: Macmillan, 1986.
Tworek, Heidi. "Peace through Truth? The Press and Moral Disarmament through the League of Nations." *Medien und Zeit* 25, no. 4 (2010): 16–28.
"Uncovering the Hungarian Bank-Note Scandal." *Nation* 122, no. 3168 (March 24, 1926): 323.
United Nations and Inter-organization Board for Information Systems. *Directory of United Nations Information Systems*. New York: United Nations, 1980.
United States and League of Nations. *Mandate for Palestine*. Washington: GPO, 1927.
Upthegrove, Campbell L. *Empire by Mandate: A History of the Relations of Great Britain with the Permanent Mandates Commission of the League of Nations*. New York: Bookman Associates, 1954.
Valery, Paul. "The Centenary of Photography." In *Classic Essays on Photography*, edited by Alan Trachtenberg, 199–216. New Haven, CT: Leete's Island Books, 1980.
van Maanen-Helmer, Elizabeth. *The Mandates System in Relation to Africa and the Pacific Islands*. London: P. S. King, 1929.
Van Rahden, Till. *Demokratie: Eine gefährdete Lebensform*. Frankfurt: Campus, 2019.
Veblen, Thorstein. "On the Nature of Capital: Investment, Intangible Assets, and the Pecuniary Magnate." *Quarterly Journal of Economics* 23, no. 1 (November 1908): 104–36.
Versluis, Arthur. *The New Inquisitions: Heretic-Hunting and the Intellectual Origins of Modern Totalitarianism*. New York: Oxford University Press, 2006.
Vesey, Godfrey. *Idealism, Past and Present*. Cambridge: Cambridge University Press, 1982.
Viktorin, Caroline, Jessica C. E. Gienow-Hecht, Annika Estner, and Marcel K. Will. *Nation Branding in Modern History*. New York: Berghahn Books, 2018.
Vismann, Cornelia. *Files: Law and Media Technology*. Stanford, CA: Stanford University Press, 2008.
"Volksgemeinschaft / Nazi Propaganda." Britannica.com. https://www.britannica.com/topic/Volksgemeinschaft, accessed May 9, 2018.
Voorhees, Dayton. "The League of Nations: A Corporation, Not a Super State." *American Political Science Review* 20, no. 4 (November 1926): 847–52.
Vossler, Karl. *The Spirit of Language in Civilization*. New York: AMS, 1977.
Wagner, Kim A. *Amritsar, 1919: An Empire of Fear and the Making of a Massacre*. New Haven, CT: Yale University Press, 2019.
Wainewright, Will. *Reporting on Hitler: Rothay Reynolds and the British Press in Nazi Germany*. London: Biteback, 2017.
Walden, Scott. *Photography and Philosophy: Essays on the Pencil of Nature*. Oxford: Wiley-Blackwell, 2010.
Wallerstein, Immanuel Maurice. *Centrist Liberalism Triumphant, 1789/1914*. Berkeley: University of California Press, 2011.
Wampole, Christy. *Rootedness: The Ramifications of a Metaphor*. Chicago: University of Chicago Press, 2016.
Wasson, Haidee, and Lee Grieveson. *Cinema's Military Industrial Complex*. Berkeley: University of California Press, 2018.
Weber, Eugen. *Peasants into Frenchmen: The Modernization of Rural France, 1870–1914*. Stanford, CA: Stanford University Press, 1976.
Wedeen, Lisa. *Ambiguities of Domination Politics, Rhetoric, and Symbols in Contemporary Syria, with a New Preface*. Chicago: University of Chicago Press, 2015.

Welch, David. *Propaganda, Power and Persuasion: From World War I to WikiLeaks*. London: I. B. Tauris, 2015.

Wennerlind, Carl. "Money Talks, but What Is It Saying? Semiotics of Money and Social Control." *Journal of Economic Issues* 35, no. 3 (2001): 557–74.

Wenzlhuemer, Roland. *Connecting the Nineteenth-Century World: The Telegraph and Globalization*. Cambridge: Cambridge University Press, 2013.

Werner, Jean-François. "The Archives of the Planet: The Life and Works of Albert Kahn." *Visual Anthropology* 28, no. 5 (October 20, 2015): 438–50.

Wheatley, Natasha. "Mandatory Interpretation: Legal Hermeneutics and the New International Order in Arab and Jewish Petitions to the League of Nations." *Past and Present* 227, no. 1 (May 1, 2015): 205–48.

White, Michael V., and Kurt Schuler. "Retrospectives: Who Said 'Debauch the Currency,' Keynes or Lenin?" *Journal of Economic Perspectives* 23, no. 3 (2009): 213–22.

Williams, Philip L. *The Emergence of the Theory of the Firm: From Adam Smith to Alfred Marshall*. New York: St. Martin's, 1979.

Wilson, Woodrow. *The Politics of Woodrow Wilson: Selections from His Speeches and Writings*. Freeport, NY: Books for Libraries, 1970.

Winkler, Jonathan Reed. *Nexus: Strategic Communications and American Security in World War I*. Cambridge, MA: Harvard University Press, 2008.

Winter, Jay. *Dreams of Peace and Freedom: Utopian Moments in the Twentieth Century*. New Haven, CT: Yale University Press, 2008.

———. *Sites of Memory, Sites of Mourning: The Great War in European Cultural History*. Cambridge: Cambridge University Press, 2014.

Willis, Henry Parker. *A History of the Latin Monetary Union: A Study of International Monetary Action*. New York: Greenwood, 1968.

Wittgenstein, Ludwig, and G. E. M. Anscombe. *Philosophical Investigations: The German Text, with a Revised English Translation*. Malden, MA: Blackwell, 2008.

Wittgenstein, Ludwig, Gilles Gaston Granger, and Bertrand Russell. *Tractatus logico-philosophicus*. Paris: Gallimard, 2009.

Wohlfarth, Irving. "Walter Benjamin and the Idea of a Technological Eros: A Tentative Reading of 'Zum Planetarium.'" *Benjamin Studien/Studies* 1, no. 1 (2002), 65–109.

Wolfe, Martin. "The Development of Nazi Monetary Policy." *Journal of Economic History* 15, no. 4 (1955): 392–402.

World Zionist Organization. *The Establishment in Palestine of the Jewish National Home: Memorandum Submitted . . . to the Secretary-General of the League of Nations for the Information of the Permanent Mandates Commission, October 1924 . . . L'etablissement du foyer national Juif en Palestine; memorandum presente . . . a M. le Secretaire General de la Societe des Nations pour la gouverne de la Commission Permanente des Man*. London: White, n.d.

Wright, Alex. *Cataloging the World: Paul Otlet and the Birth of the Information Age*. Oxford: Oxford University Press, 2014.

Wright, Quincy. *Mandates under the League of Nations*. Chicago: University of Chicago Press, 1930.

———. "The Proposed Termination of the Iraq Mandate." *American Journal of International Law* 25, no. 3 (July 1931): 436–46.

Wright, Susan. *Anthropology of Organizations*. London: Routledge, 2004.

Zimmern, Alfred Eckhard. *The League of Nations and the Rule of Law, 1918–1935*. London: Macmillan, 1936.

Žižek, Slavoj. *The Parallax View*. Cambridge, MA: MIT Press, 2009.

Zweig, Stefan, and Michel Tremousa. *Adam Lux*. Rouen: Publications de l'Université de Rouen, 1993.

Index

absolutists, ix, 2–3
Adorno, Theodor, 38, 94–95, 101, 146n24
affaire des faux billets, l', 76–84
"Age of the World Picture" (Heidegger), 23
Albania, 29, 46, 59, 135n18, 136n36
Alderson, William, 43–44
alphabets, 7, 15, 28–29, 40, 43, 54–56, 59, 75, 126n57
Amen (Costa-Gavras), 97
American Civil War, 20, 68–69
Ames, Herbert, 30, 32–34
Amicucci, Ermanno, 107
Anderson, Benedict, 10, 140n32
Antiochus Epiphanes, 103–4
anti-Semitism, 77, 96–97
Arabic, 51, 55
Arbuckle, Roscoe "Fatty," 62–63
Arbuthnot, C. C., 62
Arendt, Hannah, 91–93, 111, 113–14, 116, 118–19, 145n17
Ariès, Philippe, 103
armistice, 1, 33, 79
arts of illusion, 35
Assyrians, 52
Austin, J. L., 8
Austria, 32, 49, 75, 88, 96, 112, 135n18, 145n1
Avenol, Joseph, 32, 96, 99, 101, 145n8, 147n75, 148n89
Azcárate, Pablo de, 34–35

Bagehot, Walter, 70–71
Baker, Ray Stannard, 6
Ball, Hugo, 1, 59
Bank for International Settlements, 84–85
banking, 11, 61, 67, 69, 126n63

barbarism, 25–27, 36
Barthes, Roland, 31, 35
Bartlett, Vernon, 112
Baudelaire, Charles, 83
Belgium, 6, 21, 54, 62, 73, 82, 116, 136n36
Beneš Edvard, 79
Benjamin, Walter, 91–95, 101, 117, 143n124, 146n24
Bernays, Edward, 9
Bethlen, Istvan, 77
bills of exchange, 74, 83
Blanck, Guillermo de, 115
Bloch, Marc, x, 107–8
Bochet, Paul du, 96, 99
Bolivia, 115
Bolshevism, 2, 4, 58, 84
Bourdieu, Pierre, 131n83
Bourgeois, Leon, 12
Boxer Rebellion, 128n113
Brazil, 17, 46
Briand, Aristide, 76, 78
Bright, Charles, 10
Britain, 95, 112; Cecil and, 6; currencies and, 44, 53, 62; Edsall and, 62; Graves and, 11; language and, 48, 51, 53, 59; world picture and, 17, 26, 29
British Foreign Office, 48, 99
bubbles, speculative, 64
Bulgaria, 52, 135n18
Burrows, Arthur, 19
Bush, George W., 118
Butler, Montague C., 45

cabals, 110
Camera Lucida (Barthes), 31, 35
Capital (Marx), 69

capitalism: Anderson on, 10, 140n32; Benjamin and, 91; currencies and, 63, 67–71, 82; Jung on, 2; language and, 46–47; print, 10, 140n32; storytelling and, 91; symbolic, 22–23 (*see also* symbolic capital); world picture and, 24; World War I and, 10, 14
Carr, E. H., 7, 13
Case, Holly, 12
Cassel, Gustav, 64–66, 74–75, 85–86, 140n28, 142n85
Cecil, Robert, 6, 45, 48
censorship, 10, 13, 106–7, 111, 120
central banks, 66, 71, 74–75, 78, 142n90
Chicago Daily Tribune, 96–97, 102
Chile, 136n36
China, 12, 17, 32, 37, 46, 128n113, 136n36
Chinese characters, 55
Churchill, Winston, 59
"Civilisation, Le: Le mot et l'idee" (Ellis), 26
civilization: currencies and, 71, 75, 81; Koyré and, 113; language and, 52; standards of, 25–27, 36, 52, 104, 116; storytelling and, 93; Western, 14, 24–30; world picture and, 17, 23–30, 36
Cmiel, Kenneth, 11, 115
Colban, Eric, 51
Collaboration of the Press in the Organization of Peace (League of Nations), 105
collective force, 114–15
Colombia, 136n36
Columbia University, 58
Coming Scrap of Paper, The (Edsall), 62
communism, 47, 86, 118
Conant, Charles, 67, 69
concentration camps, 57, 111
confederate money, 69
Conference of the Directors of Press Bureaus, 106
Conference on False News, 90
Congo, 25
Contemporary Jewish Record (Koyré), 113
Cosmoglotta, 44
Costa du Rels, Adolfo, 115
Costa-Gavras, 97
counterfeiting: *l'affaire des faux billets* and, 76–84; Briand and, 76, 78; currencies and, 15, 60–86, 90, 143n109; extent of, 69, 76–81; gold, promotion of, and, 76; Hungary and, 75, 77–78; International Conference for the Suppression of Counterfeit Currency and, 59; laws, strengthening, and, 69; Mixed Committee and, 78–79; Nazis and, 86; printing press and, 59, 69, 80, 86, 143n109; technology and, 68; as terrorism, 82
"Counterfeit Money" (Baudelaire), 83
credibility: Bourdieu on, 131n83; currencies and, 72, 76, 80; failures to act, 111, 117–18; reputation and, 22, 29, 117; world picture and, 22, 24–30, 131n83; World War I crisis of, 14
Croats, 135n18
currencies: *l'affaire des faux billets* and, 76–84; bills of exchange and, 74, 83; Britain and, 44, 53, 62; Brussels Financial conference and, 66, 73; capitalism and, 63, 67–71, 82; Cassel and, 64–66, 74–75, 85–86, 140n28, 142n85; civilization and, 71, 75, 81; confederate, 69; counterfeiting and, 15, 60–86, 90, 143n109; credibility and, 72, 76, 80; dematerialization of, 63, 66–67; dollar, 61, 80, 86; fascism and, 86–88; fiat, 60, 62–63; florin, international, 73; France and, 73, 76–78, 80; Freud and, 88; Genoa conference and, 66, 74; Germany and, 63, 75, 77; gold, 15, 60–80, 83–88, 126n63; inflation and, 61–63; information and, 67–68, 70, 80–83; Jews and, 77, 84, 86–88; Keynes and, 63–64, 83, 85, 140n39; liberalism and, 62, 64, 71; mercurial mediums of, 60–62; nationalism and, 81; Nazis and, 86–87; paper, 15, 61–86; peace and, 63, 71–78, 85; phantom, 73–76; Pound on, 86–88; printing press and, 60, 63, 69, 75, 80, 84, 86, 88; propaganda and, 62, 86; reality and, 60, 64–66, 81; reform and, 61; securities and, 28, 83; silver, 60, 70; social life of, 139n10; stabilization of, 15, 32, 61, 70–72, 75–77, 80, 82, 86; Swiss franc, 73, 85; symbolic capital and, 68, 76; truth and, 61, 65, 68–69, 72, 74, 76, 80, 83, 85–87; United States and, 68–69; value and, 60–64, 70, 77, 80–81, 85–87, 141n72; world picture and, 60, 66, 71; World War I and, 62–64, 66, 72
Cyrillic script, 56
Czechoslovakia, 29, 49, 79, 82, 89–90, 96–98, 102, 135n18, 136n36

Dadaist Manifesto (Ball), 1, 59
Dadaist Manifesto (Tzara), 40
Dadaist performances, 8, 13, 40
Darkness at Noon (Koestler), 89
Dauzat, Albert, 41–42
Debabelization (Ogden), 59
Decline of the West (Spengler), 25
Dell, Robert, 104–5, 108
DeMille, Cecil B., 98
democracy, 2, 105
Dickinson, B. B., 30
dictatorships, 2, 118
Dodd, W. J., 58
dollar, 61, 80, 86
doublespeak, 78
Douglas, C. H., 86–87
Dowleh, Prince Arfa ed-, 47

INDEX 185

Downfall of the Gold Standard, The (Cassel), 85
Durkheim, Émile, 89, 124n17

Eco, Umberto, 3
Economic and Financial Committee, 31, 64–65, 150n55
Economist (journal), 70–71
Economic Consequences of the Peace (Keynes), 63
Eden, Anthony, 96, 99–100, 111
Edsall, Edward W., 62
Edward VIII, 96
Egypt, 12, 17
Eichengreen, Barry, 66
Ellis, Charles Howard, 26, 28
English, 18, 26, 42, 45, 47, 49, 51, 53, 59, 80–81, 99
Erkin, Feridun Cernal, 115
Ernst, Wolfgang, 63
Esperanto: communism and, 47; ICIC and, 48; language and, 15, 44–51, 54–59, 73, 90; neutralist aims of, 59; power, natural basis of, and, 48; Privat and, 47–48; Saussure and, 73; symbolic capital and, 48–49; universality of, 45–47, 49, 57
Estonia, 29, 135n18
Ethiopia: Italy's invasion of, 36, 96, 99, 112, 119, 134nn148–49; slavery and, 133n147; world picture and, 17, 32, 36, 128n6
ethnic cleansing, xi, 16, 34, 117
eugenics, 61, 139n11

false news: *l'affaire des faux billets* and, 76–84; Amicucci and, 107; Bloch and, 107–8; censorship and, 10, 13, 106–7, 111, 120; Conference of the Directors of Press Bureaus and, 106; Conference on False News and, 90; Copenhagen conference and, 106; fascism and, 107, 112; Hitler and, 105, 110; information and, 105–12; Jews and, 105, 107, 110, 112; liberalism and, 105; Lux and, 15–16, 90, 109, 111; lying and, 15, 35, 90, 105, 110, 113, 117, 145n17; modern use of, ix; Nazis and, x, 105; peace and, 105–8, 111; prevarication and, 68, 106, 108, 113, 117–18; propaganda and, x, 105–12; *Protocols of the Elders of Zion* and, 110; reality and, 111; scapegoats and, x; Streit and, 108–10; truth and, 105–11; Valot and, 106–7; world picture and, x, 110; World War I and, 41, 90; World War II and, 107, 112
fascism: allure of, 2–4, 10, 13–16; anomie and, 40; Carr on, 13; currencies and, 86–88; defeat of, 118; Eco on, 3; false news and, 107, 112; Foucault on, 16; genocide and, 114; information and, 4, 10, 14, 39, 120; Italy's invasion of Ethiopia and, 36, 96, 99, 112, 119, 134nn148–49; Jung on, 2; language and, 40; media and, 3–4, 38, 114, 124n19; Nazis and, 14, 38, 112–13; neologisms

of, 15, 40; Paxton on, 3–4; Pound and, 86–88; pseudoscience and, 113; truth and, 4, 14, 36, 118–20; Ur-fascism and, 3, 59; world picture and, 36, 38–39
Fascist National Syndicate of Journalists, 107
Febvre, Lucien, 26
financial crisis of 2008, ix
Finland, 136n36
Firth, J. R., 57
Fisher, Irving, 61, 80–81, 87
Flandreau, Marc, 21, 66
florin, 73
Foucault, Michel, 16
Fox, David, 63
France: *l'affaire des faux billets* and, 76–84; Benjamin and, 73, 76–78, 80, 101; counterfeiting and, 76–84; currencies and, 73, 76–78, 80; Latin Union and, 73; League of Nations and, 17, 29, 73, 76, 78, 91, 101, 112, 136n42; minorities and, 54; Nazis and, 112; Paris Chamber of Commerce, 47; Paris Peace Conference, 31, 42–43, 47, 135n24; Resistance and, 107; Vichy, 101; world picture and, 17, 29
French (language), 9, 18, 41–42, 45–47, 49, 52, 99, 103, 127n85
Freud, Sigmund, 24–26, 60, 68, 81, 88, 123n2
Future of an Illusion, The (Freud), 60, 81

Genesis, Book of, 89
genocide, 114
Geographical Teacher (journal), 30
Germany, 135n18; appeasement of, 114; currencies and, 63, 75, 77; Hitler and, 38, 40, 57, 86–87, 100, 104–5, 110, 118 (*see also* Nazis); hyperinflation of, 75, 77; Jews and, 45, 57–58, 86, 91, 96–97, 101–2, 104, 147n64; language and, 57–58; League of Nations and, 14–17, 29, 54, 57, 75, 77, 89, 96–102, 105, 112, 114, 125, 128; Lux and, 89, 96–97, 100–5; Minority System and, 54; Nuremburg Laws and, 89; Weimar Republic and, 57, 86; world picture and, 29, 39
Gestapo, 91
Geyer, Michael, 10
Ghost Dance movement, 128n113
globalization, 3, 8
Goedsche, Herman, 110
Goeschel, Christian, 101
gold: artificial, 84–86; Cassell on, 85–86; currencies and, 15, 60–80, 83–88, 126n63; Ethiopia and, 32; Freud on, 68; Japan and, 141n76; melting of, 67–72; peace and, 85; as standard of exchange, 15, 60–61, 66, 68, 70–72, 74–75, 83–85, 88, 141n76, 141n78, 142n88; symbolic tangibility of, 68–70
Gold Delegation, 84–85

gold rush, 67, 141n53
grammar, 15, 41, 44, 49–50
Gramsci, Antonio, 47
Graves, Robert, 3, 11
Great Britain. *See* Britain
Great Depression, ix, 61, 78, 84–85
Greece, 33–34, 103, 135n18
Gregory XV, Pope, 22
Gutenberg, Johannes, 3, 89

Haiti, 17, 136n36
Hanotaux, Gabriel, 46
Hardt, Michael, 22
Hebrew, 51
Heidegger, Martin, 14, 23, 25, 38, 57
Heller, Arthur, 98
Hertz, Heinrich, 57
Hitler, Adolf: abolishment of individual and, 40; false news and, 105, 110; Jewish German Press and, 104–5; *Mein Kampf* and, 57, 105, 110; Nazis and, 38, 40, 57, 86–87, 100, 104–5, 110, 118
Holocaust, 109, 117, 149n149
Horkheimer, Max, 38, 94–95, 101, 146n24
Hungary, 29, 32, 75, 77–78, 96, 98, 135n18, 143n104
Hymans, Paul, 54

idealism, 6–7, 13, 60
ideals, 12, 26, 45
Ido, 44
"Illusion of a Return to Gold, The" (Cassell), 85–86
immobility, 34–35
imperialism, 5, 10–11, 14, 24–28, 41, 72
impulses, 2–3, 24, 67, 125n29
India, 17, 25, 29–30, 47, 53, 132nn99–100, 136n36
inflation, 61–63, 77, 86
information: big data and, x; currencies and, 67–68, 70, 80–83; false news and, 16, 41, 80, 105–12; fascism and, 4, 10, 14, 39, 120; knowledge, promiscuous, and, 11; language and, 41, 50; League of Nations and, 5–14, 17–23, 28–30, 34, 38–39, 41, 50, 81, 83, 90–91, 105, 109, 115–16; libraries and, 19; Lux and, 90–91, 102; McLuhan on, 3, 11; management of, 5, 20, 22, 28, 34; newspapers and, 9, 11, 14, 19, 21, 40, 95–96, 102, 109; overload of, ix–x; printing press and, 7, 37–38, 59–60, 63, 69, 75, 80, 84, 86, 88; radio and, 2, 11, 13, 19, 21, 37–38, 44, 113; storytelling and, 91–95, 117; telegraphs and, 2, 7, 10–11, 18, 44, 60, 98; telephones and, 2, 7, 11, 18, 44, 57, 60; truth and, 10, 12–14, 38, 83, 90, 92, 95, 106, 108–11, 120; typewriters and, 19–21, 37–38, 57; world picture and, 18–23, 28–34, 38–39
Institute for Social Research, 58
Inter-governmental Conference for the Adoption of a Convention concerning the Use of Broadcasting in the Cause of Peace, 37
International Association of Journalists Accredited to the League of Nations, 104, 108
International Committee on Intellectual Cooperation (ICIC), 48, 54, 56
International Conference for the Suppression of Counterfeit Currency, 59
International Criminal Police Commission, 79
International Federation of Journalists, 106
International Labor Organization, 31, 150n55
international organizations (IOs), 24, 134n166
Iraq, 52, 53, 118–19
Israelite Community of Geneva, 104
Israelitisches Wochenblatt, 100, 102–4
Italian Chamber of Commerce, 47, 136n56
Italy, 17, 36–37, 54, 73, 99, 107, 114, 119, 136n36

Japan, 17, 46, 55, 82, 109, 114, 136n36, 141n76
Jay, Martin, 35, 125n33
Jespersen, Otto, 56
Jevons, William Stanley, 70
Jewish German Press, 104–5
Jews: anti-Semitism and, 77, 96–97; cabals and, 110; currencies and, 77, 84, 86–88; expulsion of, 51; false news and, 105, 107, 110, 112; final solution and, 14; genocide and, 114; Germany and, 45, 57–58, 86, 91, 96–97, 101–2, 104, 147n64; Hebrew and, 51; Holocaust and, 109, 117, 149n149; international finance and, 77; Jung and, 2; language and, 45, 50–52, 57–58; Lux and, 15 (*see also* Lux, Stephen); Minorities Section and, 50–51; Nazis and, 57, 86, 97, 101–2, 112; newspapers and, 87–88; persecution of, 2, 96, 96–105; *Protocols of the Elders of Zion* and, 110; Yiddish and, 45, 51–52; Zamenhof and, 45; Zionism and, 51, 56, 103, 110
Joffre, 9
Jung, Carl Gustav, 1–2, 4, 124n17
Justice (film), 98

kanji, 55
Kemal, Mustafa, 55–56
Keynes, John Maynard, 63–64, 83, 85, 140n39
Khan, Albert, 31
King of Kings (DeMille), 98
Kittler, Friedrich, 20
Klemperer, Victor, 58
Knapp, Georg Friedrich, 70
Koestler, Arthur, 89
Koyré, Alexander, 113, 117–19
Kurds, 52–53

language: Alderson and, 43–44; alphabets and, 7, 15, 28–29, 40, 43, 54–56, 59, 75, 126n57; anomie and, 40; Arabic, 51, 55; Babel and, 43; borders and, 42; Britain and, 48, 51, 53, 59; capitalism and, 46–47; civilization and, 52; community from, 40–41; Cosmoglotta, 44; Dauzat and, 41–42; determinism and, 9, 15, 135n30; disordering/reordering and, 40–41; doublespeak and, 78; English, 18, 26, 42, 45, 47, 49, 51, 53, 59, 80–81, 99; entente cordial and, 42; erasure and, 54–59; Esperanto and, 15, 44–51, 54–59, 73, 90; ethnographic approach to, 52; fascism and, 40; French, 9, 18, 41–42, 45–47, 49, 52, 99, 103, 127n85; grammar and, 15, 41, 44, 49–50; Gramsci and, 47; Hebrew, 51; hegemony, fluid, and, 41–43; ICIC and, 48, 54, 56; identity, fixed, and, 41–43; information and, 41, 50; Jews and, 45, 50–52, 57–58; Latin, 44, 48, 51, 54–56; law, criminal, and, 80; League's official, 42–43, 45; liquidation and, 27–28; local/global dichotomy of, 41–43, 56; Lux and, 99, 103–4; Maccabees and, 103–4; maps of ethno-linguistic territory and, 42–49; media and, 9, 15; minorities and, 42, 49–54, 57, 75; nationalism and, 45, 48, 51, 55; Nazis and, 40–41, 57–59; neologisms and, 15, 40, 56, 58; Newspeak, 59; Nitobe on, 46, 55, 73; Occidental, 44; Parlamento, 44; peace and, 42–44, 54; Polish, 45, 50–51; power of, 6–8; propaganda and, 58; reality and, 42–44, 51–53, 57; reform and, 40–41, 43, 51, 54–57, 138n103; revision and, 54–59; rhetoric and, 4, 14, 20, 24, 26, 53, 67, 75, 110; Roman characters and, 54–55; Sanskrit, 44; Sapir and, 56–57; Saussure and, 7, 61, 73, 87; science and, 46, 135n26; Spanish, 45–46; speech-act theory and, 8; standardization of, 41, 51–52, 57; sword and, 44, 60; symbolic capital and, 49, 116; truth and, 43, 47, 51; two faces of, 41–43; United States and, 57; vocabulary and, 15, 41, 43–44, 56–58; Volapük, 44; vowels and, 57; Wittgenstein on, 49–50; world picture and, 41–43, 49, 58; World War I and, 43–44; Yiddish and, 45, 51–52

Language of the Third Reich: LTI: Lingua Tertii Imperii (Klemperer), 58
Latin (language), 44, 48, 51, 54–56
Latin Union, 73
Latvia, 135n18
Laval, Pierre, 112
League of Nations: Covenant of, 6, 17, 28, 114; failures to act of, 111, 117–18; First Assembly of, 6, 19, 117; France and, 17, 29, 73, 76, 78, 91, 101, 112, 136n42; General Assembly, 6, 17, 118; Germany and, 14–17, 29, 54, 57, 75, 77, 89, 96–102, 105, 112, 114, 125, 128; as global planetarium, 3; information and, 5–14, 18–23, 28–30, 34, 38–39, 41, 50, 81, 83, 90–91, 105, 109, 115–16; as information factory, 18; library of, 19; Lux suicide at, 15, 89–90, 95, 101–4, 112, 815; membership criteria of, 23–24; Minority System and, 50, 52–54, 75; peace and, xi, 2–3, 6, 12–13, 16, 21, 31, 33, 37, 39, 45, 52, 54, 73, 78, 85, 90, 96, 105–6, 108, 116; Permanent Mandate Commission (PMC) and, 10, 27–28; production process of, 18–19; publications of, 19; scholarship on, 5–13; Secretariat of, 17–19, 44, 46, 48, 52, 99–100, 106, 127n93; Third Assembly of, 48, 136n52; United Nations and, 114–18; United States and, 17; Wilson and, 5–6, 9, 21, 125n42, 131n84, 135n17, 135n24

Lebovic, Nitzan, 58
Lenin, Vladimir, 25, 63
Leopold, 25
Levy-Wallisch, 104
Lewis, Geoffrey, 56
liberalism: credibility crisis and, 14; currencies and, 62, 64, 71; discrediting, 24; false news and, 105; Lux and, 104; world picture and, 24
libraries, 19
linguistic determinism, 9, 15
Lippmann, Walter, 9
liquidation, 27–28
literacy, 10, 55, 75
Lithuania, 29, 32, 53, 135n18
Los Angeles Times, 97
Lusinchi, Victor, 111–12
Lux, Adam, 145n1
Lux, Joseph August, 145n1
Lux, Stephen: Adorno and, 95, 101; Avenol and, 96, 99, 101, 145n8, 147n75; Benjamin and, 91, 95, 101; Bochet and, 96, 99; Dell and, 104–5, 108; Eden and, 96, 98–100, 111; false news and, 15–16, 16, 90, 109, 111; Germany and, 89, 96–97, 100–5; Heller and, 98; Horkheimer and, 95, 101; information and, 90–91, 102; Jewishness of, 101–3; letters of, 96–100, 104, 145n8, 147n77, 148n111; liberalism and, 104; linguistics and, 99; Lusinchi, 112; Maccabees tradition and, 103–4; as martyr, 103–4; media and, 5–6, 90, 95–97, 99; motives of, 96–97; nationalism and, 111; Nazis and, 89, 96–105, 112, 145n1; newspapers and, 95–99, 102; peace talks and, 96; photography and, 145n1; poetry of, 97–98; *Prager Press* and, 98, 100; reality and, 97; Sargent and, 95–99, 101, 104, 147n77; as Strumbursh, Peter, 97–98; suicide of, 15, 89–90, 95, 101–4, 112, 815; truth and, 89–90; world picture and, 90
lying, 145n17; acceptance of, 113, 117; Bush and, 118–19; Koyré on, 113, 117–19; media and, 15, 90, 105, 110 (*see also* false news); prevarication and, 68, 106, 108, 113, 117–18; Valery on, 35

Macartney, C. A., 53
Maccabees, 103–4
Macedonia, 52
Macleod, Henry Dunning, 70
Madison, James, 113

magic lanterns, 35
Manchester Guardian, 95–96
Manchuria, 55
mandates, 6, 10, 27–28, 31, 51–56, 127n91
Manning, Clarence Augustus, 41
Marconi Wireless Company, 19
Marx, Karl, 69
Maurois, Andre, 18, 36–37
Mazower, Mark, 10
McLuhan, Marshall, 3, 11
media: Adorno on, 146n24; Benjamin and, 91, 94; false news and, 106–7 (*see also* false news); fascism and, 3–4, 38, 114, 124n19; genocide and, 114; Hitler on, 104–5, 110; Horkheimer on, 146n24; Jews and, 87–88, 104–5; linguistics and, 9, 15; linking social processes and, 124n17; Lux and, 5–6, 90, 95–97, 99; photography and, 19, 30–32, 35–37; reality and, 4, 7–14; sword and, 13; truth and, 4–5, 10, 15; world picture and, 20, 26, 31, 35, 38; World War I and, 1, 9–12, 14. *See also* newspapers; *individual publications*
Meillet, Antoine, 52
Mein Kampf (Hitler), 57, 105, 110
Miller, Mark Crispin, 22
minority systems, 50, 52–54, 75
Mitchell, Timothy, 23
Mitchell-Innis, Harold, 70
Mixed Committee, 78–79
Moody's Investment Services, 28
Mukerji, Dhan Gopal, 25
Mundaneum, 21, 31
Muslims, 53, 55

nationalism: currencies and, 81, 143n103; India and, 25; language and, 45, 48, 51, 55; Lux and, 111; super, 2; world picture and, 25, 29–30, 131n84
Nazi-Deutsch (Paechter), 119
Nazis: art, German, and, 86; counterfeiting and, 86; currencies and, 86–87; false news and, x, 105; fascism and, 14, 38, 112–13; final solution and, 14; France and, 112; genocide and, 114; Gestapo and, 91; Heidegger and, 38; Hitler and, 38, 40, 57, 86–87, 100, 104–5, 110, 118; Jews and, 57, 86, 97, 101–2, 112; language and, 40–41, 57–59; League of Nations and, 14–15, 57, 96–98, 101–2, 112, 125, 128; Lux and, 89, 96–105, 112, 145n1; propaganda and, x, 13, 38–40, 43, 58, 86, 119; volkic doctrine of, 13, 38, 40, 43, 58, 86, 119; *Wehrwirtschaft* theory of, 86; world picture and, 38–39
Negri, Antonio, 22
Nelson, Harold, 135n17
neologisms, 15, 40, 56, 58
newspapers, 40; false news and, 109 (*see also* false news); increased media flow and, 11, 14, 19, 21; Jews and, 87–88, 104–5; Joffre and, 9; language and, 9; Lux and, 95–99, 102. *See also* media; *individual publications*
Newspeak, 59
New York Herald, 17
New York Times, 89, 96, 102, 108, 112
New Zealand, 83
Nitobe, Inaz, 46, 55, 73
nominalism, 126n59
Norway, 51
Nuremburg Laws, 89

Occidental (language), 44
Office of Strategic Services (OSS), 58
Ogden, C. K., 59
On Tyranny (Snyder), 119
On Violence (Arendt), 116
Opium Board, 32
order of things, 1, 5, 10, 14, 23, 37
Origin, Structure and Working of the League of Nations, The (Ellis), 26
Orthological Institute, 59
Orwell, George, 59
Otlet, Paul, 21, 31
Ottoman Empire, 55

Paechter, Heinz, 58, 119
Paris Chamber of Commerce, 47
Paris Peace Conference, 31, 42–43, 47, 135n24
Parlamento, 44
Paul-Boncour, Joseph, 78, 114–15
Paxton, Robert O., 3–4
peace: century of, 25; cold war and, 116; currencies and, 63, 71–78, 85; false news and, 105–8, 111; gold and, 85; international, 2, 9, 12–13, 18, 21, 37, 43–47, 71, 73, 85, 104–5, 108, 117, 134n157; keeping, 3, 114, 117; language and, 42–44, 54; League of Nations and, xi, 2–3, 6, 12–13, 16, 21, 31, 33, 37, 39, 45, 52, 54, 73, 78, 85, 90, 96, 105–6, 108, 116; Lux and, 96; nuclear power and, 115; Paris Peace Conference and, 31, 42–43, 47, 135n24; perpetual, ideal of, 116; propaganda and, 105–6; treaties for, 2, 31, 52, 54, 77–78; world picture and, 18, 20–21, 25, 31, 33, 37
Pedersen, Susan, 5, 10, 27–28
Pella, Vespasian, 82
Pelt, Arthur, 32–33
Pemberton, Jo-Anne, 12, 20
Permanent Mandate Commission (PMC), 10, 27–28, 31
Persia, 17, 47–48, 136n36
Peters, John Durham, 11
Philosophical Investigations (Wittgenstein), 49
photography: Ames and, 30, 32–34; Barthes on, 31, 35; international order and, 12; Khan and,

INDEX

21, 31; League's slides and, 30–37; Lux and, 145n1; magic lanterns and, 35; mass reproduction of, 68; media and, 126n59, 126n70; Mundaneum, 21, 31; realism and, 35; storytelling and, 94; truth and, 31, 35–37, 132n108, 133n141; world picture and, 19, 30–37, 132n108, 133n141
Pierce, John R., 120
Poland, 17, 32, 47, 50–53, 57, 135n18, 136n36
Polish, 45, 50–51
political economy, 140n32
Pollock, Sheldon, 44
Pospíšil, Vilém, 82
Pound, Ezra, 86–88
Prager Press, 98, 100
Prashad, Vijay, 116–17
prevarication, 68, 106, 108, 113, 117–18
Price, Burr, 17
printing press: counterfeiting and, 59, 69, 80, 86, 143n109; currencies and, 60, 63, 69, 75, 80, 84, 86, 88; Gutenberg and, 3, 89, 109; information and, 7, 37–38, 59–60, 63, 69, 75, 80, 84, 86, 88
Privat, Edmond, 47–48
propaganda: Anderson on, 10; currencies and, 62, 86; false news and, x, 105–12; Gregory XV and, 22; language and, 58; Nazis and, x, 13, 38–40, 43, 58, 86, 119; peace and, 105–6; volkic doctrine and, 13, 38, 40, 43, 58, 86, 119; world picture and, 22, 38; World War I and, 8–9; World War II and, 38
Protocols of the Elders of Zion, 110
psychoanalysis: Freud and, 24–26, 60, 68, 81, 88, 123n2; Jung and, 1–2, 4, 124n17
psychology, 1, 4, 11, 60, 79, 92, 100, 124n17, 133n137
public opinion, 6–7, 9, 18, 20, 100, 105, 115, 118
Putsch, Kapp, 98

racism, ix, 4, 118; anti-Semitism and, 77, 96–97; ethnic cleansing and, xi, 16, 34, 117; genocide and, 114; stereotypes and, 15–16, 95, 97, 101–2, 110
radio, 2, 11, 13, 19, 21, 37–38, 44, 113
Raestead, Arnold, 37–38
railways, 44, 87, 138n100
realism, 7, 13, 35, 60
reality: currencies and, 60, 64–66, 81; false news and, 111; language and, 42–44, 51–53, 57; Lux and, 97; media and, 4, 7–14; photography and, 132n108; storytelling and, 93, 95; sword and, 114, 116; truth and, xi, 4, 12–13, 15, 31, 38, 43, 93, 111, 132; world picture and, 31, 38, 132n108
reductionism, 16, 92–93
reform: currencies and, 61; language and, 15, 40–41, 43, 51, 54–57, 138n103; Lux and, 96

Reformation (religious movement), 38
religion, 13, 25, 33, 39, 53, 114
Remington Company, 20
"Report of the Gold Delegation," 84–85
reputation laundering, 29, 117
rhetoric, 4, 14, 20, 24, 26, 53, 67, 75, 110
Rio Branco, Raul de, 46–47
Rogers, Walter S., 21
Romania, 53, 82, 135n18, 136n36
romanji, 55
Rosenberg, Alfred, 39
Rosenfelder, Fritz, 101
Russia, 12, 17, 46, 56, 118, 124n14

Salle de la Reformation, 18
Sanskrit, 44
Sapir, Edward, 8, 56–57
Sargent, Betty, 95–99, 101, 104, 147n77
Saussure, Ferdinand de, 60
Saussure, René de, 7, 61, 73, 87
Schildkraut, Rudolph, 98
science: entropy and, 120; Esperanto and, 46; forensic, 93; Freud and, 81; language and, 46, 135n26; pseudoscience and, 113; racial purity and, 4
Scraps of Paper (film), 62–63
securities, 28, 83
security, 38, 64, 78–79, 97, 100, 118
Segel, Benjamin W., 110
Seleucid Empire, 103
self-determination, 10, 17, 42, 52, 131n84
September 11, 2001, attacks, 82, 118
Serbs, 52, 135n18
Servais, Paul, 82–83
sexism, ix
silver, 60, 70
Simmel, Georg, 67, 70
slavery, 9, 12, 36, 57, 105, 133n147
Slovenes, 135n18
Smith, Jeremiah, 77
Smuts, Jan, 26–27, 32
Snyder, Timothy, 119
socialism, 25, 63
sovereignty, 25, 27, 36, 41, 54, 78–79, 87, 103, 143n104
Spain, 91, 96
Spanish (language), 45–46
speculation, 64, 69
speech-act theory, 8
Spencer, Herbert, 69
Spengler, Oswald, 24–25
Spirit of Geneva, The (Traz), 17–18
spirituality, 1, 4–5, 39, 81, 128n113
stabilization: currencies and, 15, 32, 61, 70–72, 75–77, 80, 82, 86; Fisher on, 61; world picture and, 118, 120

Stalin, Joseph, 118
statehood, 10, 17, 24, 28–29, 69, 83
State Theory of Money (Knapp), 70
Stavri, Stavro, 59
Steiner, Zara, 66
stereotypes, 15–16, 95, 97, 101–2, 110
"Storyteller, The: Reflections on the Works of Nicolai Leskov" (Benjamin), 91
storytelling, 91–95, 117
Streicher, Julious, 101
Streit, Clarence, 108–10
Stürmer, Der (tabloid), 101
Suicide in Nazi Germany (Goeschel), 101
Swiss franc, 73, 85
Switzerland, 8, 47, 73, 101, 136n56
sword: collective force and, 114–15; language and, 44, 60; media and, 13; reality and, 114, 116; return of, 113–17; sparing, 6; truth and, 14, 113, 117–20; world picture and, 17, 24, 26, 116–18
symbolic capital, 14; currencies and, 68, 76; Esperanto and, 48–49; language and, 49, 116; world picture and, 21–24, 26, 29–30, 36–37, 39, 116–17, 130n49
Syria, 103, 151n44

Tanakadate, Aikitu, 54–55, 138n103
tariffs, 133n137
telegraphs, 2, 7, 10–11, 18, 44, 60, 98
telephones, 2, 7, 11, 18, 44, 57, 60
terrorism, 82, 118
Traz, Robert de, 17–18, 36
Treaty of Tordesillas, 32
Treaty of Trianon, 77
truth: Arendt on, 145n17; competing, 4–5, 10, 15; currencies and, 61, 65, 68–69, 72, 74, 76, 80, 83, 85–87; economics of, 127n95, 130n47; false news and, 105–11; fascism and, 4, 14, 36, 118–20; fragile economics of, 127n95; information and, 10, 12–14, 38, 83, 90–95, 106, 108–11, 120; language and, 43, 47, 51; Lux and, 89–90, 93, 95, 99–101; lying and, 15, 35, 90, 105, 110, 113, 117, 145n17; media and, 4–5, 10, 15; Paxton on, 4; photography and, 31, 35–37, 132n108, 133n141; political, 4, 13, 21, 35, 38, 51, 61, 65, 89–93, 95, 107, 110, 113, 118, 150n5; reality and, ix, xi, 4–5, 10, 12–13, 15, 31, 38, 43, 93, 111, 132; scientific, 125n33; storytelling and, 92–93, 95; sword and, 14, 113, 117–20; world picture and, 21–22, 24, 31, 35–38, 132n108
Turkey, 17, 33, 55–56, 135n18
typewriters, 19–21, 37–38, 57
Tzara, Tristan, 40

Union Now (Streit), 109–10
United Kingdom. *See* Britain
United Nations, 114–18
United States: currencies and, 68–69; Ghost Dance movement and, 128n113; language and, 57; League of Nations and, 17; Schildkraut and, 98
Universal Esperanto Association (UEA), 45–46
Ur-fascism, 3, 59

Valery, Paul, 35
Valot, Stephan, 106–7
Venezuela, 136n36
Vismann, Cornelia, 14
vocabulary, 15, 41, 43–44, 56–58
Volapük, 44
Voltaire, 8
Von Keller, 57
vowels, 57

Weimar Republic, 57, 86
Weltbühne, Die (*The World Stage*; newspaper), 98
Western Union Company, 67
What Is Money For (Pound), 87
Whort, Benjamin Lee, 8
Wiart, Count Carton de, 116
Wilson, Woodrow, 5–6, 9, 21, 125n42, 131n84, 135n17, 135n24
"Wire and Radio Communications" (Rogers), 21
Wittgenstein, Ludwig, 8, 49–50
world picture: Britain and, 17, 26, 29; capitalism and, 24; civilization and, 17, 23–30, 36; credibility and, 22, 24–30, 131n83; currencies and, 60, 66, 71; decline of West and, 24–30; false news and, 110; fascism and, 36, 38–39; France and, 17, 29; Germany and, 29, 39; Heidegger on, 23; information and, 18–23, 28–34, 38–39; language and, 41–43, 49, 58; liberalism and, 24; liquidation and, 27–28; Lux and, 90; media and, 20, 26, 31, 35, 38; nationalism and, 25, 29–30, 131n84; Nazis and, 38–39; peace and, 18, 20–21, 25, 31, 33, 37; photography and, 19, 30–37, 132n108, 133n141; propaganda and, 22, 38; reality and, 31, 38, 132n108; stabilization and, 118, 120; sword and, 17, 24, 26, 116–18; symbolic capital and, 21–24, 26, 29–30, 36–37, 39, 116–17, 130n49; truth and, 21–22, 24, 31, 35–38, 132n108, 132n117; World War I and, 18, 20–23, 26–29, 32, 34, 38; World War II and, 112
World's Monetary Problems, The (Cassel), 64–65
World War I: credibility crisis of, 14; currencies and, 62–64, 66, 72; false news and, 41, 90; Jung on, 1; language and, 43–44; media and, 1, 9–12, 14; propaganda and, 8–9; psychological effects of, 1–2; world picture and, 18, 20–23, 26–29, 32, 34, 38
World War II: destruction of, 114, 117; false news and, x, 107, 112; French Resistance and, 7;

Koyré on, 113–14, 117–19; League of Nations' failure to prevent, 5; propaganda and, 38; world picture and, 112
World Zionist organization, 56
Wright, Alex, 21

xenophobia, ix, 4, 15, 77, 83

Yiddish, 45, 51–52
Yugoslavia, 52, 54, 135n18

Zamenhof, Ledger Ludwik, 45
Zimmern, Alfred, 12
Zionism, 51, 56, 103, 110
Zweig, Stefan, 145n1

www.ingramcontent.com/pod-product-compliance
Lightning Source LLC
Chambersburg PA
CBHW051358290426
44108CB00015B/2067